sarah vowell

a listener's diary

St. Martin's Griffin ✽ New York

Design by Pei Loi Koay

Library of Congress Cataloging-in-Publication Data

Vowell, Sarah.
Radio on : a listener's diary / by Sarah Vowell.—1st ed.
p. cm.
ISBN 0-312-18301-1
1. Radio programs—United States—Miscellanea.   2. Vowell, Sarah,
1969–   —Diaries.   I. Title.
PN1991.3.U6V68   1996
791.44'75'0973—dc20   96-23288
CIP

10   9

"I only conceived this diary as a means to say I'm *just* as confused and overwhelmed as my elders, just as ill-informed and worried and perplexed and lacking in answers (but willing to look) as people twice my age."—Sarah Vowell

to my mother, my father, and my sister

JOURNALIST—Didn't you have anything on?

MARILYN MONROE—I had the radio on.

Radio is a landscape, a place inhabited by heroes and villains. And I should know. I spent a year in the broadcast badlands of 1995, which is 325 days longer than Christ suffered in the wilderness (and he didn't have to take notes). But this book is not just a road map of radioland, but of love and hate. My love. My hate. I was twenty-five years old.

I had been living in San Francisco, working at a gallery and writing for art magazines. An assignment to review a collection of essays called *Radiotext(e)*, edited by Neil Strauss, got me thinking. Strauss opens his introduction with these words: "You will never understand radio by listening to it."

In some ways, he was right. The more I read about radio's possibilities—theories of what it could be or do—the less I tuned in to the real-life black box, that dreary, intelligence-insulting, ugly, half-assed, audio compromise lorded over by the stultifying FCC. But if Strauss wasn't listening, and I wasn't listening, someone was. Someone with a vote. In those horrifying days after the 1994 congressional elections, people started pointing at conservative talk radio as the major force which fueled the so-called Republican Revolution that gave the right wing a majority for the first time in four decades. I began to understand what Bob Dylan meant when he sang, *"Is there a hole for me to get sick in?"*

Then I noticed that no one was keeping score: While American magazines and newspapers employ armies of critics to dissect the content and influence of television, movies, art, and music, radio is rarely covered. Its presence is intimated with skeletal listings that can't begin to hint at the medium's diversity. Glancing at the "Radio Highlights" section of any metropolitan daily, you'd think that all we hear is Puccini or public policy—Rush Limbaugh was never born and Kurt Cobain never died.

More than simply confronting programming, I wanted to dig deeper, to think about how one listens to the radio, or at least how I listen. Hence the diary format. Sometimes, all of America seemed to be hashing it out inside my stereo. Just as often, a song, a voice, or a throwaway remark sparked a memory or spoke to a newspaper in my hands in such a way that I felt less alone. Then again, the venom and mediocrity got to me, leaving me deeply sad. There were days that I carried around my sense of humor like a picket sign.

In order to help the reader to decipher my personal geography, a few David Copperfield facts. First, a confession: I do not know how to drive. While many people's radio memories are bound to their automobiles, mine are not. A hick twice over, I grew up in Oklahoma and Montana, graduated from Montana State (where I did college radio, of which more later), and in the course of this book, moved from San Francisco to Chicago, where I attended a graduate program in modern art history at the School of the Art Institute. As a student/freelance writer, I kept very irregular hours. Thus, the famous "drive time" had little bearing on my listening. These other occupations—taking seminars with titles like "Anti-art Since the '60s," writing book and record reviews, and teaching first-year students about Roman architecture— not only saved my soul, they made the radio a part of a life, not a separation from it.

As you can imagine, I heard a lot of crap—numbing,

malevolent examples of the worst kinds of filth. This why I often joked to myself that the book's title would be *Amber Waves of Pain*. Eventually, however, I settled in with some friendly voices: Ian Brown and Ira Glass redeemed public radio; Reverend Ivan Stang of the Church of the SubGenius became a beloved weirdo; writers Bill Wyman and Jim DeRogatis routinely bit the evil hands that fed them; and Courtney Love, more than anyone, screamed how I felt.

But it is Cobain who haunts the wasteland most of all, which is why we begin with a ghost story.

A Note on the Paperback Edition

Lately, it seems like years take on the weight of decades, which is why 1995 feels more like twenty years ago instead of two. And if the following pages faithfully capture the mean spirit of that year, then this distance is no bad thing. When I asked a friend how to introduce this paperback edition, he said in one breath, "Why don't you just say that people still listen to Rush Limbaugh, even though they no longer talk about him, and Bill Clinton still can't get a break. The end." The thing is, listening to the radio every day in 1995 has probably lowered my standards of public life—to the point that not reading Rush's name in the paper every morning strikes me as a solid improvement. And two years ago, I seriously thought I'd now be living in a country with a president named Newt.

People ask me if radio has changed, but I couldn't really say. I don't—can't—listen much anymore, though I still have enough faith in the *idea* of public radio to contribute stories to *This American Life*. Some of these pieces have even been replayed, to my surprise, on *All Things Considered*, a target herein. So I've decided that National Public Radio is just like capitalism: It will suck every dissenting voice into its vortex and claim it as its own.

As for Kurt Cobain, his voice sounds as present tense as ever, but his status as an oldies icon grows likelier every day. Like John Lennon and Elvis before him, he'll always be on the radio, just like he'll always be dead.

Sarah Vowell
Chicago, July 1997

COPPING A FEEL IN '94

San Francisco

December 31, 1994.   **11 a.m.–7 p.m. KITS-FM.**

Number 23. That's it. Decent, but not monumental. The song on the radio is Nirvana's "About a Girl." It was the loveliest, safest piece on their otherwise jagged first album, *Bleach*, and this year it is the sunniest cut on their dark beauty *Unplugged in New York*.

Packing up, looking back—December 31 is the sappiest day of the year. To stuff what's left of my belongings into cardboard boxes, to move, is always an exercise in nostalgia; but today I have a soundtrack for it: the KITS-FM 1994 Modern Rock Countdown. "Live 105," as this alternative commercial station is known, advertises itself in a deep monster voice as the "modern rock revolution" and is playing what it deems to be the top 105 rock 'n' roll anthems of the past twelve months.

Trudging through a checklist with good (but not great) songs by the likes of Sonic Youth, Pavement, and R.E.M., 1994 sounds downright respectable, polished, just fine, cool.

The thrilling lurch of the Beastie Boys' "Sabotage" and Courtney Love's gritty wails on Hole's "Doll Parts" excepted, if
this is revolution, long live the King. In this forum, even
Nirvana sounds wholesome. But sometimes, as a friend always
tells me when I'm going soft, nice just doesn't cut it.

To Live 105, "About a Girl" is just a number, twenty-
three to be exact. The DJ plays it without commentary, not
even a word about the voice from the grave that sings it. The
catchy-but-nothing-special pop group Weezer merits more
talk time, probably because they played at the station's listener appreciation Halloween concert at the Fillmore. It was
the station I turned to on the afternoon of April 8 to confirm
the hearsay of Nirvana songwriter Kurt Cobain's suicide. I
got drunk to it, singed my hair to it (as I lit up cigarettes on
the gas stove), and turned up "All Apologies" full blast so
that I didn't have to hear the sound of my own weeping for
a man I never even met. Today, though, I guess they want
to keep it light.

It was a year ago today that I attended a New Year's Eve
Nirvana concert at the Oakland Coliseum. That night now
seems so long ago, a distant memory of the way their music
once made me feel: invincible, passionate, violent, pissed. I
might have looked like a five-foot-three-inch, rosy-cheeked
Nice Girl sitting harmlessly, if not ladylike, next to you on
a city bus, but, "Lithium" on my Walkman, I was thinking,
"Don't fuck with me." In the days after Cobain's death, I
felt like a parasite, one of thousands who had taken so much
courage from a man who didn't have enough left over for
himself. In Nirvana's version of "Jesus Doesn't Want Me for
a Sunbeam," Cobain sang the line *don't expect me to die
for you* with a true conviction. No, I didn't expect him to
die for me, but listening to his lyrics, I did expect him to
die. The most terrifying aspect of his suicide was that it made
so much sense.

And it was the words, as sung and screamed in Cobain's
sincere voice, that overpowered Nirvana's furious sound on
the radio April 8. Some lyrics became a sick joke—*I swear
that I don't have a gun* or *"I'm not gonna crack"*—but most

were too-lucid declarations of despair, and to the point: "A *denial.*" It would be months before I could play a Nirvana record at home again. On April 9, the only sound I wanted to pierce my weary-eyed hangover was Neil Young's "Rockin' in the Free World" and I played it over and over. Bleak but persistent, it was encouraging, hinting that I could still face the future with rock 'n' roll songs, that the meanness of life at least offers an amplified painkiller. I heard Nirvana songs only on the radio or MTV, which is to say that I heard them several times a day all year long. Krist Novoselic's primordial bass faded low and even the frightening vengeance of the gods that is Dave Grohl's drumming ground to a whisper. I noticed only Cobain's voice and I heard only pure pain.

But that was after.

Before April 8, to hear a Nirvana song on the radio was to feel as if I knew a secret. Of course, I was deluded. The group became no more clandestine than Elvis after the release of their breakthrough album *Nevermind*. By the beginning of 1992, a Nirvana fan was as common as a bike in Amsterdam, but listening to the songs alone (and they were the reason headphones were invented), you wouldn't know it. They were that immediate, almost embarrassingly personal and so smudged with black humor that they appealed not just to the solitary adolescents who snapped up the record from day one, but to the solitary adolescent in all of us. And even though the überhip, shunning as they must what's popular in popular music, abandoned them after they became well-liked, they were too good, too funny, and too loud to stay underground.

I was sitting in the campus cafeteria at Montana State University in October of 1991, trying to scan through some French novel before class. The book was a bore and not half as interesting as the noisy redneck roundtable discussion the next booth over. They were reading aloud the record reviews in the school paper, *The Exponent*, the literary pride of a university with the breathtakingly inspirational motto "Education for Efficiency." All of the reviews were written by a DJ at KGLT, the campus station where I worked and one of

about three reasons why I endured the cow-college educational voyage with assholes like these. They were making fun
of the station as unlistenable, irrelevant, run by stoners who
actually had the gall to think that anyone with half a brain
would care about their depraved little purveyors of noise, if
I may paraphrase. They also mocked the band names. "Like
this one," whined the mustachioed one in a cowboy hat,
"check this out. Near-vain-uh. I mean, who the hell are they?"
I giggled and could hardly wait to get home and tell my
roommates. Klee, also a KGLT DJ, had played "Smells Like
Teen Spirit" on his show days earlier, and Katie, listening,
drove straight to the record store and bought *Nevermind.* She
brought it home, we listened to the whole thing, she walked
straight to the phone, called her brother, and left this message: "Have you heard the new Nirvana? It's really great"—
and hung up. It was filed under the category called Records
We Like.

Weeks later, it became A Cultural Phenomenon. Gina
Arnold, in her book *Route 666: On the Road to Nirvana,*
captured what it felt like. And it felt like revolution:

> *Nirvana's music—grunge music—reflects a time, my time.
> And my time has its own history, its own leaders, its own
> rules. It's not merely that I'd rather hear good music on the
> radio than bad: It's that I think people liking good music
> is indicative of better things. . . . Nirvana's being on the
> radio means my own values are winning: I'm no longer in
> the opposition.*

You could hear what she meant if you listened, but I'm
guessing that most of the millions who bought *Nevermind*
ignored the irony in "In Bloom"—*"He likes his favorite song
and he likes to sing along"* but *"he knows not what it means."*
Even my own cafeteria dimwits, eventually noticing that the
record rocked, most likely went out and bought it. It was one
of the reasons Cobain put a gun to his head, writing in the
liner notes to 1992's *Incesticide:* "Last year, a girl was raped
by two wastes of sperm and eggs while they sang the lyrics

to our song 'Polly.' I have a hard time carrying on knowing that there are plankton like that in our audience."

Despite the numbing Bush administration lip service to values, family or otherwise, Cobain's statement illustrates Nirvana's unpretentious example of ethics, denouncing violence against women by organizing a benefit for Bosnian rape victims and standing up to homophobia by French-kissing each other on national TV. At the Oakland concert, Cobain threw down his guitar midsong and stopped the band. He was outraged that a man up front spent the first few minutes of the new year groping a fellow female mosher. He summoned Novoselic and they stood up, pointing at the molester in ridicule, yelling, "Copping a feel in '94!"

It was a relief to know that someone like that was on the radio, on television, part of American public life. And if the other actors on the national stage, such as Andy Rooney of *60 Minutes*, couldn't see beyond Cobain's drug problem or his fans' ripped jeans enough to catch a glimpse of the beauty of their beliefs, then I will hand over my anger and trade it in for pity.

In the fall of 1994, I published a eulogy to Kurt Cobain in *High Performance* magazine, disguised as a column about Joseph Lanza's *Elevator Music: A Surreal History of Muzak, Easy Listening, and Other Moodsong,* a book that I felt represented a love letter to boredom and complacency. I finally lost my temper at Lanza's send-up of the way an easy-listening group called the Alan Copeland Singers turned a song by bluesman Leadbelly into a "sweet suburban incantation." At the Oakland concert, I wrote, "Singing Leadbelly's ballad 'Where Did You Sleep Last Night?' Cobain started off with a gently scratchy drawl. For an instant, he sounded like the greatest country singer who ever lived. Suddenly, he was screaming through the rest of it, claiming the words as his own and spewing them out of his tortured belly with more profound passion than I have witnessed in my short life. Remembering what that moment meant to me as I read Lanza's statement that 'not every musician should be obligated to reassure us that we are not zombies' made me sick."

You can hear all of that in a Nirvana song on the radio, if you care to listen. To some of the people who grieve him, Kurt Cobain was a great artist, to others he was the medicine man of their rock 'n' roll tribe, but, finally, he was simply a friend. And in the days after his death, his most honest tribute was spoken to Arnold by Seattle's Kurt Bloch of the Fastbacks in the *San Francisco Chronicle*: "I just can't stand to think of him being that sad."

Radio crept up on us under cover of silence. It belongs today to the inventory of a household like a fancy wardrobe and potted plants. Seemingly uninvolved, obscured by spools, wires, and hard rubber disks, the magical boxes sit in their corners. You adjust the steel ring, and charming melodies resound. A violin hums, an older gentleman sings "In the Month of May," a farmer speaks of synthetic manure. The world is vast and its tones are manifold.

—Otto Alfred Palitzsch

San Francisco

January 1, 1995.   **2:29 p.m. National Public Radio.**

I took back the night. And it's all mine until I get stabbed, raped, mugged, shot. I've walked alone the darkened streets of tough towns from Palermo to New York, but the congenial Midwest makes me tremble. I know for a fact that the steam rises from the gates of hell in downtown Fargo and the Antichrist, laying low, shovels snow off the sidewalks of Dubuque for extra cash.

Forget the Big Bad Wolf, the fear of God, the hands of time—they can't stand up to Minnesota Nice.

The Prince of Darkness, tied up stirring the fiery cauldrons of *Prairie Home Companion,* has dispatched his demon helpers to do his dirty work with a good-humored twang. Michael Feldman, dark angel / host of the heartland's *Whad'Ya Know?,* queries a farmer from Superior who reveals his voodoo: "Usu-

ally, we have the radio on and it calms the chickens." On
their way to the chopping block, that is.

January 2.   **8:55 a.m. KSFO-AM.**

"Out: political correctness, liberal media, the Democratic
party. In: KSFO Hot Talk 560." Today, this San Francisco
AM station gives the people what they want, chucking its
formerly liberal talk format in favor of an all-right-wing
lineup, beating Congress to the flip-flop by a full two days.

I turn it on just as J. Paul Emerson, recently fired from
another Bay Area station for making allegedly anti-Asian
remarks, orates his sign-off with a version of the Pledge of
Allegiance that's more "Try me" than salute.

A few minutes later, Ray Charles' fine version of "America
the Beautiful" is replaced by strip-club music hailing the
voice of former cop Tom Kamb. In the nine-to-noon spot,
Kamb is up against his maker, trying to emphasize his hometown agenda in opposition to Rush Limbaugh's national focus
on a competing station. "We like to think of it as our Contract
with the Bay Area," claims an ad that winks at the Republican
platform which plans to change the world.

"Whatever it is that's got you hot in the Bay Area, let's
talk about it!" Kamb barks. "But let's not just talk! Let's
fight back!" (He only speaks in exclamations.)

Issue number one concerns a man named Raphael Joseph,
convicted for murdering eight people in the Virgin Islands
and soon to be pardoned by the territory's governor. Here's
the rub: Joseph plans to settle in Santa Cruz to study to
become a counselor, of all things, at the University of California.

"You should be outraged! We've got to scare this guy
off! And by the way, Congress, our beautiful friends in the
Congress [remember the Democrats are, for a few more
hours, still in control], are the ones who gave the Virgin
Islands governor the power to free this loser! God bless
America!"

The first caller, Joe from Santa Cruz, claims that the

answer lies in the Santa Cruz Armed Militia, a vigilante group. Kamb likes what he hears: "Is that not the power of the people coming back? If they decide to grab this guy, beat the crap out of him in an alleyway, so be it!"

Impressed by this awesome display of peace-officer guidance, of problem-solving and community outreach, I turn up the volume. The callers are almost exclusively male, indulging themselves in a little locker-room bull session. When Kamb asks Brad from Campbell what he would do if Joseph came to his town, Brad responds, point-blank, "It's called a Remington 870."

"Are you a good shot?" snickers Kamb.

"I don't have to be," Brad answers, riding off into the sunset with the other boys in the Gym Shorts Gang.

And into the swirl of idealism that distinguishes male adolescent bravura walks a small boy. Patrick, no more than eight or nine, hasn't had the chance to turn into a stooge. Yet. He's been to school; he suggests writing to his congressman to influence the situation, speak his mind.

"What if that doesn't work?" probes Kamb, bored.

"You could protest," is Patrick's cheerful reply.

"Where are you going to protest?"

"I don't know," Patrick utters, growing frustrated. Then he gives up. "I don't know. My brother says to just get out a shotgun."

"Well, whatever it takes," insists the voice of wisdom conducting this impromptu Civics 101.

Interstate 5, near Albany, Oregon

January 4.   **10:33 a.m. KXPC-AM.**

Hungover and getting over a fight, my friend Katie and I leave San Francisco for Seattle. En route, we scan the AM, settling down for a while here at "Pure Country" just in time for this morning's segment of "Strange Question." Today's quiz: "Other than agricultural or business concerns, what is the one thing that Iowa leads the nation in, hands down?"

The caller with the correct response will win a "family pack" of tickets to a movie called *House Guest*.

"Is it auto manufacturing?" guesses the first caller, a good listener. Sorry, business concern.

"Is it beauty pageants?"

"Can I give you a creepy one? Is it small little towns?" suggests a woman who's watched *Blue Velvet* too many times.

"Is it teen pregnancy?"

Earlier this morning, on NPR in Eugene, a BBC journalist reported that the Thai electorate just lowered the voting age from twenty-one to eighteen, expanding the suffraged population by 2.25 million young people. CBS News attended a press conference for ascending Speaker of the House Newt Gingrich, who gushed that he is proud to be involved in "such a romantic, mythic part of America" and can only describe the way he feels as "overwhelmed."

My lips are chapped from the winds of change. What will it mean? What's romantic about Gingrich's unmerciful scorn for teenage women? What's mythic about the fact that Jesse Helms, ambassador of fear, will chair the Senate Foreign Relations Committee and represent America to the United Nations, and thus the world? I, too, am overwhelmed. One country confides in the future, trusting its youth, while another slams down its fists and demands an old package in a different wrapping.

Is a little Oregonian trivia supposed to ease your mind, save your soul? Can a family pack of *House Guest* tickets really cheer you up when your son will die invading Cuba, museums you loved will close their doors, and your grandmother perishes of hypothermia when the Social Security checks dry up? I think not. My head is jammed with meaningless data. Oh sure, I can wow my friends with my in-depth knowledge of *Archie* comics characters and the *Happy Days* television program, but what good is that?

And the answer to the question "Other than agricultural or business concerns, what is the one thing that Iowa leads the nation in, hands down?" We drove out of range before I could find out.

January 5.

Yesterday, Portland made me nervous and the radio didn't help. I spent a few pointless months there when I was nineteen, and hadn't been back since. The town looked shabby and sad in the sunlight, as I tuned in an AM sermon hosted by a singsongy preacher with an ironic bent.

"Why, if man is basically good . . . ?" he begins the next twenty-three sentences. "Why, if man is basically good . . . ?" did a man in the choir get mugged last night, did a woman he knows get raped, did thieves break in and steal a family's belongings, did he hear on the news that two teenagers killed their parents, and so on. Man is basically evil, he cries, that's why. He didn't convince me, but Johnny Cash tried.

This morning before everyone else woke up, I went through my friend Chris's records and played a really rise-and-shine, high-voltage album by sunshine chanteuse Nico before I switched to the Man in Black's last effort, *American Recordings*. A dreary little ballad, by Mr. *Pure Pop for Now People*, Nick Lowe, called "The Beast in Me" stopped me cold.

It's slow; though it's not the tempo but rather Cash's bleak and painful voice that forced me to face my own ugliness. *"God help the beast in me,"* he moans.

That Portland preacher bought a ticket on the wrong guilt trip, relying on examples of commandments broken, of killing and headline crime. By drilling his congregation with dramatic case histories, he neglects the smaller, infinitely more suitable acts against goodness and decency. Most likely, his average listener had never mugged another pedestrian, shot her husband, or robbed from the poor, but what if, like the beast in me, she had just abandoned her best friend in a time of crisis to ward off her own paranoia by getting drunk alone?

January 7. 9:51 a.m. KKDZ 1250-AM "Kidstar Radio".

"That was the Supremes, from—now this is scary—way back in 1964," bellows the condescending voice of "Kidstar" DJ Great Scott. The station's ads sum up its mission: "Radio just for kids and kids are great people."

If kids are great people, then Kidstar aims to keep them great, or at least well-behaved, balancing its intermittent fun facts with brainwashing tolerance-building songs that claim *"my mother's Jewish, my father's a Buddhist"* or even Robert Palmer's yawner, "Every Kind of People."

Yesterday, I heard a silly little song about a huge sandwich and this morning I enjoyed an old Steve Martin routine about his cat who embezzled $3,000 to buy cat toys, but most of the programming falls flat, Paula Abdul's version of "Zippity Doo Dah" being a good example.

My friend Lucy listens with me. She teaches first grade at an inner Seattle elementary school. I ask her if her students listen to this station and she replies, "They listen to KUBE 93," which has a Top 40–rap format. "They want to listen to what they see on TV," she continues.

I can't imagine anyone over the age of four becoming halfway engaged with this perkiness, with sugary readings of school lunch menus and the lame hawking of Kidstar merchandise as "Absolutely Hot!"

Great Scott reads a tidbit that the universe is so vast and empty that it resembles a building twenty miles high, twenty miles wide, and twenty miles deep, which contains only a single grain of sand. "Wow!" he hollers. "Does that make you bamboozled or what?" That depends—is "bamboozled" a synonym for *nauseous*? Or what?

3:45 p.m. KUOW-FM 94.9 NPR.

Sometimes the only way to be surprised by National Public Radio is to miss the long-winded, topic sentence–laden introductions to their stories. Driving through town, Lucy turned on the radio as a female NPR news voice (somehow they all seem to sound alike in their sober nasal condescension) finishes a sentence. ". . . one of the city's trendiest neighborhoods. The espresso bars and cafes are thriving even by Seattle standards." As she goes on to describe high-rent Capitol Hill shops with art deco furniture, I'm thinking it's another "gentrification of Seattle" story. This morning I read in *Rolling Stone* that Sub Pop—standard-bearer of American independent record labels, Nirvana's first home, and fountainhead of the Seattle Sound—just sold 49 percent of its holdings to the Elektra corporation. While it's unclear if the move is a sale or a sellout, on a symbolic level it's the signal of an era's end. Thus, art deco fails to shock. Then suddenly the reporter, Beth Fertig, swiftly crosses the street. Good-bye boutique, hello junkies. The first two boys she meets, unemployed and wearing various forms of facial piercing, "say heroin, or dope, as they call it, is all over Capitol Hill."

After citing a recent Seattle public-school survey which reported that 6 percent of local eighth-graders claim to have tried the drug, Fertig drops in on three user/dealers. Bob, Evelyn, and Steve, now in their midtwenties, began shooting up as teenagers. Evelyn came from an abusive home and explains the root of her addiction: "Oh, and it's, it's marvelous. When I, first time I did it, I was just so excited . . . you lay on your ass, and you sleep and you dream. It's an escape. It's oblivion. It's the easiest way in the world to avoid all those big emotional problems that you've been expending all your emotional energy to keep in the back of your mind." When I heard Fertig's response—"This may be part of the reason why heroin is so popular"—I was thinking, "Well, duh."

Her elaboration is even more frightening. I can understand

the desire for oblivion, but to hear that overdose deaths have risen by 60 percent in the last three years as a fashion statement becomes an unspeakable horror. Bob, Evelyn, and Steve claim that most of the younger users are middle-class kids from the suburbs who "just show up on weekends, trying to look cool." "They say heroin is almost as trendy as cocaine was in the eighties," Fertig continues, "only heroin is the antipower drug, the choice of outsiders and grunge rockers, like Kurt Cobain." Evelyn concurs. Calling them "puppy junkies," she maintains, "They obviously come to Seattle hoping to see rock stars. They want to know where the rock stars buy their dope so they can buy it from the same dealer, you know what I mean? 'I go to so-and-so, and that's who sold, you know, Kurt his last shot.'"

Cobain's considerable contribution to art will always be shadowed by this other legacy. While his music led so many young people to freedom, his habit has induced others into the prison of addiction. But Sasha, a young user, doesn't see it like that. If it's not one prison, it's another: "I don't have to listen to somebody's authoritarian rule. I've gotten rid of the car loan, the rental payments, the insurance payment. I've gotten rid of the credit card. I've gotten rid of, you know, the electric bill, and it's like, surprising how little you need to actually live and be happy. And today if I get spun or junked, or drunk or high, or stoned or whatever, great, and if I don't, I don't.''

Bozeman, Montana

January 9.   **9:30 a.m.**

I leap up the familiar granite steps to KGLT, polished for the new semester. The first time I climbed them, I was seventeen, invited to read my eleventh-grade odes to angst on a short-lived poetry program called *Bards Anew*. "I am the tree that grows amidst the rocks," I read, with all the teenage torment I could summon, "twisted, but strong, admired but not loved." I was thrilled to be imposing my pain on the world that caused it.

A few days later, the program aired and I sneaked out of the underage section of a Steel Pole Bath Tub show to listen, for the first time, to my own voice coming out of a friend's car radio in the Sundance Saloon parking lot. I went back into the bar, once again, just some kid, a threat to somebody's liquor license, another unstamped hand. I was used to being in the way. But that night, things were different. I had been ON THE AIR.

Plus, I had seen it, that day at the station—Utopia, Shangri-La, El Dorado—the KGLT record library. Albums I had only imagined, from reading John Rockwell's *All American Music*, checked out from the public library the previous summer: John Cage, Harry Partch, Ornette Coleman. If it was noisy, I cared.

I finished high school a semester early, tree that grows amidst the rocks and all, in January of 1988. I started college at Montana State two months later, signing up for the KGLT apprentice class before I got around to registering for my courses. Three months after that, I was FCC-licensed, hosting my own show, *The Twentieth Century*, at age eighteen. My slogan: "Tune in to the twentieth century. After all, it's almost over."

I took over the Wednesday-afternoon "classical" slot, home for ten years to midday Mozart. I made enemies fast, playing mostly American composers from Elliot Carter to Jimi Hendrix. To sandwich Bartók's *String Quartet No. 5* between the Velvet Underground's "Black Angel's Death Song" and the Shangri-Las' "I Can Never Go Home Anymore" seems silly, cute even. But as sound, as an appreciation for the violence of which violins are capable, it worked.

I had the religion called "art of our time." As an orchestral composer then myself, I took on each complaining caller (and there were several every show) with a zealot's tirade against the long-dead. "Don't you want to hear out your compatriots?" I would plea. "Not really," was their inevitable reply. My radio philosophy was terribly simplistic; I played the music I wanted to hear. I soon learned that afternoon office workers would rather type to Schubert or Cheap Trick than Partch's *Delusion of the Fury*. My most common request was not for a particular piece of music but this: "Make it stop." And after a year of needling bassoons and cracking clarinets, I was worn out. Besides, I had figured out once and for all rock 'n' roll was a lot more fun.

But there was more to KGLT than music. I joined the news staff in the summer of 1988, when there were two big stories, the Olympics and the Yellowstone fires. Mostly we collaged together bits and pieces from the AP wire or features from strange little organizations such as Mother Earth News. Once, at the local Holiday Inn, I attended the big Department of the Interior press conference about the fires. All the networks showed up with their vans and equipment and I arrived on my bike (bearing a KGLT bumper sticker), yanked my little cheap-ass tape recorder out of my backpack, and stuck it next to the CBS microphone.

Our newscasts bordered on the incompetent, often sounding as if we should give up collecting news on our bikes and just use them to deliver papers. Anyone who relied on us as their primary journalistic source was pushing the limits of citizenship. We massacred the reading, cracked up frequently, and blatantly shaped the presidential election coverage in the favor of Michael Dukakis (or at least against George Bush). Dave Wendel, the fiercest editorialist among us, turned into a two-headed media/media-critic monster, often countering some White House press release with eloquent commentary along the lines of "What a bunch of crap!"

It was news delivered with a punk ethic: Do it yourself. We sounded like members of the audience who had walked in off the street, and of course we were. We even had punk theme music, Gang of Four's slicing "I Found That Essence Rare," with the line *you always get what you ask for.*" And with us you got . . . well, you never quite knew. In later years, the news team cleaned up its act and actually attempted to be informative broadcasters. It was better; it just wasn't as funny.

A job on the news staff warranted a spot on the station's executive staff. I don't recall that we accomplished that much at those meetings, hiring new people, reading apprentice applications, or occasionally chucking or choosing syndicated programs. We hung out, we argued, we talked about records. While the general manager ran the show, each one of us had a voice, a vote. We weren't exactly running a business; it was more like running an art project. The point is, we were running something. And people listened. It was remarkable. Don Yates of Seattle's KCMU criticized the feeling in *Option* magazine: "It's like [KCMU station manager] Chris Knab told me, when you put a person behind a microphone, they all of a sudden develop this sense of power, this sense of ownership."

As I reach the third floor, I wait until the ON AIR light is turned off before I burst into the KGLT studio. Barrett Golding, DJ, producer, audio artist, and my good friend, turns around to give me a hug and barely shuts up for the next couple of hours of his show and straight through lunch. If I were photographing him, I would use long-exposure film to capture the speed of his motormouth.

Barrett, like a lot of brilliant people, is a mess, and so is his show in a wonderful KGLT sort of way. He tells me that Marvin Grainger of KEMC (the Billings NPR affiliate) characterizes KGLT's spontaneity with a little irritation: "You guys are so damn live."

Barrett jolts around the studio like a hyperactive child. He's an instinctive collaborator, feeding off other people incessantly, pumping them for information, for stories, for jokes, and firing back his own opinions and anecdotes twice as fast. His voracious attention span, or maybe lack thereof, allows him to cue up one record, listen to another, answer the phone, and hold a conversation in a ten-second period, crash-landing onto the mike when he figures it's time.

When he has a visitor, his show abruptly begins to reflect the conversation. I mention my visit to Olympia last weekend to hear a mutual friend's band and he lurches for a Hole CD and puts on "Rock Star." "*Well I went to school in Olympia,*" it begins, and he successfully manages to censor out all four

of Courtney Love's screeching *fuck*s in the name of radio
friendliness.

Our crony Ben Lloyd, architect and KGLT DJ/producer,
comes in and sits down, complaining about a proposal he
has to write for a design job. I commiserate about the
graduate-school applications I was suffering through this time
last year, and *voilà*, Barrett's scouring the spoken-word section.
He airs Hugh Gallagher's "3A Essay" about a college applica-
tion. ("I know the exact location of every item in the supermarket. I have performed covert operations for the CIA. I
sleep once a week. When I do sleep, I sleep in a chair. While
on vacation in Canada, I successfully negotiated with a group
of terrorists who had seized a small bakery. The laws of physics
do not apply to me. I balance, I weave, I dodge, I frolic, and
my bills are all paid." He just hasn't gone to college.)

Michael Weaver, the station's music director, walks in as
Barrett plays the Silver Jews. Barrett offhandedly comments,
"Hey, Michael, I think you'd like this group." But Michael,
a wiry encyclopedia of indie records, knows more than I
ever cared to learn about the Silver Jews, clearing up their
connection to his favorite pop group, Pavement. Suddenly,
everyone's bouncing around the studio, pulling CDs and
talking too much, making me terribly homesick for such
indulgent recordspeak, which always begins with the simple
but magical phrase, "Listen to this!"

January 10.   **1:45 p.m. KGLT 92-FM.**

Radio is the playground of coincidence. Just as I rip myself
away from my paperback copy of Stanley Booth's *The True
Adventures of the Rolling Stones*, I turn on KGLT and hear
"You Can't Always Get What You Want." Afterward, the
DJ announces his stunningly creative set, ushering in the
Stones with Bob Dylan and Van Morrison sixties standards.
Still, it prompts me to look up a passage I read this morning
concerning Booth's life thirty years ago, in 1965:

I had left Tulane and was in Memphis, working for the Tennessee Department of Public Welfare, an outfit that confirmed every fear I'd ever had about the social system. I would come out of a house that stank with the ammonia smell of poverty, start my car, turn on the radio—there was interesting music on the car radio for the first time since 1957—hear the Beatles or the Supremes and have to turn the radio off. The happiness of popular music was unbearable at such times, but I could always listen to the Stones. I sensed the strong blues truth that underlay their music.

From the looks of things, "You Can't Always Get What You Want" is turning into the national anthem. Problem is, what if you can't get what you need?

January 13.

Faced with a choice of boring and dumb or boring and high-brow, which would you pick? *Baywatch* is the most popular television program on the same planet that turns away half a million Wagner groupies per year clamoring for Bayreuth Festival tickets. *"Here we are now, entertain us."*

I am opposed to Gingrich and company's proposal to sever government support for the Corporation for Public Broadcasting (CPB), but it's not because I find myself responding to NPR's *Morning Edition* with "Gee, I never thought of that" gestalt shifts. Not to mention the fact that it's old news that every self-respecting, non-pod child in America wishes Barney would fuck off and die, preferably painfully, in a fiery, tortuous mass ritual. Though nonurban public television stations (such as Bozeman's KUSM, Montana's only PBS affiliate) rely heavily on CPB funds, many small, listener-supported radio stations, such as KGLT, receive no CPB money, because they channel their resources into programming instead of the full-time staffers required for CPB aid. Still, even though a goodly portion of public programming is lifeless, dull, and occasionally pretentious, pulling the plug on the CPB, thereby requiring those stations to either fold or succumb to commercial sponsorship, effectively closes the door on the minute amount of adventurous work that seems to squeak by the complacency patrol.

Today's edition of the *Bozeman Daily Chronicle* contains an editorial by local columnist Marjorie Smith, identified as a "Bozeman arts advocate and a former member of the Foreign Service," titled "Public TV, Radio, the Antithesis of Elitism." She claims to only watch public television and, "given a choice," to listen only to public radio. She has a problem with the accusation that public broadcasting has been called elitist, arguing that the commercialization of public broadcasting would lead to audience-supported satellite superstations only available to those who can afford a satellite dish. She may be right, but she also claims, "According to my dictionary, the first definition of 'elite' is 'the best or most skilled members of a given social group.' If we take the 'given social group' to be music lovers, this definition of elite would fit my understanding of classical music and jazz. They are my favorite forms of music because they are the most difficult for the performers and the most challenging for the listeners." (She has obviously never sat through the deafening noise, disgusting film backdrops, and blinding light of a Butthole Surfers show, the very essence of "challenging.") "This music stretches people as well as entertaining them," she continues.

"Difficult"? In that case, maybe there should just be only one channel constantly spitting out a tape loop of Yo Yo Ma's version of "Flight of the Bumblebee." I mean, that is one tough song. This whole "challenging and difficult" argument not only completely misses the point about the greatness of art, but it is downright un-American. Lester Bangs, who always argued for real rock 'n' roll, once wrote, "It's not about technique. It's not about virtuosity, twenty-five years at Juilliard, contrapuntal-counterpoint, the use of ⁶⁄₈ time in a Latin-tinged context. *This stuff is not jazz. . . .* This stuff is dirt bikes doing brodies: How long does it take to learn how to start up and ride one?"

The fact is, NPR is so devoid of dirt bikes doing brodies I'm still trying to decide if I'd miss it at all. To argue for its rescue by lamenting the loss of the Metropolitan Opera fails to convince me further. Maybe now that it's being led in handcuffs down the death-row corridor, NPR will take a look at its programming—safe stories and orchestral warhorses— and think about ways to hep it up.

January 14.   **12:00–3:00 p.m. KGLT.**

I spent this afternoon back in the DJ saddle, subbing my friend Megan's rock show on KGLT. I passed the first two hours all alone in a swirl of music, studio monitors cranked to bursting. Around two o'clock, two scruffy college boys showed up. They were about twenty years old, with their eyes peeled, mostly on the CDs lining the shelves on the studio walls.

"Can I help you?" I asked, glancing at one of the many flyers bemoaning recent album thefts.

"We just want to see what you have," alleged the taller one.

Now they had my attention. I watched their fingers as they mooned over the hundreds of recordings. They were transfixed.

As it turned out, they had never before seen a radio station. They were just walking through the student union building, got curious, and climbed up the stairs. They didn't say much, but they sat down and watched. I played boy-rock songs by Neil Young, the Melvins, Pure Joy, and the Sweet, but they surprised me by requesting the female yelps of PJ Harvey.

"You can do it too, you know," I mentioned, and told them about apprentice class and when the applications were due. One of them wrote it down and asked me to turn up the volume. We sat there for a while longer without talking, just listening. They smiled, thanked me, and left.

A few hours later, buying some wine at the Community Food Co-op, at a friend's party, at the Filling Station bar listening to an over-the-top punk band from Missoula called the Banned, I was treated to the gracious immediacy of small-town feedback. About seventeen people approached me with "Heard your show" or "Loved that James Brown," one acquaintance rolled his eyes and hissed "eclectic," while another enjoyed my discussion of Hole's predatory song "Plump" as a celebration of the reintroduction of wolves into Yellowstone Park. If there is one thing I miss about living in Montana, it is this unwavering possibility of connecting with the community, and, through radio, quite literally having a voice.

January 16.   **12:42 a.m.**

I came home at midnight, restless. I rummaged in my parents' basement, dug out my cross-country skis, and took off around town. It must have snowed four inches and it was still coming down in huge flakes. It was so quiet you could hear them hitting the ground. I sped around the streets, completely alone. It was my first snowstorm in a year.

Wearing a dopey après-ski grin, I turn on the radio and hear, "What you do is, you get all the welfare moms a scope on a tripod, shooting all the illegal aliens." And at that moment, my snowy peace melted into a dirty pool of ugliness and shame. I flick off the radio and stew. "Try again," I tell myself a few minutes later, and this is what I found moving through the dial: ". . . seeking the death penalty . . . An American woman from Austin, Texas, has been killed in Cambodia. . . . Relax and enjoy, it's a whole new adventure waiting for you. . . . *Playboy's* playmates' private pleasures . . . 1-800-34-NO TAX . . . They shot you in the back. . . ." And finally, a country singer chimes in, *"This ain't no place for children."*

9:15 a.m. KGLT.

Turn on the radio, and hear THAT VOICE on this, his day. He's talking about how he wants to be remembered: "I'd want somebody to say that Martin Luther King Jr., tried to love somebody."

January 17.

Ben Lloyd and I walk around town interviewing people about their memories of listening to the radio. The cashier at Joe's Parkway market talks about driving to work and hearing that Kennedy was shot, while my father, who swapped tall tales with my friends for four solid hours last night, shied away from the microphone, only saying that listening to the radio "helps me not to be so lonesome." A boy behind the counter of the Pickle Barrel sandwich shop screamed, "Radio sucks! Those DJs really piss me off!" A guy on the street remembered calling a station to win Van Halen tickets and when he lost, being rudely asked to "get off the line, asshole."

Our friend Jim Kehoe calls radio "the soundtrack for my life" and remembered "one time being in Los Angeles and I used to scoot around the dial and I heard Bob Seger, the same song, on eight different stations at the same time. And then once, driving through Chicago, it was really hot and we were kind of stuck there on the Dan Ryan. We were listening to all the Jeffrey Dahmer stories. We had only AM radio because my sister and I couldn't agree on tapes and the FM didn't work. Then we came across this gospel station. It had really good music and great ads for the South Side Meat Shop, which sold everything that I'd never eaten on a cow. And great ads for faith healers like Sister Cross. You know, if someone put a mojo on you kind of stuff."

January 19.   5:00 p.m.

They could be "just the facts," a who-what-where-when info whirlwind: Red Cross blood drive, Thursday, noon. The public-service announcement has a time-honored tradition of boring exposition and cutesy connections, like Jerry Garcia's spot on forest-fire prevention spoken over the Grateful Dead's dreary "Fire on the Mountain." But at KGLT, in-house PSAs can turn into sixty-second exercises in obtrusive silliness and obnoxious exercises in comedy, the point being to fill people in without putting them to sleep.

My friend Drake Socie (a local rock promoter for Mothlight
Productions), Ben Lloyd, and I make a PSA for one of Drake's
upcoming shows featuring the bands Kill Creek and Mule.
The script:

SARAH.   My grandpa used to have a mule by the name of
Buster.

DRAKE.   Well what the shoo-fire happened to him?

SARAH.   He died. *(Music starts: Mule.)* All the king's horses
couldn't bring Buster back to life, but Mothlight
Productions is doing the next best thing.

DRAKE.   Please welcome Detroit's Mule to Cow Town
Wednesday, February 8, at the Filling Station.

SARAH.   And if that's not a carrot sweet enough to gnaw
on *(Music segues to Kill Creek.)*, Kill Creek from
Lawrence, Kansas, will whinny and kick your
dreams come true. *(Music segues back to Mule.)*

BEN.   That's Mule, Kill Creek, plus Bozeman's own
Snuffy's Impala on Wednesday, February 8, at
the Filling Station for anyone eighteen and older
at nine o'clock.

DRAKE.   You can lead a horse to water . . .

SARAH.   But you have to be twenty-one to drink.

January 20.   **3:26 p.m. KGLT.**

In the middle of listening to a rock show hosted by Jon
Moreau, aka Johnny Hot Wheels—a sometime engineering
student / mining demolitions expert from the logging town
of Libby, Montana—I hear Hole's "Doll Parts" with Courtney
Love's abrasive repetitions of the phrase *"Someday, you will
ache like I ache,"* to which Hot Wheels replies as the song
ends, "That may or may not be true."

January 24.   **4:30 p.m.**

And lo, having descended into the bowels of the Midwest, do I ascend the staircase to my new apartment, and thus my new life. After Marion, my Scottish angel landlady, closes the door behind her, I am left alone with two suitcases and a radio. Unsure exactly why I just left behind a community, a half-dozen true friends, three encouraging mentors, and my fiercely doting parents for this self-imposed exile, I turn it on. I hear two friendly voices: The first is Martin Booksban's, over the applause for a New York Philharmonic stab at Wagner. As a teenage trumpet player, I spent a lot of time with announcer Booksban, the guide to the Philharmonic season. Just hearing him talk, I feel that old adolescent gawkiness coming back. The second is Kurt Cobain singing "Lithium" and I think that if I'd had a voice like this sucking on the words *"I'm so ugly, that's OK 'cause so are you"* and then hurling them back across the room at age fifteen, I might not have cried myself to sleep every night until college.

9:00 p.m. NPR.

I listen to the first half of the State of the Union address on the radio, with Marion and the neighbor, Jorge (who says that radio in his native Honduras attempts to "talk about the life"), before we switch to TV. On the radio, dealing only in the Southern-statesman drawl of Clinton's voice, it all makes sense, even sounding eloquent in its measured phrases punctuated by the smatterings of applause that echo with consensus-building and friendship. On the tube, however, the eye sees what the ear can't hear: Al Gore's narcotic gaze, Newt Gingrich's sarcastic grin, Bob Dole's arching eyebrows, and the women of Washington plopped into the audience in bright dresses the colors of plastic Easter eggs.

January 26.

Standing at the Walgreen's drugstore checkout line, nonchalantly buying gum and lightbulbs, I glimpse the face that nags at my conscience, provoking me with vicious eyes through a cloud of smoke, the *Time* magazine logo stamped across his forehead like the mark of the beast. "Is Rush Limbaugh Good for America?" demands the headline. His throat pinched by a garish tie, he grips a smoldering cigar turning into ash. They say that inhaling secondhand smoke pollutes the lungs worse than the act of smoking itself and there's no heavier breather on American radio than Limbaugh, who huffed and puffed and blew the House down, not to mention the Senate.

I buy the magazine and take it home. He tells interviewer Margaret Carlson, "I'm not a hater, not one of the angry radio guys. I'm an entertainer with a conservative agenda who wouldn't have twenty million listeners if I spewed venom."

The fact that Limbaugh—and radio talk-jocks of his ilk— is almost universally recognized as a catalyst in overturning the November congressional elections, offers me, a woman he might categorize as a "feminazi," one small bright side: His influence confirms, for better or worse, the continuing power of radio in the United States. Sixty years after Hitler wrote, "Without the loudspeaker, we would never have conquered Germany," he is the noisy announcer to the silent majority. But as Mr. Crowley, my high-school French teacher always warned, "It's the quiet ones who get you in the end"— the way neighbors of serial killers tend to comment, "He was such a quiet man."

I'm not afraid of Limbaugh, the P. T. Barnum of the conservative circus—where there's smoke there's hot air. I'm not even truly afraid of Congress, which has an inefficient track record, to say the least. What scares me most are the voters. Limbaugh's flock, as characterized by the psychofans who call his program not to discuss ideas but to anoint his feet in the oil of their worship, lack their leader's passion for theater. Just as a good sideshow actor can make an audience forget about the stage and draw them into a story by the power of his voice, Limbaugh's listeners will not wake up until the lights go on. It's just a show, folks. It's just a show.

January 27.   **11:00 a.m. WLS 960-AM.** *The Rush*
                                              Limbaugh Show.

Well, maybe not. The House just passed the Balanced Budget Amendment and Limbaugh can't shut up about it (not that he can shut up, period). This, he tells us, is only the beginning. Newt Gingrich has phoned him this morning. Limbaugh refers to the speaker affectionately as "Mr. Newt," which sounds like the name of a cartoon salamander instead of one of the two most powerful men in Congress. Mr. Newt tells Rush that he plans—for April 15, 1996—to call a vote on the Constitutional amendment which would require a three-fifths supermajority to raise taxes. "I suggested to Mr. Newt," chuckles Limbaugh, " 'Why don't you call it the "Rush Amendment"?' He laughed. I laughed."

And the country was nervous that JFK would seek counsel in the Pope?

Limbaugh belongs to a long line of unofficial political puppeteers in American history. Just think of that presidential Fozzie Bear, Ronald Reagan, voicing the opinions whispered in his ear by the Jim Henson of first ladies, Nancy. Rush is one of the loudest Hillary bashers clogging the airwaves, skewering Rodham-Clinton for exerting exactly the sort of unelected influence that he enjoys.

But Rush wants it both ways, to be a political darling and a populist maverick. In case you were worried, he sets the record straight:

I told you people yesterday. Somebody called here and asked about allegiance to politicians and so forth and I said that my allegiance has never been to politicians. My linkage is always and has always been and will always be with you, The People, the audience, the people of America. That's to whom I'm tuned. And I have things that I agree with and

*I like and I have my passions and I fight for 'em, Republican
or not.*

He then plunges into a long tirade condemning the "mainstream media" for failing to foresee the fall of the Berlin
Wall and the collapse of the Soviet Union (which is true,
Tom Brokaw was probably just as surprised as everyone else).
Limbaugh's problem is that he starts with a grain of truth,
sometimes a mere droplet, then proceeds to riff like some
sort of pompous jazz soloist who hasn't noticed that the band
went back to the melody without him. He goes a little nuts:

> *To them, the Soviet Union was a great place.... To the
> mainstream press, our problems in getting along with the
> Soviet Union were strictly our fault. Did they predict
> the downfall of the Soviet Union? No. Did they predict
> the falling of the Berlin Wall? No. Because many in the
> mainstream press didn't think that either of those were any
> big deal.*

That's right. As I recall, the cover of *Time* the week the Wall
fell read, "Wall Comes Down, No Big Whoop."
    With an apocalyptic flair, Limbaugh speaks to his faithful
listeners as Noah must have addressed his pious family on
the ark, amidst the screams of drowning sinners:

> *The equivalent of the Berlin Wall has fallen. Liberalism
> in America has actually been written out as a dominant
> ideological governing force in the United States. You ought
> to feel good about this, folks. In the broad sense, it is some-
> thing to celebrate and feel extremely smug and good about.*

If by "liberalism" he means a shared responsibility, a belief
in civil liberties and pure and simple kindness, I fear he may
be right.

January 28.   **9:00 p.m. WBEZ 91.5-FM. Joe Frank:**
In the Dark.

It's been a while since I gnawed on Joe Frank's gristle of embarrassment. Tonight's story, "Insomnia," is told by Dana Gould over a bed of inane, mildly disquieting synthesizer music that pushes a little too hard on the Flute button.

Gould grew up in the dead-end New England small town of Hopedale, Massachusetts, where, he deadpans,

Everyone in my family, at one time, drank. Every adult I knew, growing up, drank. Everyone in Hopedale drank. When I became a teenager, and my friends started to drink, every weekend I was faced with a simple social choice: I could go out and watch my friends drink or I could stay home and watch my family drink.

He says he's always had trouble sleeping because he's Catholic. Like me, like probably every Christian child in America, he suffered through this nightly call to the grave:

> *Now I lay me down to sleep*
> *I pray the Lord my soul to keep*
> *If I should die before I wake*
> *I pray the Lord my soul to take.*

I remember trembling as my twin sister and I performed this little daily duet, both of us eyeing the strange picture on the wall of the guardian angel guiding two small children (who, I thought, mixing mythologies, were Hansel and Gretel) in the dark, mentally asking her, "Can you help me out?" Or, as Gould sarcastically intones, " 'Good night, son. Try not to die in your sleep.' Because I actually thought as a kid, if I went to sleep, I could just slip into death."

His next sentence ties his childhood vistas of alcohol consumption and the Christian death cult to his dark humor: "I'm a comedian by trade. And I had built a wonderful reward system in my life where the more miserable I would be, the funnier I would get. And what I discovered, that by dwelling on the pain and the misery of my life, the more successful I became."

Now living in Los Angeles, he returns to Hopedale to visit his family over the Fourth of July weekend. It is excruciating. He returns to L.A., doesn't sleep, and suffers an emotional breakdown.

I had this one T-shirt I bought in Seattle at the Sub Pop record-label store. On the front of the shirt, in big letters, it said 'Loser.' And I always thought that it was so funny. I wore that on the plane the day I went to visit my parents. Something inside me wanted to show up at their house with 'Loser' written across my chest. I was on the floor and I spotted it and I picked it up and I walked down the beach, and crying, ripped it up and threw it in the ocean.

He finally restores himself after a three-hour phone call to his parents, telling his father, for the first time, that he loves him. That night, he says, "I became a member of my family."

I couldn't get Gould's voice out of my head. His story, lacking any sugary emotion, and delivered in a plainspoken, almost drastically simple manner, haunted the radio as I scanned past mambo and Tom T. Hall waxing about *"old dogs and children and watermelon wine."* I settled on an AM talk show where a little girl's voice cried, "I've never seen my father and he's never seen me and I feel sad inside." "Do you want to see him?" asks the host. "Sure. I just want to tell him that I love him."

January 29.   **9:58 a.m. WJMK-FM 104.3.**

I was listening to this computer-programmed oldies station (which plays brainless sets of Elvis, Gladys Knight, the Beach Boys, and Neil Sedaka) last night. I turned the radio off at Petula Clark's dippy "Downtown"—everything's great!—a song I have loathed since I was forced to practice it at trumpet lessons in junior high. Strangely, the song is still playing as I turn on the radio this morning, as if WJMK's power is hooked up to my stereo and all of Chicago has been waiting for me to get out of bed so that Petula can finish the song.

January 30.

This morning on the subway, on my way to my first day of graduate school at the Art Institute, I realize that I don't know when to get off. I panic and detrain. Above ground, I ask directions to Wabash Avenue. I find it, but turn the wrong way, north instead of south. Already five minutes late for class, I lose my mind. Just as I find the school, I stop dead. A radio screams through the windows of an empty Volkswagen Rabbit parked out front. It's Elvis singing "All Shook Up." "You got that right," I say to myself as I stand there and listen, falling deeper into the hole of tardiness. I figure that the King is a good omen, and go to my class, Art and Ritual. Not only is the professor five minutes later than me, but she announces that she has a voodoo shrine to Elvis and his dead twin standing in the middle of her living room. Welcome to art school.

January 31.   11:25 a.m. WLUP 97.9-FM "The Loop".

Wendy, the DJ, on Van Halen's new album: "You know, they show what happens with drunk driving and stuff, but they still rock."

January 31.   9:35 p.m. WDCB-FM 90.9 *Introduction to Poetry.*

The featured poet has written a depressing little tribute to the painter Edward Hopper. "The word that I was drawn to most in this poem about Hopper was 'stranger,'" intones the woman hosting the program. The poet responds, "That sense of being a stranger in your own landscape. . . . What you're getting is a private person in a public space, alone and vulnerable." This makes sense remembering any Hopper image that comes to mind, especially the Art Institute's warhorse, *Nighthawks*. But tonight, on the subway, I watched a teenaged white boy and a middle-aged black woman come together in an animated conversation, because he had the guts to break the ice with the wildly original opening line, "Did you ever get an infection?" He had just gotten his nose pierced this afternoon; she did hers a few months back. They talked for a while, politely. Maybe they were still strangers but they weren't alone. And yes, she's avoided infection: "So far."

> *If enough people think studying the media is a waste of time,*
> *then the media themselves can seem less influential than*
> *they really are. Then they get off the hook for doing what*
> *they do best: promoting a white, upper-middle-class, male*
> *view of the world that urges the rest of us to sit passively*
> *on our sofas and fantasize about consumer goods while they*
> *handle the important stuff, like the economy, the environment,*
> *or child care.*
>
> **—Susan Douglas,** Where the Girls Are

February 2.

Ad in today's *Chicago Reader* for radio station WXRT: "Last night, we snuck into your home, stole your CD collection and we're playing them right now." I walk over and turn on the station; they're playing Counting Crows (or as the guy standing behind me at the Fillmore last fall called them, "Counting Sheep"). Funny, I don't remember buying that one.

February 4. 6:00 p.m. WBEZ. *A Prairie Home Companion.*

I know people who love this man, this mellow throat, this chuckling raconteur of the upper Midwest. Why, why, why do I hate him so? Hate every breath he draws, every last tinkle of every last ivory he sings over? Garrison Keillor, obviously adored by thousands, rubs me raw.

He sings "Let's Fall in Love." Fine. We hear a corny, joking commercial for duct tape. We hear a polka. Okay.

Then he celebrates the birthday of Charles Lindbergh, "always a quintessential Minnesotan."

Describing Lindbergh's parents, Keillor notes that

> *they undoubtedly loved each other. But they were so entirely different. She was effusive and emotional and talkative. The father was [pause] a Minnesotan. He said once himself, "I find it impossible to express pleasure."*

And maybe that's it with Keillor—people love him because he's lacking in pain, but there's no real pleasure either, just a seamless, toothless, smug kind of smile. He goes on about Lindbergh:

> *Now if those Lindberghs up in Little Falls had just had a good record collection, and young Charles A. had access to a guitar and a harmonica, he'd been able to listen to Robert Johnson 78s, he might have become as this man on stage . . . John Hammond.*

Nothing could make my skin crawl more than hearing the self-satisfied Keillor even utter the *name* Robert Johnson— unless it's hearing the gooey rococo mess Hammond makes out of Johnson's "Come on in My Kitchen."

February 5.   **"Sound" column for *High Performance***
magazine.

"Why did you tell me that?" a German acquaintance asked me recently, after I had told a childhood anecdote.

"It was just a story," I answered, suddenly defensive.

"Americans are so damn narrative," he sighed.

Maybe it's the hick in me, this compulsion for punchlines and biography. It was fueled by hymns and ballads, heard in a sanctuary, on the radio. *I'm proud to be an Okie from*

Muskogee but take me back to Tulsa, I'm too young to marry. Because of your cheatin' heart, there's one cigarette in an ashtray and since some kill you with a fountain pen, are you washed in the blood of the lamb? Living in cities, up North, back East, out West, I couldn't hear my uncle's winking yarns as he sat on his porch, holding a banjo, saying "winda" when I guess he meant window. That could be why I can't get Terry Allen's sound collage *Dugout* out of my head, not to mention out of my cassette deck.

If Bill Clinton backs off every promise he made and walks away from every oath, it will hardly lessen this one small thrill—to hear the State of the Union address, however vapid its content, delivered with an Arkansas inflection. Terry Allen and his wife, Jo Harvey Allen, talk Texas as they narrate, and don't tell stories as much as they recount telling moments. *Dugout*'s family history is less an unbent timeline than it is a box of yellowed photographs dumped out on a floor. Allen picks them up, piece by piece; *Spring of 1959* says the first one, *1892* is marked on the next. Each tale becomes a landmark: a thirteen-year-old girl lies in a barn, drunk, with bloody knickers, a boy's father shoots his dog caught up in a fence, a doctor burns out a child's tonsils with an iron poker in the middle of a blizzard. These small narratives become familial common knowledge: "Daddy, tell me again about that dog," asks a son.

A man and a woman lie in the dark. As the crickets drone and a train passes by, they recollect. He played baseball, she played the piano. "She says a person has to dig into the heart of everything, and what little gets dug out is all there is, or all there will ever be. He says he remembers every game. She says she remembers every single song, and it no longer is just about the two of them. It's all of it, most of which can never be said."

• • •

Telling stories is a kind of digging, as is listening. Holding
hands in the dark like that just may be the sweetest, most
profound way to do it, but it can happen sitting on chairs
in a room full of strangers, all of whom are paying for the
privilege.

When my friend Barrett Golding told me about an audio
collage he was working on, recording a therapy group in
Bozeman, Montana, discussing their dreams, I quoted him
the old line, "If there's one thing people want to hear less
than other people's problems, it's other people's dreams."
The expected strange images surface: a woman taught to fly
by dolphins, a man who climbs a giant stethoscope listening
to the heartbeat of the world. But, listening to a tape of
Barrett's finished work, each voice is in awe of what they've
seen, becoming deeper over the crouched reverie of Joe Howard's score, played on the electric bass. The way these people
talk to each other, listening to what seem more like prophesies
and legends, warnings and visitations, than anything as everyday as dreams, takes on the religious function of congregation
as their stories turn into conversations. As one man put it,
"You don't exist separately." He speaks of the Old Testament,
that Joseph interpreted the Pharaoh's dream of seven fat
cows and seven lean ones as seven years of plenty followed
by seven years of famine, prompting the Egyptians to store
food. "The whole civilization was able to survive," he says,
"based on one dream." And so thousands lived because one
man listened to another.

Who, now, should we listen to, in order to live? Lately, I've
been listening to the radio, but I haven't heard the Texas
passion of Allen's couple or the communion of Barrett's Montana dreamers. What I've been hearing is Washington politicians—one who can't keep his word and a whole mob of
others whom I fear just might. Not only do they want to take

the babies from young mothers, they want to take the stories from us all. Not that we'll run out of narratives—paper's cheap and talk is free. Tape, production time, and recording equipment are not. *Dugout* and *Dreamtime* were aired on *New American Radio*, a program supported in part by the National Endowment for the Arts. For now.

Barrett funded his piece with an NEA grant. Without it, he claims, "It never would have gotten made. I couldn't even find the money for that much tape, much less the music." There is enthusiastic support for privatizing public radio, cutting off the already minimal government support of the arts. Barrett maintains that he would continue to find financial support for his work, but only pieces with a standard documentary format, unlike the barrage of voices and viewpoints in *Dreamtime*. He alleges that "the stories that are a little deeper, frequently need to be told through a sleight of hand, away from linear perception. That's the way the brain works, you have to trick it."

Deep and *different* don't sell. Or as Allen's ball player, lamenting the introduction of foul lines into baseball remarks, "Men who can hit on the extreme left or extreme right will be eliminated for those who can hit within the confines." In 1994, the major-league strike effectively eliminated, at least on the national level, the entire game. And if you can rob America of baseball and get away with it, who knows what will be taken next?

February 7.   **10:00 p.m.** *AP Network News.*

The weary, beaten voice of President Clinton announces that he was unable to settle the Major League Baseball strike and that he will turn the problem over to Congress for further negotiation: "Spring training is just nine days away and I think many Americans consider this pressing. At least when the bill goes to Congress, the American people can make themselves heard one way or the other." Should the American people be more angry at the fact that the man whose index finger we trust with the red button cannot solve even a sports crisis or that our most beloved act of play (not to mention primary metaphor of community and courage) has been turned into a greedy sham? As Terry Allen narrates about old-time baseball in *Dugout*, "That's the only way the game is played—with heart and for blood. Nobody made any money."

February 8.   **10:28 a.m. 97.9-FM WLUP**

Two buddy-movie types describe the sort of rhymes Dr. Seuss would be writing if he were still alive. One pal comes up with this little racist lyric:

> *Crackhead Jack sat on a bicycle rack, trying to sell his*
> *   big bag of crack.*
> *Crackhead Jack had pushed his stack to anyone named*
> *   Tyrone, Jose, or Mack.*
> *When along came a homey saying, Hi-diddle-dee. Hey*
> *   Jack! You're in my territory.*
> *I beg to differ, said Jack in a tiffer. You sell coke and*
> *   that is for a sniffer.*

And yet: the most famous crackhead in America right now is not Tyrone or Jose but none other than Fawn Hall, Ollie North's loyal, blonde aide-de-shred. According to a TV reporter from *Inside Edition* on a WJJD-AM talk show two days ago, Fawn has recently undergone rehab for crack addiction. It seems she married rock 'n' roll, a writer and drug buddy of Jim Morrison's who turned her on to the substance. As if that's not enough to bear, North doesn't return her calls. She's "crushed."

February 9.   **10:32 p.m. Dial scan.**

As if I wasn't depressed enough about the Republican sweep through Congress, Senator (and presidential contender) Bob Dole cheers me up further by reminding me, "Thirty Republican governors—think about it. And think about all the state legislatures that we took over, all the county courthouses, all the offices up and down the line. This was not just a victory at the top. This was a victory from the bottom up."

Change station. A heavy-metal singer is talking about how his band has taken the high road, resisting selling out like so many other rock bands that evidently aren't as cool as his:

You know, we never have written music for money. That's why we've taken the long route. . . . But you know what? It's status with symbol. [What?] There's a lot of bands that come out that sell three to five million records their first record—that's status with no symbol. [Again—what?] I mean, can you live with yourself at the end of the day? Do you think that you're really that good that your record sells that much, because it's not just a passing trend?

Interviewer: "Obviously some bands weren't able to live with themselves after that kind of success."

Metalhead (*understanding the allusion to Cobain*): "Yeah. You break up or you end up firing people or even worse, ultimately, you kill yourself."

Change station. Two men discussing support for the arts. Commentator number one: "Grants! We hate 'em! Nobody subsidizes plumbers [who happen to make more than $50 per hour but who's counting]! We think grants suck! They want to do away with the NEA, go right ahead!" Commentator number two: "I don't hate artists, you know, only the artists who are professors and you know who you are and I will find you, dammit!"

February 10.   **7:30–9:00 a.m. WBEZ-FM. National**
                        Public Radio's *Morning Edition.*

Today on *Morning Edition*, a cultural field trip to that stately
marbleized un-funhouse called the National Gallery of Art.
This is a cozy pairing, in that the National Gallery is the
NPR of museums, which is to say, loaded with an inflated
sense of its own stately importance. Luckily, today's tour
guide is longtime NPR host Susan Stamberg, who, refresh-
ingly, can be a bit of a goofball.

So can Claes Oldenburg, whose Pop retrospective (he prefers to call it an "anthology") she walks us through.

Stamberg describes her first Oldenburg experience, driving
by the famous spoon-and-cherry sculpture outside the
Walker Art Center. Her response? "Wow! Then there's the
giant outdoor clothespin in Philadelphia. Wow!"

Letting us in on a vaguely screeching noise in the museum,
Stamberg notes, "You know, I can't think of the last time it
was that I recorded a piece of sculpture."

Oldenburg replies, "That's right. This sculpture has a
voice. I've heard it do more groaning, but they're keeping it
very well greased here." (I bet they are.)

Though Stamberg ends her essay with the cliché line, "He
helps us see in a new way," she does communicate some of
the delight at seeing a big, funny sculpture of a Swiss Army
knife in such stuffy digs, "doing something we don't often
do in big serious art museums: we smiled."

It is a nice, quiet little piece of cultural substance. They'll
cover Oldenburg now that he's a textbook dweller, old news,
and has one foot in the grave. He comes off like a cute old
man who attends cloth-napkin receptions, not the crazed
freak of thirty years ago calling for an "art you can blow your
nose with." On second thought, the National Gallery has a
long history of supporting all kinds of snottiness.

February 11.   **12:00 p.m. WZRD-FM. Church of the**
                          SubGenius: *Hour of Slack*

The Church of the SubGenius, a religious parody group that worships a godhead named J. R. "Bob" Dobbs, airs a lovably wicked weekly broadcast of "sermons," media criticisms, musings, and just plain noise. This week, the Reverend Ivan Stang ponders his oppressively multimedia lifestyle after he "decided to surf the Internet, flush Bob Dobbs down the digital sewer, and take advantage of the virtual global-village idiots of the damned. . . . The other day," he continues,

this information overload just all avalanched at once. I was late to pick up my kids. I was charging the video batteries up so I could tape the school play. . . . I was listening to the CD player and the answering machine at the same time and trying to read the e-mail and pay the electric bill and the phone bill, when the family phone downstairs rang and the dogs started barking because the UPS man had come at the same time as the postman. And then the paper started spewing out of the fax machine and a tornado warning came on the TV.

Memphis

February 16.   **6:25 a.m.**

If Muslims have their Mecca and Catholics plot that Vatican visit, White Trash girls like me get misty at the mention of Memphis, and here I am just passing through. I wake up from a troubled sleep on the *City of New Orleans* train on my way to Mississippi to visit my twin sister, Amy. (Her husband, Jay, a soil scientist, is working near Natchez for the next few months.) I turn on my radio and watch Beale Street go by, scanning the dial for Elvis, of course, but even mythic Memphis sounds like everywhere else: Soundgarden for Pete's sake. Now, I like Soundgarden fine and all but I sure as hell do not want to hear "Black Hole Sun" in the King's home-town. No Jerry Lee, no Al Green, only . . . Bruce Springsteen's

"Born in the U.S.A." Making the best of it, I pretend El is singing. This isn't far-fetched, considering that had he lived, he probably would have added this one to his Vegas set. In fact, the song has Elvis all over it, encompassing seemingly irreconcilable viewpoints, pissed off about being forced to murder the Vietnamese in the name of God and country, but still a "cool rockin' daddy in the U.S.A." By the time this song was written in the 1980s, Elvis could have put together a big red, white, and blue light show to go with this, perhaps displaying all those cute photos of his Private Elvis years on huge video monitors, maybe ending the show with a kiss and a wave, walking offstage as a stars-and-stripes-motif curtain drops, then coming out to do an encore of the "Star-Spangled Banner" and "How Great Thou Art."

A group of dozens of men in cowboy hats boards the train, ruining my little fantasy. One sits down next to me and I grouchily move my stuff. Two minutes later his buddy comes and gets him to move to another car. He gets up and (I swear) tips his hat to me, saying, "Have a nice trip, little lady." I do not reply, though I do find the Soundgarden station again and happily listen to Hole, one of those "little lady" bands that all the little ladies seem to like so much.

Natchez, Mississippi

February 17.

Amy and Jay drive me around all day. We visit Christ Episcopal Church just outside of Natchez and traipse through its ancient, muddy graveyard. There's a sign inside the foyer that reads

Interrupted by the Civil War which desolated its churches— our own being no exception, for in 1864, it was entered by a band of Yankee ruffians belonging to an Illinois regiment stationed at Natchez who danced in the chapel, played lewd aires on the organ and wound up their sacrilege by stealing a part of the silver plate, composing the communion service.

"Lewd aires"! I laugh to myself, picturing drunken boys in blue demolishing the church's silence with a scorching chorus of the Civil War equivalent of "Louie Louie."

We continue through the Natchez Trace and the fabled Highway 61, visiting Civil War ruins, an Indian burial mound, watching the plantation houses go by, enjoying a lunch of collard greens and corn bread, and passing a little house where the snake handlers hold their meetings. I was primed for some devil's music as we turned on the car radio. I wanted songs about asking for water and getting gasoline, about fear of the future and regretting the past, about things going from bad to worse and getting bitter about being done wrong sung with guts and spit and wood and sounding like dirty floors and kindhearted women. Here's what I got: "99 Luftballoons"—mideighties German synth-pop clean enough to eat off. Where's a lewd aire when you need one?

Chicago

February 21.   **5:00 p.m. WRCX-FM 103.5.**

All day long, this station, which plays straight-ahead rock 'n' roll and heavy-metal music interspersed with lame, macho repartee (even from the female announcers), has hyped a "press conference," guarding some BIG secret that will change all our lives.

At five o'clock, "Mancow" asks for a drum roll. "You gotta be kidding me," he quips. "Is this right? It's right?"

I'm getting excited. What? A Beatles reunion—with John? Michael Bolton's finally dead?

"Ladies and gentlemen," he booms, "this will happen Friday, April 14, 1995. Ladies and gentlemen, Rock 103.5 presents Balance Bash '95 with Van Halen!!!!!!!!!!!!!!!! [*Cheers and clapping heard from studio.*] Yes!! Van Halen is coming to town! This is unbelievable!"

George Bush getting elected president after Iran-Contra was unbelievable. This is called a concert tour. Happens every day.

February 24.   **10:00 p.m. Dial scan.**

President Clinton: "Unless I miss my guess, a bill doesn't
become law until I sign it." Announcer: "Yeah! That's Bill!
He's still there saying he's got a pair!" And down the dial:
"Three industries make money on Valentine's Day—cards,
candy, and detectives." Says one private eye, "For us, it's like
Christmas," going on to describe how one of his female
clients went to a hotel where her husband was cheating on
her, knocked on his door, and handed him two dead roses.

February 28.   **"Rush Limbaugh's America"**
                      (*Frontline* documentary, PBS-TV).

I'll admit I was looking forward to this, thinking that good ol',
soon-to-lose-its-federal-funding, commie PBS wasn't above a
little good-humored character assassination. I still hate Rush
Limbaugh, but after watching this downright balanced documentary, however, I have to guiltily live with the fact that I
hate an awkward loner of an underdog who, according to his
mother, didn't even have a date for the prom. Tracking Rush's
professional career from Cape Girardeau, Missouri, high-
school DJ to middle-aged media monarch, he is labeled a
"new kind of star."

   Some of the most compelling tape comes from the (fright-
eningly) self-proclaimed "dittoheads," Rush's fans who don't
so much agree with the host as genuflect in front of him.
"Megadittoes, Rush," they frequently begin their calls. Not
content to worship solely in the electronic temple, they con-
gregate at restaurants called "Rush Rooms," such as the
Limbaugh-themed café called Ditto's. The dittoheads defend
their autonomy: A woman named Ann Reynolds exclaims,
"We all are freethinking people." But a young man named
Richard Lewis gets all wispy as he tells the camera, "Finally,
there's someone who's speaking for me."

   Though Limbaugh refused to be interviewed for the program, the producers have dug up some vintage Rush, including that dashing figure of a man making cute, enlightened

quips such as, "Feminism was established so that unattrac-
tive, ugly broads could have access to the mainstream."
(What's *his* excuse?) He "honors" Hillary Rodham-Clinton
because she "single-handedly destroyed her husband's presi-
dency." We watch him addressing his television audience
with, "Is this the best-looking audience in America?" (They're
all bleach white.)

Still, to his followers, he is a kind of savior who wrenched
the Republican party "out of the country club and made it
the people's party." (The mean, megalomaniacal, dangerous
kind of savior, but that's just me.) "No matter how scared
you are," according to Rush's e-mail pen pal Hazel from
Brooklyn, he makes you feel like "it can get better." Even
the nondittohead talk-show host and failed Bush campaigner
Mary Matalin claims that it was Rush's show that got her
through her post–1992 election depression.

Despite pointing out Rush's blatant homophobia (he says
his views are "in the mainstream"), and describing his disgusting former practice known as "caller abortions," a sort
of "there's no stopping him now" veil hangs over the entire,
hour-long description: PBS that even Rush might watch.

But as noon rolls around, WBEZ always slaps me in the face
with Marian McPartland. So today, instead of a CBC feature
I was anticipating on reactions to gangsta rap in the black
community, I get McPartland's *Piano Jazz.* I go take a shower
and when I come back some boring jazz guitar guy introduces
a piece he wrote about artist Joan Miró. It goes plink, plink,
chord; plink, plink, chord.

March 7.

Something Rush Limbaugh said the other day has been eating
at me. He was bragging about being invited to "The Big
Smoke," a cigar smokers' protest in Lafayette Park across
from the White House. He waxed thus:

> We in our society, ladies and gentlemen, have an ever-
> increasing bunch of ninnies who are dead set against
> anybody enjoying themselves. If you have a good time, some-
> body's going to be upset. If you have a good time doing
> something somebody doesn't think you should be doing, then
> they're going to be angry and they are going to use whatever
> clout, political or otherwise, they can get you to do to stop
> it. . . . Do you know why people smoke cigars? They like 'em!

Do you know why some men have sex with other men, Rush,
you homophobic reactionary? They like to!

March 10.   **9:55 p.m. Q101-FM.**

Ad for an upcoming Weezer concert: "The hottest bunch of
geeks goin'. . . . They might not be cool, but they're popular."

March 12.

Perfect cup, perfect hairbrush, perfect sink, perfect lamp.
And what's the perfect music on the radio? Italian opera.
California-born artist Andrea Zittel's sculptural environ-

I'm standing again tonight on a roof top looking out over London, feeling rather large and lonesome.

—Edward R. Murrow, London Blitz broadcast, September 21, 1940.

March 1.   **11:00 a.m. WLS-AM 960. The Rush Limbaugh Show.**

Rush did not watch the PBS portrait, though he does clear up that, yes, he did too date in high school.

March 3.   **9:30 a.m.**

In a cab through downtown Chicago, the driver is tuned in to an AM sports talk show in which a commentator discussing the baseball strike shoots down the claims that the whole seedy enterprise is un-American, reminding us that it's *more* American to go for bigger bucks.

March 5.   **10:00 a.m.–1:00 p.m. WBEZ. *CBC Sunday Morning.***

Invariably, funny and intelligent Canadian host Ian Brown's hinting at what's on tap for that mythic "third hour" and how he'll be "back in five" after the news whets my appetite.

ments—she calls them "perfect units"—in the Art Institute of Chicago's *About Place: Art of the Americas* exhibition are pared-down, architectural machines for living. Sleek, cubic, and portable, as if an International Style architect decided to design a trailer, it's hard to decide if these are oppressive, claustrophic spaces or cozy tributes to life on the go. The educational pamphlet asserts, "Zittel designs little 'buildings' intended to improve—to simplify and thus purify—the lives of the individuals who inhabit them. . . ." In that case, they should switch off *La Traviata* and scan the dial for something more pure and simple, like Bach or Chuck Berry.

March 19.

The biggest story in Chicago is the return of Michael Jordan to the game of basketball, and more importantly, the Chicago Bulls. The past week has witnessed much "will he or won't he and if so when and where?" speculation. But as this morning's *Tribune*'s front-page story notes, under the headline "Court is Back in Session," "One caller to a sports radio show Saturday had this to say about the scheduling of Jordan's first news conference: 'When Jesus comes back, you going to ask what time mass is?'"

9:23 p.m. WLS-AM. *The Jake Hartford Show.*

Concerning a local news story in which ten-year-old paperboy Jeremy Palmer saved his earnings and bought a bike that was promptly stolen, talk-show host Jake Hartford opines, "I think he should get a gun."

A caller sarcastically grumbles, "And what's this kid doing working anyway? He's supposed to sit home and whine and write letters to Bill Clinton about a summer jobs program." He recalls being harrassed on his own boyhood paper route by another boy with a BB gun who stopped bothering him after he fired back with a gas-powered pellet gun.

"See," Hartford notes, "weapons work."

"Yeah, they do," agrees the caller. "It was wonderful. I didn't have to call the police. I didn't have to whine."

Hartford says, "By the end of the night, either we should get this kid a bike, or we should get him a gas-powered pellet gun."

Fine advice, for 1955. I don't know what kind of guns the crack-dealing kids in my neighborhood are toting, but I'm sure a snazzy air rifle would really scare them off.

March 21.   **11:35 p.m. WNIB 97.1-FM.**
Adventures in Good Music **with Carl Haas.**

Bach's *Tocatta and Fugue in D minor* is the baroque equivalent of "Satisfaction" in its archetypal, full-throttled hugeness. Performed by Marie-Claire Alain on the pipe organ at a church in Helsingborg, she drives at the climax, sounding like some gorgeous brass band dispatched from heaven instead of one solitary Frenchwoman. Haas, celebrating tonight the 310th anniversary of Bach's birth, evokes what it must have been like for the Leipzig kapellmeister, always dealing with choirs and orchestras and their inherent variables, to sit alone behind the keyboard in self-possession: "Here he would get the sense of power and freedom that he could get from no other sources." If much of Bach seems too solemn and pared-down on the radio, this one was practically built for broadcast, filling up my sad little apartment and melting the frost off the windows.

March 23.   **10:38 a.m. WXRT 93.1-FM.**

An ad for the Museum of Science and Industry reassures the modern rock crowd that they've changed their image from "slide rules and dusty old bones." Now, "You can hear the music of Sting on seventy-two speakers!"

March 24.

At nine-thirty, I was listening to NPR's broadcast of the House Subcommittee on Employer-Employee Relations' affirmative-action hearing. Congressman David Welding (Republican–Florida) says,

There's a disproportionate amount of white males who are successful writers of novels, composers of popular songs, composers of symphonies, inventors of major products, creators of new enterprises, discoverers of major medical breakthroughs, major scientific breakthroughs in physics and chemistry.

Interestingly, the *only* male *anyone* cares *anything* about today happens to be black. He's not making scientific breakthroughs (though he does defy gravity) and he's about the least political figure you could imagine: Michael Jordan. He plays his first home game tonight and he is revered like some sort of messianic figure, as best expressed in this morning's *Tribune*, which runs a strange photomontage with the huge, omnipotent head of Jordan floating over the city of Chicago. All the sendups in the paper contain biblical metaphors from the cautious (prodigal son) to the miraculous (second coming).

The *Mike and Dan* sports talk show at eleven o'clock on WSZR (live from Michael Jordan's Restaurant downtown) sounds like some sort of *Saturday Night Live* parody in its relentless enthusiasm-gone-berserk. Says Mike, "We're gonna spank Orlando tonight. We're gonna spank 'em, Dan. . . . They should wear diapers on the court tonight." Dan fantasizes: "Here's the perfect scenario for me. Michael Jordan gets forty, hits a jumper from outside, three-pointer to win the ball game and Horace [Grant, of the Magic and former Bulls star] has six points and three rebounds."

They're joined by TV sportscaster Doug Collins who waxes, "It will be one of those nights that really, the game is secondary to me. I very seldom ever say that. It's an event. It's all the things that go with the greatness of an athlete like Michael Jordan."

That we can agree on something, anything, even this, is a relief.

March 25.   **12:00 p.m. WZRD 88.7-FM. Church of the SubGenius:** *Hour of Slack.*

SubGenius Reverend Susie the Floozie, who has "a metric ton of Jezebel spirit bursting out a ten-pound bag," delivers this interpretation of her religious archenemies, the fundamentalists: "Fundamental is right. You take out the fun, then you take out the mental, and all you're left with is the *duh.* The carrot they dangle in front of you is the promise of inheriting the kingdom of God. Well, I'm not sticking around waiting for that old fart to die!"

March 26.   **9:21 p.m. WRCX-FM 103.5.**

I crave, at times, simplicity—a honed-down ¼ rock 'n' roll song, heartfelt, well-scrubbed, and lacking decoration. Scanning the radio past repetitive ethnomusicological drumming, blues guitar masturbation, and an "alternative" DJ asking for local bands to send in their CDs, especially instrumental tracks so she can talk over them, I come across the ballad that begins this tale, "About a Girl." It sounds honest and to the point. But whatever distilled pleasure I derive from it is spoiled by a segue into the lame-ass intro I instantly recognize as the Spin Doctors' "Little Miss Can't Do Wrong," which is your basic "Grateful Dead for the nineties" crap. Every time I hear this song, I picture one of those neohippie girls I went to college with dancing to it in a circular fashion, thus fanning her patchouli oil aroma into my already polluted world. "I hope you hear this song and it pissed you off," cracks that scraggly, smiling lead singer. Congratulations, man, you succeeded.

> Radio happens in sound, but sound is not really what matters
> about radio. What does matter is the bisected heart of the
> infinite dreamland/ghostland, a heart that beats through a
> series of highly pulsed and frictive oppositions: the radio signal
> as intimate but untouchable, sensually charged but technically
> remote, reaching deep inside but from way out there, seduc-
> tive in its invitation but possibly lethal in its effects.
>
> *—Gregory Whitehead*, Wireless
> Imagination

April 1.   **10:30 p.m.**

Just as Anthony from the West Side, the ninth caller, is
winning tickets to a Bobby "Blue" Bland–B. B. King concert
from the soul DJ on 1390 AM, my mother calls. My grandmother, Pearlette Parson, is dead. I called her Ma.

I pour myself a whiskey; she would not approve. She would
in fact get down on her knees and rebuke the devil himself
if she knew that I was toasting her memory with Jack Daniels.
When I tell people "my grandfather was a moonshiner during
Prohibition," I always wait a moment before adding, "until
my grandmother found out." Feeling liquor-guilt, I turn off
the sex-saturated blues radio and dig out my *Bristol Sessions*
tape—a 1927 country-music recording session—and sing
along with the hillbillies warbling "Washed in the Blood
of the Lamb," one of the gospel showstoppers from Ma's
repertoire.

It's been fifteen years since she lost her mind for good. I
remember what it felt like for me at age ten to watch Ma

wandering the halls of her nursing home, gone to the world but hollering a selection of old-time church songs.

She no longer remembered me, much less my name or face, but she could belt out "Bringing in the Sheaves" word for word. She built a little room inside her head made out of hymnals and paced around in there, singing the words on the pages as if there were nothing else to do. If Sunday is the day we practice our religions, which is to say that we succumb to the rituals of our passions, then my grandmother drew her own calendar by scratching out every other day of the week. Listening to her was no longer listening to the woman I once loved and feared. Her body became a metal rod, a transmitter stabbed into a hill for a radio station with a ten-song playlist. Tuning in, it was always Sunday.

Webbers Falls, Oklahoma

April 4.   **12:42 a.m. KBOO-FM.**

When I arrive at his house in Braggs tonight, Uncle John A., Ma's eldest son, who fought in the Pacific during World War II, shows me a book that a distant relative put together of Parson family history, beginning with the Trail of Tears. Our Cherokee name, he tells me, was "Ah-kee-la-ni-ka."

He points to an ancient photograph of my grandfather's cousins. "That there is Carl Parson," he says, touching the sepia face of a small boy. Carl was just a teenager in the 1920s when he and his buddies—all of them drunk—accidentally killed an old man they meant to rob down by the Arkansas River. This put Carl behind the bars of the Oklahoma State Prison in McAlester (an institution dear to my own heart because the first concert I ever attended was country singer Webb Pierce backed by the McAlester Prison Band). After a few years of good behavior, my incarcerated relative was entrusted with greater responsibilities and freedom of movement, so much freedom, in fact, that he simply walked away one day, never to be found.

Carl traveled around for a while, assumed an alias, and settled down not far from his family, across the Arkansas state line. He remained a wanted man and figured that contact with his brothers through the usual means endangered his identity. So they devised a code: Carl kept his radio tuned to one station for the rest of his life and when his brothers needed to reach him, such as when their father died, they would call the station and request a certain song. Lord knows what the song was—"There's No Place Like Home"?

And now, lying here in this wet Oklahoma air with the radio on, this line jumps out of a song: "The blood still runs down Cherokee Highway."

Muskogee

April 4.   **11:11 p.m.**

The funeral was this morning at the Pentecostal Holiness Church in Braggs. To travel back in time to my childhood, to sing those old Christian songs like "I'll Fly Away" and "I Will Meet You in the Morning" with my cousins, and watching my mother see her mother for the last time ripped me apart. Muskogee radio, on the other hand, is devoid of any real pain. "Richard Nixon's supposedly a great hero, because he opened up China. Boy, did he open up a can of worms," claims an AM station. "If you need special treatment to treat itchy skin, you're not alone," encourages another. The Red Hot Chili Peppers sing "Give It Away" on the FM and its pulsating groove resides so far away from here, so far away from weeping and preaching and "I'll Fly Away," that I turn from my sleeping mother and picture the strange bass player Flea wearing his hilarious pants made out of dozens of stuffed animals sewn together.

Cincinnati Airport

April 5.   **8:00 p.m.**

The doo-wop stalker love song on a Cincinnati oldies station—you broke up with me because I was an obnoxious jerk and now you're dating *him*, so I drive by your house and stare in your window every night, thereby proving that I'm an even bigger creep than you thought—is overpowered by a huge noise. Taking off my headphones, I recognize "Achy Breaky Heart" and join my slack-jawed fellow travelers watching a group of perky, thirtysomething bartenders, smiles so wide they must smear their teeth with Vaseline, perform a rousing line dance in the middle of the airport.

Chicago

April 7.   11:00 a.m. WLS-AM. *The Rush Limbaugh Show.*

Rush celebrates the first 100 days of the Republican-led Congress and its most notable achievement—that, according to a recent poll, "at the end of the year 47 percent of the [American] people had never heard of Mr. Newt and now that number is down to 6 percent."

April 8.   7:00 p.m.–12:00 a.m. Q101-FM.
"Suicide Prevention Special."

I paid $6.66 for the beer and cookies I bought earlier to get through this, which could be an omen—you would think that five hours of uninterrupted talk about suicide might induce people to kill themselves.

Kurt Cobain's body was found a year ago today.

At seven o'clock sharp a Pearl Jam song, "Better Man," ends. There is no Seattle significance here; Pearl Jam fills up one-fourth of Q101's playlist. A recording of a needle raking across a record introduces the promo they've been hyping all week: "Q101 stops the music." The program will benefit the Center for Suicide Research and Prevention at Rush Presbyterian Hospital here in Chicago.

DJ Robert Chase is joined by a few of his modern rocking coworkers, as well as Rush doctor David Clark. After some lame, inter-DJ chitchat ("I never see you at this time!") they list the celebrities who will be offering their "Don't do it" two cents' worth. At least one name would have made Cobain cringe—Pauly Shore.

Chase was on the air last April 8: "The kids calling in trying to deal with that problem was amazing to me. I had one girl on the phone for an hour and a half who said, 'If he doesn't have anything to live for, my God, what do I have to live for?'"

Throughout the evening, callers—mostly teenagers— phone in to describe their suicide attempts and friends who killed themselves; they receive counseling, either on the air from Dr. Clark, or from other volunteers. The most gut-wrenching testimony comes from fourteen-year-old Jeannette, whose twin sister killed herself last month.

I am afraid to hear this. As a twin, I cannot contemplate the loss of my own sister. Jeannette, whose sweet, young voice grows increasingly quiet, sobs, "She was my twin. My identical twin. We were real close."

She describes what it was like to face her sister's death: "It's kind of like looking at yourself die. . . . I feel like half of me is missing now. [*Crying.*] It's just . . . I . . . really miss her."

A remarkable Nirvana fan named Josh, who is fifteen, is in the studio with his counselor and reads a rambling, touching analysis of Cobain's life and death:

It was just such a let-down. I can't describe it. . . . Kurt was labeled unmasculine in school by jocks. And they thought he was, like, feminine but he just happened not to be gay. And when he got famous, he saw the same type of people in his audience and he tried to drive them away, like for one example, by jokingly kissing Krist on Saturday Night Live. *. . . I thought this was real admirable and people like Mickey Rooney* [This is a great slip; he means Andy Rooney but who could blame him for mixing up one boring, grouchy jerk with another?] *seemed to call him a loser and this is wrong.*

Josh wanders beautifully for a few more minutes, ending his soliloquy with thoughts on Cobain's demise: "It was a total waste of talent. I wouldn't encourage it."

Dr. Chase offers kindhearted, levelheaded counsel to dozens of people in pain. Over and over, notables from Tori Amos to the singer for Candlebox invoke various warnings against self-inflicted death. It all makes me a little uneasy. On the one hand, the tortured side of Kurt Cobain would understand the callers' hurt and pain. On the other hand, his funny and sarcastic side would have laughed at the entire "I'm okay, you're okay" process.

As I listen to Dr. Chase tactfully tackle the depression of the 1990s, I crack open Michael Lesy's look at depression—economic and psychological—in the 1890s, *Wisconsin Death Trip*. He wrote, in 1973,

> Today, public health officials actually believe that if a potential suicide would just take the trouble to pick up his phone and call a prevention center, he could be talked out of his ill-considered opinions. In the 1890s, a man was offered no imaginary hope that he could be charmed from his despair by a few well-placed words of sympathy or perception. Rather the newspapers reminded him that quite a few others, perhaps even people he'd met, had taken two from two long enough to know that their remainder was always zero and that his problems had nothing to do with his opinions or attitudes, but with the conditions of his capture at birth.

You can hear this bleakness in Nirvana's darkest songs, in the echoes of the sick laughter Cobain must have spewed when he titled one of them "I Hate Myself and I Want to Die." And one year later, his mixed message is still as mysterious, as stained with pain and glee, as the lyrics of "Smells Like Teen Sprit."

Unlike this special, there was nothing sappy and "You're gonna make it!"–inspirational about Cobain's voice. After five hours of this, if I hear the phrase "get help" one more time, I'm going to smash something. Chase spoke earlier with Anthony DeCurtis, the *Rolling Stone* editor, who tells a story about one of the reasons we liked the band in the first place: "When the city of Aberdeen talked about putting up a statue of Kurt Cobain, Krist said, 'Well if they do, I'm going to personally go and just knock it down with a hammer.'"

So maybe that's the best advice. Knock down the statues. Turn up the records. Which is exactly what Q101 does—to its credit—playing two hours of the band's songs, commercial-free.

April 15. **Record review for *City Pages*, Minneapolis.**

On a recent installment of the talk show *Leeza*, a middle-aged man was introduced, for the first time, to his thirtyish daughter whom he never knew existed. Ten minutes into the program, she announced her impending wedding and asked her newfound father to escort her down the aisle. He looked frightened and stunned; she was ready to progress to grown-up events and matrimonial specifics while he was, in essence, witnessing her birth. It seems that the field of audio art is received with similar shell-shock—longtime practitioners are already issuing retrospectives when the public at large missed out on their first words.

Combining music, sound, and speech (from narratives to non sequiturs), audio art falls between the cracks of broadcasting, not reportage, not song, not drama, but sometimes using all three. Since it's unlikely that any six-year-old in America answers "audio artist" when asked what she plans to be when she grows up, the field is fed from other disciplines, namely radio, music, visual art, and performance. Jacki Apple and Guillermo Gomez-Pēna represent the latter group. Both artists have recently released CDs that look back on their work from the 1980s to the present.

Gomez-Pēna's *Borderless Radio* and Apple's *Thank You for Flying American* share a celebration of collaboration, biting social commentary, some good guitar grooves, a pervasive sense of humor, and a reliance on irony that, looking back, was sometimes the only possible release from the Reagan-

Bush death grip. In radio, both artists have found a welcome ear. Gomez-Pēna insists that

> as a performance artist I must be a public intellectual immersed in the thorny issues of my times. This society pushes art-makers and cultural critics to the margins, confining us to the predictable roles of antiheroes, agonic bohemians, exotic freaks, media celebrities, or isolated academicians. Radio can still provide us with one of the few existing outlets to escape the insularity of the art and academic worlds.

As a notable, if not notorious, Latino mouthpiece, Gomez-Pēna is a sort of anti–Pete Wilson. While much politically informed art these days is humorless mush, the self-styled "warrior for gringostroika" makes his points with hilarity, wit, and a good dose of venom. He toys with radio conventions, turning the do-gooder boredom of the PSA format into saucy Spanglish collages parodying the Proposition 187 ethos: "Why don't you go back to your greasy, third-world dictatorship, jerk?" asks a bitchy shouter on "Quintessential PSA" (1993).

"Radio Pirata: Colon Go Home" (1992) commemorates the Columbus anniversary through send-ups of "man on the street" opinion polls, the serious public-radio interview, faux commercials, and a "Miss Discovery Beauty Contest" in which the winner receives a temporary green card. Here, free trade promises "no taxes . . . and lots of salsa" and those who tire of anticolonialist tirades aren't bigots, merely sufferers of "compassion fatigue."

Though Gomez-Pēna confronts and crosses the real, physical border between the U.S. and Mexico in all of these works, the idea of border as metaphor is just as crucial. For instance, the continuing introduction (some would say contamination) of the English language with Spanish vocabulary—and vice versa—is the source for both humor and concern. "Norte/Sur" (1990) offers "I Want to Hold Your Hand" in Spanish, along with the intuition that chili con carne might someday be known as pepper steak. These unions, we're told, won't go away: "This is bilingual radio, a continental infection, and there's no antidote for it."

If Gomez-Pēna's continental infection is a fiercely public continental mission, Apple's work filters America through the introspection of solitary figures. This seems accurate— ask any fellow citizen you trust what the 1980s felt like and the response might be "alone."

Narrating "Idaho" (1980), Apple explains that Boise's Main Street appears designed for Gary Cooper gunfights and that to the east, Atomic Research Center scientists are tight-lipped about their round-the-clock projects. She drives to the desert, which is "impervious to your existence. It is as if you are merely a film projection of a still photograph."

The infinity of space, like the desert's expanse, is home to the loneliest individual, the astronaut. In the series *The Garden Planet Revisited* (1982), Captain Charlie, "a paragon of late twentieth-century technological man, hurtles through time and space, stranded on a station, abandoned and alone, on a mission without end." Charlie personifies the one word that best describes this entire album—adrift. To Apple, the two great American locations of freedom—the Far West and outer space—become environments of alienation. This is not to say that *Flying American* is overtly gloomy; the humor of it, as in *Borderless Radio*, is its grace.

An audio return to the mean and lonesome eighties won't be much of a shock: Just read today's paper and it will all come back. Too easily.

April 19–May 18.

1995 marks National Public Radio's twenty-fifth year. Two recent books published by Houghton Mifflin historicize NPR's contributions. I had planned to spend the entire month of May reviewing the books for the Twin Cities paper *City Pages* and monitoring/suffering through NPR broadcasts. But I turned on the radio on April 19 and started my National Public month eleven days early.

• • •

I only hear two words: "Oklahoma" and "bomb." Carl Kassell was delivering the news on NPR the morning of April 19. His unwavering voice always maintains the same authoritative diction, whether he's talking Dow Jones or death. By the time those two words register, I lunge at the radio and turn it up as another reporter finishes a sentence about emergency vehicles clogging up downtown Oklahoma City. For a second, I'm relieved, knowing that my relatives rarely turn up that far west of Tulsa, until I realize that while my family probably isn't hurt, someone else's might be.

The NPR affiliate I was tuned to promptly resumed its scheduled program, *Performance Today*. I sat there, numb, just barely aware of the New England Conservatory Wind Ensemble and an interview with an Armenian-American violist. Obviously, at that moment, I craved more information. I didn't know at the time that the next two weeks' news would involve a constant and painful rising death toll until the number of people murdered in the blast would reach 168. *Morning Edition* and *All Things Considered*, like the rest of the national media, proceeded to obsess over the disaster in an orderly fashion. It was Waco, it was talk radio, it was the so-called patriot movement of gun-nut militias (especially the Michigan Militia, associated with bombing suspects Timothy McVeigh and the Nichols brothers).

However, the most moving, gut-wrenching radio commentary that I heard concerning that contemptible event did not originate from NPR. On the Canadian Broadcasting Corporation's *Sunday Morning*, the parents of a young woman who was killed by terrorists in the Lockerbie disaster read a letter. Addressing the families of the Oklahoma dead, they said this, simply and with loathing: that what happened will never make sense, that they will never get over their daughter's death and that there is evil in the world.

If the hearts of Oklahoma City are now full of pain and anger, compassion and disbelief, this is certain—that Tupperware containers all over that county runneth over, that if there is a breed of people built to tackle death and love thy neighbor, it's Okie women who could stare down Satan himself and shoo him out of their kitchens. At this moment, casseroles are bubbling over and prayers are being whispered onto corn bread and black-eyed peas. Heaping piles of God-knows-what and steaming bowls of buttered this-and-that are being driven to churches and houses all over town in a selfless frenzy of generous hospitality.

If you think all the reports of "coming together" and "sense of community" in Oklahoma City merely pay lip service to some idealized stereotype of heartland goodness, you weren't at my grandmother's funeral. Those Braggs churchwomen who fretted over potatoes, macaroni, ham, and cobbler, who fed my family with the warmest faces I will ever smile back at, couldn't possibly know that they are, at times, the objects of my sarcastic venom, that I blame them for obeying their husbands and serving them like slaves, that the strongest part of me indicts them for teaching me to sing Sunday-school songs of spiritual oppression like this one:

> *I will be a helper, at home, at church, at school*
> *I will be a helper, obeying all the rules*
> *When there's work for me to do, I'll do it happily*
> *I will be a helper to everyone I see.*

I have spent the second half of my life running away from those kindhearted women and their do-gooder songs and into the arms of Neil Young and Jean Genet. Maybe my most blissful moment of the past few months erased them completely; standing alone last December at the DNA Lounge in San Francisco, I watched the Fastbacks' red-blooded attack on the Sweet song "Set Me Free," and for a few minutes there was no Oklahoma in my past, no obeying all the rules, and goddamn if all the Tupperware didn't vanish from the world. In that bar, America wasn't a country, as my aunt once said about Oklahoma, "where the women take care of the men." It was a country where men stand next to women (or in jumpy guitarist Kurt Bloch's place, fly around them) screaming scratchy words of glee side by side, turning campy guitar riffs into reckless declarations of independence.

I tell that story not to escape from the pain at hand but to express my ambivalence toward my birthplace. I cannot imagine Oklahoma City's grief or even hint at its present darkness. I'm not sure what a casserole could mean to the woman whose two small sons died in the blast, but I imagine that she's been offered several. If I seek to obliterate the forces of my Pentecostal childhood, of (women especially) spending this life in a backbreaking race to the next life's reward, I still search in vain for the huge Oklahoma kindness, where thoughtful concern is not an exception but a natural fact. I believe the words I heard on NPR, Sunday, April 23, the presidentially proclaimed National Day of Mourning. Addressing the crowd at the Oklahoma City Fairgrounds, Bill Clinton declared: "If anybody thinks that Americans are mostly mean and selfish, they ought to come to Oklahoma. If anybody thinks Americans have lost the capacity for love and caring and courage, they ought to come to Oklahoma."

With those words, if only for a day, we got our president back, or rather the man whom we elected, intelligent, compassionate, articulate, warm. He uttered gentle condolences while at the same time, he firmly decreed our responsibilities toward free speech: "When there is talk of hatred, let us stand up and talk against it. When there is talk of violence, let us stand up and talk against it. In the face of death, let us honor life."

Clinton's fellow speaker at the service, the Reverend Billy Graham, was so moved by the president's moralizing eloquence that he claimed the speech "could be a sermon from a pulpit anywhere. And, uh, maybe that's what he'll do someday [*laughter*] ten or twenty years from now."

If Clinton's Sunday-morning hopespeak contained benevolent New Testament calls for redemption, his Sunday-night appearance on *60 Minutes* seethed with Old Testament wrath, unequivocally condemning the bombers' actions and seeking antiterrorism legislation in no uncertain terms. The following morning, Cokie Roberts called Bob Edwards at

Morning Edition with her analysis. While Roberts was straightforward and measured as usual, I was taken aback by what she said: "I think President Clinton has really managed to hit all the right chords since this bombing, that he's shown sympathy and anger and he's, really for the first time I think, seemed to understand the presidential role as national father and healer and preacher, and then finally, by last night, a sort of stern disciplinarian."

How long has it been since a journalist has said something, anything, affirming about the president? Granted, Clinton's denunciation of the bombers is as close to an uncontroversial statement as one could make, but I'm not picky. Right now, I'll settle for any scrap of relief I can get.

"Be well, do good work, keep in touch," Garrison Keillor always signs off his cutesy public radio segments (*Writer's Almanac* being superior to *A Prairie Home Companion* if only because it's one-twelfth as long). It's amazing how truly grating that smug little phrase has become for me, especially these days when the American national motto is turning into "Feel like shit, blow each other up, hold your tongue." Of course, Mr. Woe Be Gone, in his Mr. Rogers–style cozy pep talks, is only trying to give his listeners a cardigan sweater of the heart. Too bad what they really need is a bulletproof vest.

These are dark days, and the times, they are abominable. Lately, I'd rather skip the cup of coffee with Bob Edwards and just get drunk with Neil Young instead. In Thomas Looker's new book, *The Sound and the Story: NPR and the Art of Radio*, Edwards sums up his job as *Morning Edition* host: "Don't embarrass yourself and fuck up." When I read that telling sentence, I thought of an article Greil Marcus wrote on Young a few months back quoting novelist John Irving, who was talking about Young both as a fellow artist and as "one of my heroes—along with Bob Dylan. They're not afraid to embarrass themselves—and you've got to be able to do that.'"

Fear of embarrassment has become the NPR cancer. A friend says that he no longer listens to their programming, because he finds it "hopelessly competent," always good, but lacking in radio thunderbolts. Edwards, who Looker calls "the voice of *the news*—the knowledgeable and comfortable anchorman who sounds as if he knows more than he says and who introduces people who tell us more than we know," has accomplished his goal; he almost never fucks up. But he doesn't rock the free world, either.

Bob Edwards and NPR are growing old gracefully together: so tasteful, so reassuring, so mature, so dull. And it's paid off; Looker notes that by 1994, NPR's news shows had ten million listeners. Still, the subtext of his history, which examines *Morning Edition* and *All Things Considered* (which the comic strip *Wonk City* recently labeled *All Things Beaten to Death*) in their weekday and weekend incarnations, as well as NPR staff, contains this subtext: What went wrong?

The same can be said of *Listening to America: Twenty-Five Years in the Life of a Nation, As Heard on National Public Radio,* edited by ATC host Linda Wertheimer. Though her upbeat introduction to the dozens of transcripts is inherently congratulatory ("We have been fortunate to have the leadership we needed to grow in good times and make our way safely through other times. . . ."), the chronologically arranged contents speak for themselves. The first transcript, ATC's debut broadcast on May 3, 1971, covers anti-Vietnam protesters moving through Washington. It is a disorienting but thrilling narrative. Spontaneous and raw, reporter Jeff Kamen is immersed in the demonstration, recording the gut reactions of participants ("My eyes are burning a little bit. My skin burns. I always react this way to gas.") and arguing with an officer after making the on-air observation, " 'Here come the police. One demonstrator knocked down by a motorscooter policeman. . . . Anger now . . . anger of the young people.' "

Compare that bit of free-form journalism to Martha Raddatz's commentary that ends the book, a November 11, 1994, piece on then "Speaker presumptive" Newt Gingrich—logical, expository, nothing special. While the first essay is a cacophonous barrage of sirens, helicopters, and chanting protesters, the last presents a predictable script that volleys between reporter description and goalspeak by Gingrich and Georgia congressman John Linder. *The Sound and the Story* laments NPR's gradual evolution from challenging radio to proficient news:

> *They were innovators—even revolutionaries—not because of their politics but because of their aesthetics. They assaulted the status quo not with ideology but with electronics. They were guerrillas fighting in the media wasteland created by television against the tyranny of the visual. They were subversives who were asking Americans to close their eyes and open their ears.*

And what are they now, according to Looker? "Low-key commercial radio."

Looker's book, though concerned primarily with news, is largely art history, continually analyzing form and content so much that he probably should retitle the effort *The Sound or the Story*. While nearly every NPR staffer he interviewed shuns the term *art* in describing compelling radio, the chronicle is filled with mourning over trading creative sound work for "just the facts," bare-voiced reportage. Obviously, the best production utilizes, as Ira Glass (one of NPR's most interesting commentator / producers) put it, " 'the strengths of radio as a storytelling medium.' "

One of the most frequently used words in various indictments of the "old NPR" just happens to be "indulgent," not only because of an un-newsy obsession with beauty, but because of a true commitment to both playfulness and, as Bob Edwards claims, " 'a broader definition of the news than we have today. It was more than just wars and presidents and news conferences. . . . it was life." Or as NPR pioneer Bill Siemering is quoted as saying, " 'Public radio will reflect the joy of human experience.' "

Perhaps the most striking example of NPR's previous

whimsy is a small, trivial anecdote from former *Morning Edition* producer Jay Kernis. Required to write an introduction to a news segment for Bob Edwards which also informed listeners of an upcoming piece concerning a haiku poet from New Jersey, Kernis penned this preface in haiku form:

> *Some words hit, some hurt.*
> *Jersey poet writes haiku.*
> *News from Jean Cochran.*

"Every part of the format could be manipulated *for meaning*," Kernis reflected. The haiku might sound silly to some people, defiantly undignified, stupid even. To me, it sounds like play made audible, like not only paying attention to details but relishing in them, like celebrating the wit and humanity of the audience. It sounds like someone truly caring about what he's doing with impassioned delight, and how often do you find that? To the straight newshounds now running NPR, that little tidbit is probably the very definition of indulgent. But Edwards himself defends the Kernis approach: " 'He didn't water down the ugliness. Sometimes he made the ugliness register more.' "

Wertheimer's anthology, as a greatest-hits collection, nicely contrasts the mischievous with the weighty and is as interesting for its bits of cultural zeitgeist as its jaunts through radio history: Susan Stamberg refers to the as-yet-unnamed Watergate scandal as "the Caper of the Bungled Bugging"; an inaugural reception for Nancy Reagan elicits the comment, "I have never seen so many fur coats"; and Ian Shoales, bored with the Statue of Liberty restoration hoopla, reminds us, "It's not like she does anything."

But it is just as interesting to think about what Wertheimer left out. For instance, where is David Sedaris?

I just received a tape of Sedaris's Ira Glass–produced commentaries. I push Play and recognize the familiar voice of

Neil Conan in chipper wake-up mode, introducing *Morning Edition* listeners to Sedaris, who "cleans New York apartments for a living but spent the summer in northern France, where his boyfriend owns a run-down house in the country."

"August 20, 1993," Sedaris begins, describing the villagers' interest in the home-improvement progress he and his boyfriend, Hugh, have made on the house, walking in to exclaim, *"Bonjour, monsieur! Qu'est-ce que vous faites?"* As the accordion music starts, I'm suddenly standing in my old apartment in Washington, D.C., eating cereal and once again running late for work at the National Gallery of Art, where I had an internship in the archives. Leilani, my D.C. roommate, was a *Morning Edition* fiend and I listened with her every day; it seemed like the Washington thing to do. While I was a consistently tardy government-worker-in-training because of my double-edged love of coffee and sleep, this was the only time I was late because I couldn't tear myself away from NPR.

But that morning, the voice on the radio was smart, funny, nervous, and underemployed. He hilariously describes his attempts to make conversation with a neighbor woman in his halting Dick-and-Jane French: "I saw an old lamb in a field with a horse and they appeared to be content together." Or, in Paris, he shops for medical curiosities, asking shop owners, "How much is that wax head in the window? . . . The scabs on the face, are they illustrating the advanced stages of syphilis? . . . Was this used for torture or hairdressing and how do you heat it up?"

I was so surprised and delighted by the combination of deadpan delivery, sick humor, and childlike pathos, that when I got to work and that hour of *Morning Edition* rolled around again, I forced my museum coworkers to listen. They didn't laugh, though one woman managed to mutter, "Weird." I began questioning if the museum career was such a hot idea for me after all. Did I really want to spend the rest of my professional life working with people who didn't laugh at jokes about syphilis and torture spoken by a sarcastic but lovable apartment cleaner on vacation?

Fortunately, the tape includes most of the *Morning Edition* intros to each entry, recapturing what it felt like to move from familiar announcer to voice-out-of-nowhere. But Ira introduces one of the funniest, most poignant stories, "Quad," on the Chicago-only program he shares with Gary Covino, *The Wild Room:* He says that he originally sent this one to the NPR headquarters, but they sent it back: "*Morning Edition* has always been very, very good, but sometimes there are some things in [Sedaris's] commentaries that they just don't feel entirely comfortable with."

Sedaris immediately comes on:

> *I spent my high-school years staring at the pine trees outside my classroom window and picturing myself* [violin strains here] *on the campus of an Ivy League school, where my wealthy roommate, Colgate, would leave me notes reading, "Meet me on the quad at five." I wasn't sure what a quad was, but I knew I wanted one desperately.*

His bad grades send him to the worst of all possible state colleges instead, where he improves his grades in order to transfer: "I chose Kent State because people had been killed there. They hadn't died of boredom. That was saying something."

Here, Ira interrupts to point out that this was the phrase that troubled the morning folks because the families of the Kent State dead might listen to this and "feel really, really messed up to hear this little joke." They ask Ira to get Sedaris to pen a less offensive replacement. He comes up with several equally dark reasons why he chose the school, listing them here with a sadistic smirk. My favorite: "I examined the famous photograph of the grieving young woman, her arms thrown up in despair. The campus looked good in the background." Needless to say, *Morning Edition* chose the blandest option: " 'So where's David?' 'Kent State.' 'Ohhhhh.' How brave of me, how tragic."

The most famous and notorious Sedaris piece, his "Santaland Diaries," begins, "I wear green velvet knickers, a forest green velvet smock, and a perky little hat decorated with spangles. This is my work uniform." He says it straight, doesn't flinch through his telling of what it's like to be a grown man working as a Macy's elf under the wildly dignified moniker "Crumpet."

Crowd noises. "Twenty-two thousand people came to see Santa today, and not all of them were well-behaved." When his caustic retort to one mother elicits the threat "I'm gonna have you fired," he responds with indignant amusement that he wants "to lean over and say, 'I'm gonna have you killed.'"

An overzealous Santa commands him to sing "Away in a Manger" to a little girl on his lap: "It didn't seem fair that I should have to solo, so I sang it the way Billie Holiday might have sang if she'd put out a Christmas album." Here, he takes a barely audible breath. You expect a slow tempo, perhaps a more womanly delivery than Sedaris's boyish nasal timbre. What comes out is thrilling; it really is Holiday, slowly lurching, "Uh-waaaay in a maaanger . . . no cri-ib fora beed. . . . The-uhhhlittle lord Jesuuuuusssss lay down hiiiis sweet heaaaaaad."

Sedaris's quick-witted observation and his flair for cutting into ridiculous situations with biting remarks gives his work its surface charm, its entertainment. But nearly every piece ends in a state of melancholy—"Quad" with the assertion that "people aren't foolish so much as they are kind," and the "Santaland" realization that the holiday photo is "not about the child, or Santa, or Christmas, or anything, but the parents' idea of a world they cannot make work for them."

Despite its Sedaris deficiency, *Listening to America* still offers a number of gems: Ross Perot's pig-headed eruption at Wertheimer's reasonable line of campaign questioning, a strange little celebration of a sunset, and a sobering piece concerning the American abandonment of Saigon in 1975 in which the final, homeward-bound Americans lie to, fuck over, and leave for dead the duped Vietnamese who had helped them all along.

The most remarkable story is Alex Chadwick's portrayal
of a young Czech woman during the Velvet Revolution of
1989 whom he had hired to act as his interpreter. He soon
discovered her involvement as a student revolutionary leader,
marveled at her dedication and passion, and finally reveled
in her one small moment of peace at a rally, eyes closed and
listening to Dvořák.

One of the strengths of NPR is this willingness to tell the
stories of such unsung individuals, like talking to voters such
as Aggie Shaw the day before Nixon's 1973 inauguration.
Shaw's comments evoke an undermined democracy: "'I
didn't vote for anyone. I didn't think any candidate was worth
a vote.'" As Wertheimer writes, "If you want to know where
the country is headed, ask." This is evidently easier said than
done.

The April 21 edition of the listeners' roundtable *Talk of
the Nation* (whose rarely publicized subtitle happens to be
Who Cares What You Think, You Paranoid Psycho), hosted
that day by NPR pantheon regulars Neil Conan and Nina
Totenberg, focused on the aftermath of the Oklahoma City
bombing just two days before. Nick, from Charlestown, West
Virginia, after unequivocally attacking the bombers' actions,
says,

> *I think that it really gives us an opportunity as a nation to
> see that the real threats to national security in this country
> are internal. . . . If you look at what's called the "mainstream
> political debate" in this country, it's become perfectly okay.
> The coverage loves people like Newt Gingrich and . . . Rush
> Limbaugh's become a superstar. And it's clear from their
> rhetoric, from their propaganda—*

Nick is rapidly interrupted by an incredulous Totenberg, who
butts in with, "Now, you don't really want to say that. You
don't want to really stick Rush Limbaugh with the bombing,
do you?"

Not letting anyone tell him what he does or doesn't really
think, Nick responds:

*Well, let me put it this way: The whole political debate has
been put so far to the right that it's understandable that if
you tell enough people that the government is the focus of
evil and that everything wrong in this country is due to the
federal government and you portray the president as some
kind of a satanic figure who murders people and you know—*

Conan cuts him off with, "I'm not sure that any of the people
you've identified have talked about the president as a satanic
figure or that this has to do with the political debate in this
country."

Besides the fact that to say the bombing of a *federal*
building has nothing to do with politics is slightly unbelievable, if Conan had listened to *Morning Edition* earlier in the
day, he would have heard Bob Edwards introduce a story on
the Pierce Creek Church in upstate New York, which placed
"full-page advertisements in a couple of newspapers that said
that a vote for Bill Clinton was a vote for sin, for abortion,
homosexuality, and condom distribution in the schools."

Another caller, Tom from Oakland, tells of his experience
working for Food Not Bombs in the Bay Area, a feed-the-
homeless group whose members are routinely arrested and
harassed by the authorities:

*I'd like to reflect on the fact that what happened around
the world . . . in Iraq . . . there were Oklahoma federal building–
type bombings that happened every minute, all day long,
every day in that country. The same is true even today. As
we speak, the United States is killing people in—*

Interrupted by Conan, who is practically screaming, "Tom!
Tom! Tom! Tom! Tom! Good-bye, Tom. Thank you very
much."

So much for forum, for communication and debate. Perhaps Wertheimer could amend her statement as follows: If
you want to know where the country is headed, ask, then
pull the plug and laugh at said person as if they're speaking

conspiracy-theory nonsense whether they have a point or not, reprimanding them with "You don't really want to say that."

Almost as disturbing is that for all of this, NPR is easily the best mainstream news source in American broadcasting. And connecting the phrase "hopelessly competent" with National Public *anything* just six short years after the Reagan administration is in many ways encouraging. NPR's relative achievement is even more astounding given the fact that, according to Looker, in 1993 the "annual budget for *all* its news coverage—foreign and domestic—was around $16 million . . . less than the amount of money the *Des Moines Register* spends each year to report on Iowa news. . . ." () But that still doesn't explain why most of NPR's great, early moments were the product of a budget probably less than the Des Moines paper spends covering five blocks in Dubuque. As Looker has noticed, "It has been a long time since Bob Edwards read haiku before headlines from Jean Cochran." Just maybe you don't care. Perhaps you prefer sonnets. Or you want your updates straight, no chaser. But a radio is not a newspaper with speakers. NPR, in its finest moments, remembers this, and sets aside its gutless goal of competence, giving us the loud and quiet of the world. For public radio should make life audible, should scream at terror, whisper doubts, nag at the conscience, and, if need be, resort to haiku comedy. And if Bob Edwards embarrasses himself in the process, we'll come to know him not as the voice of reason, but as a man.

May 19. 8:00–9:00 p.m. WBEZ-FM 91.5. *The Wild Room.*

"What is popular is not always right. What is right is not always popular." That said, the Velvet Underground begins to play "I'll Be Your Mirror," a song that I had never connected with the phrase "media watchdog" until now, listening to Nico drone lines such as *"let me be your eyes."*

The song ends and Gary Covino's voice reminds me that I'm listening to the radio instead of the banana-cover Velvets record. My brain, however, had already started playing John

Cale's great, scattered viola intro to the next track on the album, "Black Angel's Death Song," one of my favorites, even though I've never begun to understand half the lyrics. But I want to listen to it now because one phrase always stands out: *"Choose a side."* Like Nirvana's urging *"Hate, hate your enemies / Save, save your friends,"* it is a sentiment that I don't always agree with but frequently need to hear.

And speaking of sides ... While anyone who listens to NPR lately will notice that its coverage is blandly middle-of-the-road, it has been seen as a leftist propaganda factory. However, if I were to construct a "Radio Moscow" picket sign for Jesse Helms to tote through Lafayette Park, I'd paste Gary Covino's picture on it. The April 28 edition of *The Wild Room* involved a May Day celebration in which Covino elegized the commie girl who once broke his heart a few minutes before inviting callers to phone in and join him in singing a snazzy little anthem from (his own copy of) the IWW songbook.

Covino notes that his comrade Ira Glass, who is producing an ongoing series for NPR about Chicago elementary schools (I heard a moving one on ATC last week about the woes of transfer students) is away this evening accompanying the children on a field trip. Since Ira started his education sequences by observing the high-school experience, Covino cracks, "I figure if he stays with NPR a few more years he will be tracking the progress of a fetus in the womb." Instead, Covino is joined by Shirley Jahad of the WBEZ news department to talk about her interviews with the Southern Illinois Patriots League, a militia.

Today is the one-month anniversary of the bombing in Oklahoma City.

Jahad says that the next big event planned by these representatives of the "patriot movement" (which they simply call "the movement") is to burn the U.N. flag, which symbolizes a dangerous global threat to American autonomy.

"I've actually been to the United Nations in New York," Covino tells her. "It's really nice in there, actually. It's a nice building. . . . So maybe if we were taken over by the U.N., America would be a little more civilized."

When Jahad notes that the group's main focus is the protection of their Second Amendment rights, Covino rants that there are more than enough guns around "for the next three thousand years" and presents his solution to weapons proliferation: "My personal position is that, if we have to, we should just repeal the Second Amendment, declare martial law for thirty days, and confiscate all arms. I think these wimpy 'Brady Bills' will never do anything."

Jahad laughs and tells him that "by their reading of history . . . you would fall right into the category of a Nazi in Germany."

I feel strangely at home listening to this conversation. Growing up, this was mundane dinner-table chatter, though my father the gunsmith usually equated Covino's theory with Soviet tactics instead of fascist ones. I remember sneaking the *Communist Manifesto* into my room and reading it as a teenager. I knew very little about communists except that Ronald Reagan hated them, which seemed like a good enough endorsement at the time. When I would approach Dad with vague (I thought almost Christian) ideas about the distribution of wealth, he would plow into a tirade about how the access to firearms was the only true dike against the floods of totalitarianism that was so lengthy and tedious I would have agreed to tattoo the "Guns and Ammo" logo on my forehead to make him stop. (To his credit as a Constitutionalist, meaning that his belief in the entire Bill of Rights supercedes specific ideologies, he would always drive my sister and me to our antinuclear meetings and No Contra Aid protests in the family vehicle, a Ford Bronco emblazoned with an NRA sticker for every year he'd owned the car.)

Jahad spoke with a man named Glad Hall, the head of the Southern Illinois Patriots League, and asked if talk radio had influenced the group's activities.

Hall answers her as if she'd asked if he's of woman born:

*There's no doubt that the talk-show hosts are really the ones
who are responsible for educating as many people as to
what's going on . . . and are really the fuel that is feeding
the whole thing. We're indebted to them an awful lot. They
do a lot of research, they have a lot of researchers that work
in the background. We owe them a lot.*

Covino is surprised by the power Hall is granting radio, wondering if *The Wild Room* is "leading people to join any
whacked-out groups." When Jahad asks him what those
groups might be, he responds, "The Ambiguity League . . .
the Neurosis Cadre. The Psychosomatic Corps."

Hall identifies the he-man/G-man-turned-talk-show-barker
G. Gordon Liddy as "very, very popular," so Covino plays
the whistles-and-bells opening credits of Liddy's show, full
of sirens and bullhorns and helicopters and Liddy proclaim-
ing himself "the voice of hope and freedom" on "Radio
Free D.C."

Before reminding us that Liddy has been vilified for
encouraging listeners to gun down federal agents in light of
recent events, Covino concedes that Liddy "knows how to
start a radio show," and that "if *Talk of the Nation* started
this way, more people would stay tuned to that show past
the first three minutes."

Jahad brings up Clinton's attack on the NRA earlier this
week because of a particularly hateful fund-raising letter
describing the federal Bureau of Alcohol, Tobacco, and Firearms agents as "jackbooted government thugs" who wear
"Nazi bucket helmets and black stormtrooper uniforms,"
whose mission is to "harass, intimidate, even murder, law-
abiding citizens."

Covino plays a tape from the TV program *Crossfire* in
which Liddy claims:

*What I said was, if a federal agent comes knocking at your
door, specifically BATF, says, "I have a search warrant,"*

open the door, let 'em in, stand aside, and let 'em search. What I said is if they come shooting, they're shooting at you now, you have the right to self-defense, and in that event, if they've got a body-protection armor on, then you are best to shoot at the groin area.

Covino compares what Liddy says he said to the tape from last August 23 of his actual broadcast:

If the Bureau of Alcohol, Tobacco, and Firearms comes to disarm you, and they are bearing arms, resist them with arms. Go for a head shot, they're going to be wearing bullet-proof vests.

The Ambiguity League frowns here, finding the statement hopelessly devoid of nuance.

After a caller phones to say about the BATF, "They don't wear jackboots, they just wear brown shoes," Covino launches into a related report on Liddy's contribution to the June issue of *Car and Driver* magazine—a review of the new civilian version of the military's HMV, popularly pronounced "Humvee," and affectionately referred to as "the hummer."

Covino does not attempt to conceal his pleasure at reading Liddy's tough-guy prose:

It wasn't the absence of a gun turret, although I did notice this immediately. Nor was it the surprisingly comfortable seats, nor even the Don't Ask, Don't Tell quality of the vehicle's hummer nickname. No, the tip-off that the legendary "Humvee" had been emasculated [Here Covino interrupts to note that "Now we're getting to the real point, which is, is the civilian version of the military jeep enough of a manly vehicle?"] *by the forces of political correctness was the first thing the driver sees after climbing in. The underside of the sun visor is placarded with admonitions to "Wear seat belts" and "Don't drink and drive."*

Covino plays a country-rocker of a song that starts out inno-
cently enough. A woman sings about a stereotypical family
vacation across America. The chorus, though, is interesting,
in that the female singer reminds herself not to forget to
pack the Uzi and the AR-15, because, you just never know.

Covino whispers, in mock sincerity, "See, I'm in radio.
The microphone is my weapon. The microphone is my Uzi."

"And you shoot it off a lot, don't you, Gary?" Jahad says.
She goes on to describe her visit to the Lake County Gun
Show. She leafs through a book she picked up there at the
"education table," noting that the "Barnes and Noble just
doesn't carry that kind of stuff," and lists chapters with directions explaining "how to make a twelve-gauge shotgun with
a pipe."

They decide that the manual would be a perfect incentive
gift for the next 'BEZ fundraiser. Covino quips, "Enough of
this Garrison Keillor stuff. Let's show people how to make
pipe bombs and guns at home."

One wonders (even though one doesn't want to know)
how many new pledges they would get.

May 21.   **10:00 a.m.–12:00 p.m. WBEZ-FM 91.5.**
                    CBC Sunday Morning.

Cute: It's "Stairway to Heaven" sung by a swingin' Elvis
impersonator in an arrangement straight out of an imaginary
The King Sings Hits from His Movies songbook. Host Ian
Brown identifies the cover, by Neil Pepper, as one of twelve
versions of the Led Zep megahit on a new Australian tribute
album called *Stairways to Heaven.*

Brown notes that the song has been called the greatest
rock song in history, as well as the worst, asserting that,
"Somebody once calculated that by 1991, 'Stairway to
Heaven' had been played for twenty-three million minutes
on U.S. radio." In 1991, he says, an Albuquerque station
played it for twenty-four hours straight:

*People called the police. They thought the DJ had had a heart
attack because the station had been overrun by terrorists
dispatched by Saddam Hussein, who was apparently a Zep-
pelin fanatic. This was in fact not true ... but it does
demonstrate what happens to your brain if you listen to the
song for any length of time.*

He recounts the weirdest "Stairway" anecdote, the 1982
Consumer Protection Hearing in which the California State
Assembly was informed that part of the song, played backward,
said: "I sing because I live with Satan / The lord turns me off /
There's no escaping it / Here's to my sweet Satan whose power
is Satan / He will give you 666 / I live for Satan." Brown asks
us to "listen carefully" and plays a backward, garbled jumble
that sounds like four CDs skipping at once. In case you missed
the 666 stuff he plays it again, wryly declaring, "Perfectly obvious
to me," ending the segment with the lounge-act version of the
song from the new CD by a group called Pardon Me Boys, who
croon "doo-wah-it makes me wonder!"

May 29.   **9:13 p.m. WJJD-AM 1160.**
                                              The Tom Leykis Show.

I missed the first few minutes of this, and admittedly, I
stopped at this station because the question, "She described
childbirth as mutilation to females?" sort of captured my
imagination. But I think I can safely file the lawsuit in question under *Oh, Brother.*

A male student at a state university in California is suing
the school for sexual harassment (and $2.5 million) because
he had to sit through a guest lecture by an apparently radical
feminist who showed slides of female genitalia and spoke
explicitly about masturbation. And even if the lesson plan
were as sinister as the man's poor lawyer says it was (there
are allegations of child pornography) the plaintiff did not
walk out or speak up.

Ron, a car-phone caller from Detroit, pretty well captures
the essence: "I have never heard so much tripe in my life."

A character in one of Jorge Luis Borges's stories dreads mirrors because they multiply men. The same might be said for radios.

—R. Murray Schafer, The Tuning of
the World

June 4.   **10:00 a.m.–12.00 p.m. WBEZ-FM 91.5.**
                        CBC Sunday Morning.

The story begins simply, intelligently. I tell myself something banal, something like "Interesting idea," and pay attention. The reporter, Mary O'Connell, is talking about "john school," a new police program in San Francisco set up to educate first-timers caught soliciting prostitutes, sort of like a traffic school for sex offenders.

A lieutenant from the Vice Crimes unit addresses the trespassers in a classroom at the Police Academy. One of the men, O'Connell tells us, drives a Lamborghini with the license-plate motto SEXNFUN. Other male authority figures, an assistant district attorney and a health educator, admonish the class with threats of the consequences—jail and disease—of their actions. Norma Hotaling, the ex-prostitute who designed the program with the lieutenant—her former nemesis—describes the sexually transmitted diseases she acquired (and passed along) while on the streets.

The core of the class revolves around the testimony of

ex-hookers like herself, testimony that she admits is often
excruciating for the women to deliver. She says that on the
streets they learned to "dissociate" themselves from reality
and this ability enables them to speak to the men they disdain.

This all sounds logical, a fine idea. You expect some guilt-
inducing finger-pointing and heartfelt confession. What you
get, starting with the first woman, Shashan, is the purest,
deepest expression of hatred that I have ever heard spit out
of a radio. She sighs:

> *Hi, I'm Shashan, ex-prostitute, garbage can, filth, trash, you
> name it, you wanted it, I'll give it. Didn't give a damn. My
> pimp was crack. All you could do for me was fuck me real
> quick and give me some money so I could go get my drugs. . . .
> I've got men issues today. I don't trust you, I don't like you,
> you abuse us, you use us, you destroyed a big part of my—
> my womanhood. I hate your fucking guts.*

I squirm at the applause she receives when she finishes. Are
the men themselves clapping? Are the polite conventions of
public speaking so ingrained that one applauds being
despised?

Norma Hotaling calls it "healthy, righteous anger." This
biblical word "righteous" describes Shashan's fury; the raging
inflection with which she hurls her words could explain the
judgment of God, The Flood, the apocalyptic desire to anni-
hilate the wicked. She is stoning them with every drop of
acid her stomach can spew.

Carrie, described as "a slim, Jewish woman in her twenties
who sold sex in New York City," sounds only slightly more
calm than Shashan (anyone would). Her story makes me
want to throw up: "I was pregnant out there, this pimp made
me . . . I was pregnant and he wouldn't let me have an
abortion and I went out there on the street—nine months
pregnant. Fucking men nine months pregnant. . . ."

A man in the class has the gall to say, "I care about you. . . .
What I did is not right. But we're all victims. You're a victim,
I'm a victim."

O'Connell notices that the students start making excuses, relying on what she calls "the capitalism argument—women supply and men demand."

One star student defends his actions by nonchalantly pointing out the no-frills thriftiness with which prostitution allows him to cheat on his wife. Without it, he would have to waste a bunch of time and money in bars, buying women flowers and dinner. Paying a hooker for the service, he seems to be saying, just makes so much gosh-darn sense.

O'Connell asks Hotaling if she thought a man like that would be changed by the class forum. When she answers no, O'Connell nudges her with, "Is there a tiny part of your mind where you think, 'I'd love to call his wife'?"

"A tiny part?" she asks as her jaded laughter trails off.

Some people never learn. A man who answers the question, "What led you to purchase another human being?" with "Maybe you're making a bigger issue out of this thing than it really is," is met with applause. Still, when given the pep talk to list the qualities of a good human being—the men come up with "respect" and "kindness"—and compare them to the list of what makes a man ("aggressive," "controlling," and "as much sex as possible") maybe a few lightbulbs went on. But the brainstorms of replacements for paid sex in their lives, such as team sports and friendship, most likely inspired the sort of eye-rolling the radio listener can't pick up. It's hard to imagine the SEXNFUN guy, faced with a free afternoon, sweating over the choice between picking up a hooker or a bowling ball.

I reach for the phone and call a good male friend. "Fucking men," I employ as a greeting, making him, for a few minutes, regret being home and his gender and ever making my acquaintance, though not necessarily in that order.

Highway between Albuquerque and Santa Fe, New Mexico

June 6–22, I took part in a School of the Art Institute of Chicago course called "Looking for Land Art, Among Other Things," which involved traveling around the Southwest with

sixteen other undergraduate and graduate students looking
at large-scale artists' earthworks from the 1970s.

June 6.   **4:05 p.m.**

I haven't been on a group bus trip like this since my high-
school band went to the Moosejaw International Band Festival in Saskatchewan in eleventh grade. I'm more than a little
amused about being led around the great American landscape
by two wisecracking British instructors along with the motley
art-school types brooding alone and looking out their respec-
tive windows. As the bus pulls out of the Albuquerque airport,
I gorge myself on the huge Southwestern emptiness. I settle
into my seat and turn on my Walkman radio.

I hear a single guitar, vaguely scratchy, lean into a melody.
The drums barely nudge him for a few seconds and the band
joins in. Kurt Cobain takes a breath and starts singing "The
Man Who Sold the World," just one of the many death-
drenched ballads from the *Unplugged in New York* album.
He sighs through the I-thought-you-were-dead lyrics, and I'm
so happy to just sit that the weary oppression of his voice
escapes me for a few seconds. The song turns instrumental—
processional—with the guitar line gently doubled by the
cello. The sound turns into an easy-paced vector, perfect for
moving through the unfamiliar landscape. The (recorded)
live audience claps and Cobain, forever the admiring fan,
announces, "That was a David Bowie song."

The guest on an AM station has just written a book about
the reincarnation of animals. He tells a story about a veterinar-
ian who made a barn call to a sick horse. He was consulting
with the pony's owners and told them that he'd like to treat
their other horse as well, to prevent spreading the illness.
"What other horse?" they ask. He mentions the white stallion
he had seen running around the pasture that afternoon. The
owners press him for details and he evidently perfectly
describes their long-dead pet.

I turn off the radio: Two ghosts are enough for one afternoon. (Three—if you count David Bowie.)

June 8.   **9:05 a.m.**

We arrive at the tiny town of Quemado in the afternoon
and wait inside the bar. The bartender, a middle-aged woman,
broadcasts the town gossip. She says that a school administra-
tor just ran off with the bus driver and everybody knows it
and that the area is so sparsely populated that "when someone
dies, we all feel it."

Karen, the *Lightning Field* caretaker employed by the Dia
Art Foundation, shows up with her sticky, barefoot, small
daughter in tow. She seems like an average-enough blonde
woman at first, but once we follow her lead down the twisting
dirt roads to the site, we realize that she is in fact a death
wish on wheels, driving recklessly enough to undermine her
maternal image. She pulls up to a rustic little cabin, tells us
where to find the food, to watch out for rattlesnakes, and
speeds off again, leaving a cartoonish cloud of dust behind.

I walk out to the field. There is no escaping the wind.
The steel rods sway like emaciated skyscrapers. They wiggle,
turning the breeze into a faint hum. I put my ear to the
metal and hear a pulse. I grasp the rod with my fingers, tight,
as if it will heal me. I don't feel any better, but I don't feel
any worse.

It takes me nearly two hours to walk the perimeter. The
desert floor is punctured with hundreds of holes made by
small animals. I walk slowly, watching for rattlers. In fact, I
am so terrified of snakes that I freeze for a full two minutes
before I realize that the threatening dark coil in the corner
of my eye is a pile of manure.

The rods frame the desert and chop it into pieces. The
view of the surrounding hills through any two poles is singular,
unrepeated. Moving through the configuration is to confront
the subtle variables in the land—the changes in soil from
hard to soft, and the undulating contours made by anthills,
pale green plants, and rocks.

At the southern edge of the perimeter, an antelope bolts

past me into the field. It runs for maybe five seconds before it registers my presence, stops cold, and turns to stare at me for a while, then walks away.

The afternoon sun is so relentless and intense that the metal rods become almost invisible. After nearly two hours of the piercing heat and deafening wind, I cannot walk straight. I return to the cabin dehydrated and dizzy.

While everyone naps, I sit in a chunky old rocking chair inside the coolness of the cabin and read. Every so often, I look out the window at the field and every time, it's startling. Being out in the middle of it, looking around and through and past the metal, the piece makes sense, seems inevitable, part of the world. But looking through the rectangle of the window, it feels unreal, like the picture in the books. (It's a feeling I'm used to: The Sears Tower looms out past my window in Chicago, and every time I see it, I feel as if I live in a photograph instead of a real city of trees and trains and crowds.) I page through a three-ring binder, Dia's attempt at information. The xeroxed book is too informative, comically accurate, reducing this space of earth-meeting-sky down to measurements and statistics.

The pink-and-red sunset, which we watch from the cabin's porch, illuminates the rods, turning them white. This shift in temperature and light is a material in the piece as much as the metal spikes. The *Lightning Field* doesn't just take up space: It takes place, exists in time, and doesn't so much measure the variance of light as hand you the experience; this is the gift of the place.

I drink a beer and think of Claude Monet. De Maria was in so many ways attempting to bypass Monet's art world, the gallery system's insistence on commodification, the easel painter's attempts at representation. But Monet forces us to recognize the instability of the visible world through his serial views of haystacks. To do so involves admitting that something as solid and permanent as Rouen Cathedral—which he also painted at different times of day—changes as each second goes by: a grain of the masonry blows away, a shadow disappears for keeps, a speck of dust lodges into the eyes of a stone saint. Every evening, the seemingly enduring architecture is subtly attacked by the forces of decay. The very idea of timelessness is exposed as a fraudulent human conceit. With each sunrise, the *Lightning Field* reinvents itself; a rabbit obliterates an anthill and the place is changed forever.

We eat the dinner Karen prepared for us—too cheesy—and then go out into the dark, build a fire, set off fireworks, and tell stories under the stars as if we're only on a good old-fashioned camping trip instead of an odd, art-school adventure. We sit in the freezing cold until the fire's nearly gone and go inside the cabin and sleep in our clothes. At five-thirty, three of us get up and gape at the sunrise. To say that the light turns an eerie greenish yellow . . . the words look blank and meaningless on the page. The cold metal turns a ferocious white and we separate, take solitary walks among the poles, warmed by the gargantuan sun. Staring at the silent acres of land (the wind has, for a few minutes, let up), I don't care if I ever see Chicago again, with its noise and bodies and gunshots.

This feeling will pass.

And now, over three hours later, I sit in the desert sun (I'm warm for the first time in maybe fifteen hours) and take out my radio. The FM is dead in this magnificent wind. Feeling exhausted but a little in touch with the mysteries of the universe, I switch to AM. "Why is it," a man asks, 'brassiere' is singular and 'panties' plural?"

I move around the dial and hear an ad for an Indian jewelry–making handbook and a turquoise/lapis lazuli supplier which doesn't get much circulation in the Midwest.

I waffle back and forth between two Spanish stations; a man hosts one and a woman the other. Not speaking Spanish, I don't understand either announcer, except I notice that both of them frequently insert the word *americano* into their monologues.

A morning-guy type from Albuquerque asks his talk-show audience three questions:

"(1) Should the U.S. help the U.N. in Bosnia, yes or no? (2) Is Bob Dole right or wrong to critique the entertainment industry over content and subject matter in movies or music?"

Last week, Dole issued a crotchety statement against sex and violence in films and popular (read *rap*) music, calling for more family-oriented entertainment such as Arnold Schwarzenegger's last film, *True Lies* (which was, I hear, bursting with bombs and killing, but never mind), therefore managing to endorse censorship while at the same time insinuating that family entertainment can only be made by Republican megadonors like Arnie.

The announcer continues his enumeration: "(3) Should there be or will there be a mistrial in the O. J. Simpson trial?"

Steve calls to vote no, yes, no. Jeff says, "(1) No. I just don't think it's worth the lives of the marines and army and navy that's out there right now. (2) I think he's right. Today's entertainment's really gone down the tubes. (3) There shouldn't be but there will be." Steve number two decides, "(1) We should stay out of Bosnia. That thing could turn into another Vietnam. (2) Bob Dole is absolutely right. (3) I agree with the guy before me."

As a black beetle scours the terrain around my feet, I turn to a Navajo station. A woman, speaking in beautiful rhythms, plays country songs, including one about a Mexican immigrant living in San Antonio who was "proud and living on faith." A few minutes later, a male DJ goes on shift, booming, "Here's Jimmy Buffett!"

"You're listening to the voice of the great Navajo Nation in Window Rock, Arizona," the man announces. The faint hint of a fiddle starts playing and he launches into a disorienting language tennis match between Navajo and English, so I only understand every few words: "rodeo news . . . bull riding . . . first week . . . trophy buckle . . . second week . . . Skip Hanson . . ." etc. The rodeo talk continues for a full fifteen minutes.

At commercial time, I get ready to move down the dial, but the advertisements are as intriguing as the musical language: a car dealer courting Navajo women by promising them respect, a spot whispered in dialect that sounds so seductive and persuasive that the Sirens themselves would be oafish and brash by comparison, and a grocery-store ad that tips its hat to the area's ancient inhabitants, calling them "pretty smart to survive in the desert."

We listen to this station later in the morning as we head back to Quemado. In the midst of a swirl of Navajo words, the announcer says "Tennessee Ernie Ford" but never plays an Ernie song. Since this is a name one rarely mentions in passing, I drive myself crazy wondering why, why, why. Later in the afternoon, a Santa Fe cab driver tells us that in Spanish, *quemado* means burned.

Santa Fe

June 9.   **10:30 p.m. KSFR 90.7-FM.**

In bed at the Motel 6, I'm exhausted from the strain of Santa Fe's heat and crowds and bored by the drab interior that is my room. But then: beautiful, strange, college-station noise. I hear two creepy Beatles covers. The first, a sparse, Hawaiian/surf version of "Day Tripper" sung by a drunk Elvis impersonator from Arkansas (or so he sounds), grows progressively quiet and staccato as if hordes of bloodthirsty insects have murdered the singer and now buzz happily around his corpse. The second, an instrumental shot at "While My Guitar Gently Weeps," could only be a bootleg recording of a perpetually cranked-up jack-in-the-box sputtering in a toy warehouse where a clerk unpacks boxes of Slinkys. This is followed by something even stranger, a thumb-piano (no, a guitar) accompanying a depressive woman singer; they appear to be playing two different songs at once. ("It figures," I think as this one is identified as a release from Albuquerque's Nonsequitur Foundation, a nonprofit noise distribution center run by my pen pal Steve Peters, one of the unsung heroes of American audio art and new music.)

"No, there's nothing wrong with you, me, or our radios," the DJ assures the—I'm guessing—small audience.

Chimayo

June 10.   **11:00 a.m.**

Four of us ride out to this charming, tiny village. The hole
in the church floor contains hallowed dirt that is said to heal
the sick. We arrive just as a pilgrimage group from Santa Fe,
dressed in matching green souvenir T-shirts, is filing into the
yard, led by a young man in a wheelchair. The interior of
the chapel reeks of candle wax. I tiptoe over to the holy hole
and run the sand between my fingers, a little unnerved by
the scores of crutches lining the walls. As we pull back onto
the road toward Taos, Bob Dylan's "Like a Rolling Stone"
flies out of the car radio with so much spiritual force that
not only could the lame walk again if they heard this, they
might just dance around urgently enough to drill their own
sacred holes in the ground like human tornadoes.

"Like a Rolling Stone" isn't a song. It's an argument for
living.

Highway between Albuquerque and Gallup

June 11.   **10:50 a.m.** *Casey Kasem's Hot 20 Extra.*

Casey slobbers on and on about some pretentious-sounding
guy named Steve who (are you allowed to do this?) rides
his horse out to Stonehenge and supposedly communes so
completely with the spirits of ancient mystics that he can
feel their power and (Casey pauses dramatically)"even hear
their music." There's a lot of static. The creepy, oppressive
Police song "Every Breath You Take" starts playing. "I'll be
watching you," Big Brother—I mean Sting—threatens.

Oops, I get it. Not Steve—*Sting.*

Grand Canyon

June 12.   **2:45 p.m.**

I can only stammer. I gasp and stare and sneak up to the
edge, pull back, and gasp again. To even hint at the vastness

of this becomes impossible, and it is with no small hesitation that I turn on my radio. This is a place for silence, not the *ABC Network News*, which I listen to, perched on a rock. Attorney General Janet Reno has just announced the creation of a new television network for the U.S. prison system to "educate and provide rehabilitation for prisoners."

Even the briefest mention of incarceration here, at the edge of the most astounding expanse I have ever looked at, makes me cringe. The very idea of sitting in a small, dark cell and watching television, much less *prison* TV, constricts my throat. No one has mentioned exactly what sort of programming might be rehabilitative, but I'm guessing *Jailhouse Rock* won't be on the lineup.

With all this land and air around me, I abandon Janet Reno and everything she, at this moment, represents—problem-solving, compromise, even innovation. I don't want to hear it, don't want to think about locks and keys or mistakes or crime and punishment. I want to look at big rocks and stir up dust and shade the sun from my eyes.

Somewhere between Flagstaff and Sedona

June 14.   **9:35 a.m.**

I look at the intensely red rocks and evergreens out the bus window, so unreal and garish they remind me more of fake *Star Trek* set pieces than pieces of my own country, and turn on an FM station called "Calf Country."

All of the songs on commercial country radio have the same perky tempo and this one, just one more representative of the woman-as-nature cliché, is no exception. It's a cutesy tribute to a tattooed Texas woman branded with an image of the Lone Star State near her privates. Her body is a map of the state; elaborate double entendres are drawn between erogenous zones and specific locales along the lines of "she drives me wacky in Waco."

3:25 p.m.

Between Big Water and Big Glitz, the monument to American know-how and the town where capitalism goes on vacation, I hear this song—as small and private as one man's body. He says that he went to the movies. In the big Western sunshine, which right now makes me only blank and sleepy, the Beatles' "A Day in the Life" makes me want to sit in a bookstore and read sad novels for free. I long for, practically pray for, rain, but it never comes. If anything, the sun shines brighter and as the chaos part of the song crashes around asking questions, a gleaming subdivision comes in view as if to mock the very notion of turmoil.

Deciding that it's a bad idea to get tea-soaked in Anglo poetics on the verge of a Vegas weekend, I change stations. This is more like it: breezy, cool jazz, the sound of the dryest martini. Devoid of John Lennon's emotion, this is detached and air-conditioned. A tenor saxophone plays with such hipster apathy that it sounds like he's just killing time till happy hour. The pianist solos as the ridiculous but impressive pyramid that is the Luxor casino appears on the horizon. If "A Day in the Life" is one of those stop-cold songs that calls everything into question, this fake jazz can never inspire communication, merely eye contact between people who remain strangers.

The desert near Las Vegas: Michael Heizer's *Double Negative*

June 16.

With a name like *Double Negative*, how can you not not joke around? We didn't not want to visit Heizer's other earthwork in the area, *Complex I*, but he said, "No, no, it's not not unfinished," even though thousands of PBS viewers didn't not see the thing on Robert Hughes' documentary series on modern art.

And speaking of complex, our directions to the site imply

navigational chaos. We've heard that some visitors don't make it out there on the first try, which only adds to our determination. The instructions advise checking in at the Overton airport with a certain Mr. Winter. When we arrive there, the man who meets us sadly announces that Arnold—Mr. Winter—has been dead for five years.

I was prepared for a roughriding bout of motion sickness, of breaking away from established roads to "cross the mesa," and driving over tumbleweeds, rocks, and mud. In fact, we find the place easily and park at the edge.

The piece is smaller than I expected, mostly because I had read an interview with megalomaniac Heizer, who made endearing statements such as, "My work is independent of anybody else's, and comes directly out of myself . . . whatever I was doing I was doing it first. And whatever I was doing, I was doing it myself." The work itself was only a fraction of the size of Heizer's ego.

Confronted with this deep gash in the earth, this still-massive assault of bulldozers on an innocent, ancient table of land, I can understand feminist readings of the piece as violation. Driving up, we joke that maybe the Guerrilla Girls have filled it in and built a rape crisis center on top of it. I write a limerick:

> There once was an artist named Heizer.
> As art despots go, he was the Kaiser.
> His work was a trench
> that he thought was a wench
> and the feminists said, "We wish you would die, sir."

The radio, as usual, lends the situation a sick sense of humor. I sit at the edge and listen to Aretha Franklin—"You Make Me Feel Like a Natural Woman."

Dark humor aside, there is a sinister mood here. How ugly. How obscene. And how bloody pointless. A big art ditch. So fucking what. If, as I read somewhere, Heizer meant to evoke THE VOID, then I suppose he succeeded. Do we need one more gigantic reminder of the human obsession with oblivion, with nothingness and lack? With no small delight we play Frisbee across his void and the gesture is so ridiculous and silly, so entertaining (and Heizer loathes entertainment) that it feels like a giant fuck-you to Mr. I Stand Alone.

Evidently we're not the only ones to find alternative recreational functions for the place; shotgun shells litter the ground. We've heard a lot about militias in the area, and looking down the long hallway formed by the two facing dugouts, I realize that the space forms an ideal rifle range. When the NEA and the NRA finally plan their summit conference, this is the spot for it: Something for everyone and so close to the Vegas hotels!

Las Vegas

June 19.   **9:40 a.m.**

A talk-show host brags that he understands why O. J. Simpson would want to kill his former wife, because he fantasizes about doing away with his with the help of an Uzi. He even wrote a song about it, which he performs lounge act–style, to the tune of "Mack the Knife," ending with a scream through the lovely sentiment *"Look out that bitch ex-wife!"*

Brigham City, Utah

June 20.   **11:35 a.m. Bible Broadcasting Network.**

Last night we ate pizza for dinner in a restaurant that offered a neatly arranged display of the Book of Mormon at the counter. The serious volumes sat there, lined up like a little pew full of preachers, as if their presence was as natural as the silverware and napkins next to them. I wanted to take one back to our table, but if I've learned anything from some friends' Jehovah's Witness parents, it's never, ever, show an interest.

An announcer on AM radio pays tribute to General Douglas MacArthur, who, he quotes, said that " 'Armageddon will be at our door' " and that the problem facing America " 'is theological. All natural and cultural development . . . it must be of the spirit if we are going to save the flesh.'" These words, while eloquent, are wide open, but the man uses them as a tiny doorway into denouncing the blasphemies of religious cults, which he calls "anti-God, anti-Bible, anti-Christ." They should be demolished, he says, "if America is to be spared." His how-to-spot-a-cult recipe includes these attributes: following a human leader, deserting your family, keeping cult secrets, substituting another text for the Bible (fighting words, in these parts).

Near Lucin, Utah: Nancy Holt's *Sun Tunnels*

June 21.

It could be the loner in me: I imagine every imposing land-mark, every work of art, each pyramid and famous peak, as silent and evacuated. I had pictured myself at the Louvre, contemplating the fuss over the *Mona Lisa*'s smile in analytic quietude. Instead, I was herded past the glass-encased specta-cle in a flurry of whispers and exclamations in such an inhu-man stampede that the experience could have been the poster image for the Hell Is Other People Foundation. Similarly, I thought of Nancy Holt's *Sun Tunnels* (an X configuration of four concrete cylinders built to view the solstices) as a quiet place, meditative and spiritual, drenched in solitude, not, as we find it on the summer solstice, a combination kegger and family cookout.

One group of surly solstice watchers (who seem to agree with Holt that this is a fine spot to view the sun but couldn't care less about her art) park their two pickup trucks side by side and blast a car radio through opened doors. It's just loud enough to create an intrusive racket but not loud enough to discern any music per se. But they have just as much right to be here as anyone. More, actually, since they live nearby. Their radio hum takes on an almost benign patina compared with what comes next—a hippie family noodling around inside the sculptures playing little whiny flutes.

Salt Lake City

June 22.   **4:28 p.m. KCNR 1320-AM.**

I say good-bye to the trip kids and go on alone to California
to visit friends. With hours to kill before my flight to San
Francisco, I get on a bus downtown to kill time. I take a tour
through the headquarters of the Latter-Day Saints led by
two exceedingly clean and perky young women. I enjoy trailing around behind a French teenager wearing a backpack
shaped like a teddy bear through a chapel with trippy space
murals, which, except for the Jesus figure waiting at the top,
seem more like a Yes album cover than a religious fresco.

Back at the airport, I search the radio for LDS sentiment,
only to find an AM talk-show host named Rick Taylor spewing, "Should teens be encouraged to have sex? I think yes!";
that grating *All Things Considered* theme music (followed
by the even more grating drab haughtiness of Robert Siegel
and Noah Adams droning about welfare reform); and the
Rolling Stones' "Shattered." Exhausted, I drift off to sleep
until my flight is called. Earlier, I looked up my name on
the computer in the Mormon genealogical research center.
I found a me christened in Somerset in England in 1682.
With the desert and the universe (not to mention teen sex,
the Mormons, and the Stones) in my head on four hours of
sleep, I felt at least that old.

San Francisco

June 25.

Back in San Francisco, I'd much rather eat and talk than
hang around listening to the radio. But before leaving on my
jaunts around town this morning, I listen to Live 105's remote
broadcast from Golden Gate Park, where Pearl Jam is playing
an outdoor concert. Evidently, the ticket situation turned
into chaos and good old Eddie Vedder himself is amidst the
crowd, trying to straighten out the problem, which seems,
well, nice.

June 25.   **4:55 p.m.**

A graduating high-school senior named Jason Prince gets a chance to say something to the country. On *Weekend All Things Considered* on KQED, he announces, "You have to be idealistic to forge forward and make a difference." Ten minutes later, on KSFO ("Hot Talk 560"), talk-show host Spencer Hughes uses his broadcasting access to bitch about city bus drivers: "One thing that drives me nuts is idiots that block intersections. . . . I was on a bus yesterday that blocked the intersection. . . . Who are these idiots that drive these MUNI buses? They're impersonating professional people if you ask me."

This morning's *San Francisco Examiner* contains an article lifted from Charles Ornstein of the *Dallas Morning News*. The National Association of Radio Talk Show Hosts has honored G. Gordon Liddy with its Freedom of Speech Award. House minority leader Dick Gephardt of Missouri called it "not only wrong, but outrageous" and equated Liddy's rhetoric with "gangsta rappers who advocate violence against police." Granted, Liddy's sentiments run the gamut from hideous to vile, but unlike KSFO's host, Hughes, who wastes space with meaningless complaining that would make Andy Rooney blush, Liddy does stand up for education. (I've heard him drone on about the schools that his children have attended, though he has never to my mind mentioned that his daughter attended my art school.) He even occasionally allows for oppositional viewpoints to be represented on his otherwise over-the-top show. Which is more than you can say for that cowardly, insecure, antieducation creep, Rush Limbaugh.

Los Angeles: Los Burritos Restaurant, Sunset Boulevard

June 26.   **3:45 p.m.**

Bewildered by my first day in L.A., I devour a good burrito and try to ignore the bad radio. It's tuned to a Spanish-language station that plays only saccharine ballads interrupted by booming, cheesy announcers and exclamatory ads.

You don't have to speak Spanish to understand that every last song is straight out of the pre-Nirvana universe, full of fake, slick moaning over one lost love after another.

June 27.   **8:10 p.m. Dial scan.**

AM: A talk-show host asks a sex offender, "I want to know why you abuse kids." Isn't the answer to that one always going to be the same? Something along the lines of "I'm a sick, insane creep"? . . . Someone just bunted in a baseball game. . . . Another game, or maybe the same one (they all sound alike to me)—Cubs against Padres—3 balls, 2 strikes. . . . Ad for an automatic earthquake shut-off valve that "will stop the flow of gas going into your house," because "it's the topnotch in valves." . . . Don Rickles is talking about advising Sharon Stone to "sit down and shut up." . . . A drum machine–propelled synthesizer ballad. . . . Orange County voters are faced with a half-cent sales tax to bail out their failed city government. . . . An ad in Spanish for the Six Flags Magic Mountain amusement park. . . . The dollar is down a third of a yen at the New York close. . . . A PSA warning about motor oil working its way into the water supply. . . . A woman speaking Chinese (I think) with Vivaldi's *Four Seasons* playing in the background. . . . Los Dodgers have *tres* something or other in this Spanish play-by-play. . . . A man tries to sell something in Spanish. . . . A woman with a very small voice sings arpeggios in Italian with piano accompaniment.

FM.

Garden-variety cool jazz. . . . A duet about Bonnie and Clyde sung in French, as in "Bun-nee Per-ker." The answer, they sing, is to die. . . . "Bob Marley's become literally an industry. Every college student in America," a man claims, "has a copy of *Legend* in their collection," which I doubt. (But I remember a temp job I had at a huge bank in San Francisco where I was assigned to go with a slimy, ladder-climbing weasel-in-training to fetch coffee for some big meeting. Marley was on the tape deck at the coffee shop and while they filled our order, the corporate underling tapped his wing tips and sang along to "I Shot the Sheriff," completely oblivious to the irony of the situation, continuing the song on the street and up the elevator all the way to his small gray cubicle.) ... That song from Bizet's *Carmen*, which I first heard on the *Gilligan's Island* episode in which Phil Silvers guest-starred, directing the castaways in a musical version of *Hamlet*. ... A rap ad in which a man asks, "Open my jacket and see Nike on my chest," though it's unclear if the logo would just be stamped across a shirt or tattooed on his skin. ... A Japanese station where everybody talking sounds truly cheerful. ... A country song about—surprise!—regret. ... A sale on "select boneless rib-eye steaks." ... Pearl Jam. ... A wonderful maria-chi band with a tuba player gone mad. ... A program called *Insight for Living* promises to reveal "the hidden jewel of worship," whatever that means. ... John Mellencamp. ... A syrupy R&B ballad. ... Ditto. ... "My Guy." ... Madonna singing "Say Good-Bye"—so I do.

Figuroa Street

June 29.   **12:05 p.m.**

A Spanish station plays on the radio in this East L.A. laundro-mat. A rowdy, ponytail-wearing girl, about eight years old, occasionally drowns the music by pounding the pinball machine with the palms of her small hands. As my clothes hit the spin cycle, a little boy sits down next to me with a Gameboy, while yet another child plays a video game that puts out the noise of twelve Vegas slot machines, and an old woman wheels a screeching cart around the room. Just as I'm thinking that no one is listening to the radio (who could hear?) I see a man and woman leaning into each other next to the dryers. They start to subtly dance close as a dreamy ballad lilts out of the radio, but the way they sway and smile, you get the feeling that they could find the rhythm in a toothpaste ad.

JULY

The cards were scattered on the table, face up, face down, and they seemed to foretell that whatever we did to one another would be washed away by liquor or explained away by sad songs.

—*Denis Johnson, Jesus' Son*

LAX

July 1.   **11:00 a.m. KPFA-FM.**

You might think that the Unabomber's threat to blow up a plane here today would discourage a few people from flying. In fact, this terminal is jam-packed with nervous lines of travelers spilling out past seats and into corridors. Still, a lot of them look a little anxious to leave, especially the ones without seats who sprawl onto the floor or lean against plants and walls. Maybe the desert made me greedy for elbow room, but it's hard to concentrate on this Pacifica news discussion of the fairy-tale Los Angeles subway system with all these heaving bodies in my space.

A billion dollars it's supposed to cost.

If shiny, vapid Vegas taught me to love Chicago architecture and its grimy brick opulence, the L.A. freeways have turned me into a raving zealot for the el. As a nondriver who just spent my entire L.A. visit at the mercy of friends'

automobiles, I cannot wait to ride the train home tonight
through the Loop's grand contours, over the river and under
the ground.

St. Louis Airport

6:55 p.m.

In the short walk changing planes, A *Prairie Home Companion*
welcomes me to the Midwest. There's a peppy little marching
number about people who are bohemians because they have
no health insurance. That's one way of looking on the bright
side. It could be a slogan to reassure the uninsured millions:
Trade Your Health for Hip!

Chicago

July 3.   **9:25 p.m. WFMT-FM 98.7.**

The *1812 Overture* jumps the gun on the Fourth of July
across town in Grant Park. I turn the ending's bombast up
full-blast until the ceiling shakes. At nine-thirty, to accom-
pany fireworks, the orchestra packs up and a tape pulls in
the slack. But not just any tape—a weird collage that bleeds
Whitney Houston's decorative ooze through "America the
Beautiful" (I didn't know *beautiful* had that many syllables)
into Vivaldi, which bumps into "Born in the U.S.A.," which
waves to a military ménage à trois of "As the Caissons Go
Rolling Along," the Air Force anthem, and the Marine Corps
hymn. As the tape gets local, I can see a big pink burst out
my window: "Sweet Home Chicago" winks at Sinatra. Just
as Frank's about to lose the blues, a big white blossom erupts
in agreement. Then red. Then green. Then Disney's mock
apple pie—"A Whole New World" from the *Aladdin* soundtrack, which is erased by "Stars and Stripes Forever" in all
its mammoth spirit, decorated with little yellow dots and
shooting stars that rise again as glowing suns across the "Battle Hymn of the Republic."

I have a soft spot for Sousa only because of a misspent

youth decked out in a dorky hat in the low brass section of the marching band, not because his punchy rhythms are meant to shoot my hand over my heart. The clichéd signifiers of Independence Day, especially the militaristic anthems, have nothing to do with me, my life, or why, despite the violence this country has wrought in the name of peace and freedom, I remain somehow proud to call myself American.

In fact, I'm still a flag-waver. It's just that I wave around banners other than the stars and stripes. And in my world there's no such lame nonissue as the "flag-burning controversy" because my flags—lickety-split surf guitar or Jennifer Jason Leigh—are already on fire.

July 5.   **11:40 p.m.**

I have this tape, a two-headed monster of soul: Little Richard on one side and James Brown on the other. I've been soaking up the sheer commitment of the thing, those voices becoming a resin to rub against, to feel sticky, close up. When the tape ends, as good things must, I turn on the radio, and manically search for the same kind of guts. Nothing comes close, a meaningless progression of stone-cold synthesizers, talk-show drudgery, embarrassing ads, and Lionel Richie's brain-dead "All Night Long," which seems to last as long as its title suggests.

I yank the cassette out of the stereo so it doesn't get contaminated. A friend stopped drinking good coffee at restaurants because it made it harder to stomach the cheap shit he drinks at home. My speakers, it seems, understand the sentiment.

July 6.

Some guardian angel against grouchiness must be looking out for me, plopping a little act of God into the mail this morning—writer Stanley Booth's tapes of a radio show he and two buddies did last March to celebrate Black History

Month—three whole cassettes of all kinds of funk, jazz, blues, soul, and gospel (sometimes all of the above in just one song) made by African-Americans from the state of Georgia. One act of genius ends and three more take its place, followed not by radio babble, but something like the sound of real conversation.

What it is, is the Fourth of July, two days late.

The show, recorded in Waycross/Brunswick, is called *Jazz Tracks*, and its beginning is as lovely as it is obvious—Ray Charles' breezy "Georgia on My Mind," in which the sweet roughness of Ray's voice scratches out the string section's sugary hysterics. More Ray, then some funk and stops for chitchat as host Bill Davis introduces Stanley and Jim Pettigrew Jr., as "esteemed authors, writers, lovers of life." A few songs later, and they're all good (especially an Atlanta singer named Nappy Brown, whose midnight blue voice won't let go of the phrase *"I declare"*), the vocal pipes burst into a gusher of nonwords like *"leema"* and *"lamma."* In other words, Little Richard has arrived, rapidly and all at once, singing the hell out of "Heeby-Jeebies" for all the onomatopoeic force it's worth. Stanley will later call the singer "the original king—and queen—of rock 'n' roll."

There are old songs, about love, of course, but also dead mothers and shipwreck that come to sound older, ancient and slow. There's Bessie Smith's hilarious "Jelly Roll," James Brown's pleading autocratic fantasy, "If I Ruled the World," and the good-hearted joy of Blind Willie McTell, whose talent Stanley will elegize as global: "As Telly Savalas says, 'The Carribean, Vegas, Tahoe, Atlantic City, all over the world.'"

July 7.   **7:45 p.m. WBEZ.** *The Wild Room.*

"The studio equivalent of a homeless shelter," Gary Covino calls it when he sees the look on my face. I had pictured 'BEZ, the local NPR affiliate station as a little more slick. But the microscopic, worn-out studio, decked out in dingy brown carpet and dilapidated green chairs, oozes a sickly smell of defeat. And I thought some of their *programming* was drab.

Mere moments before *The Wild Room* airs, Ira Glass barrels in with a handful of tapes and CDs. He throws the stuff down, gets situated behind the board, and starts pushing buttons. Gary picks up the phone to instruct whoever it is that's waiting on the line, "Hello Larry. It's Gary."

A few haphazard remarks later, they're on the air:

And this is The Wild Room *and this is Gary Covino and I have a confession to make. Maybe it's because I'm an American, maybe it's because, yes, I'm a boy, but for the last couple of months, I own a computer. I've been spending a lot of time on this computer.*

This is Ira Glass. I'd also like to say that I have a shameful confession, that I, too, have been surfing the Net. I have not only visited Web pages. Last week, I wrote a Web page and it's a sorry, sorry thing. It's as bad as confessing to being a Star Trek fan, *which Gary and I will never do.*

Switch to a tape Ira made of a man who just got dropped by his electronic-mail service for transmitting pornography, or, as the company representative calls it over the phone, "graphics violations."

"Hello Chicago," the violator remarks, "I've been a naughty boy. I've been kicked off of America Online for viewing pornography—collecting, trading, and sending it to friends. I'm an adult male, thirty-four years old, happily married for eleven years with two kids. America Online has kicked me out of cyberspace."

"Did we say the name of the show?" Ira asks Gary.

"The name of the show is 'Bless me, Father, I have sinned.' We are going to talk about computers because we're Americans, we're on the radio. It's 1995. This is public radio and that's all you do. Anything, anything, anything to keep from having to talk about poor people."

Ira announces that all of the music on tonight's show was downloaded off the Internet from the computer games Sim

City and Tetris, which doesn't strike me as completely legal, though it's the sound of pure bureaucracy.

Back to the tape. Ira logs on with the alleged pornographer. They plop down into an exclusive chat room and end up talking to the man's cyberacquaintance, coincidentally a 'BEZ listener who recognizes Ira's name. When queried about his response to AOL's restrictions he says, "They violate my rights. The right to party." When Ira asks if he'll send something risqué, he refuses, because there's a "climate of fear."

Gary notes, "It's a 'BEZ listener. They're not going to go out on a limb."

The listener writes, "Is Ira Glass there now? He might be antiporn because 'BEZ kowtows to feminists."

When Ira asks the obviously cracked-up Gary how to respond to that, he giggles, "You come back on and say WBEZ kowtows to everybody!"

"Because we are the people's station!" screams Ira. "Feminists! Antifeminists!"

"You name it, we kowtow to 'em!"

Ira mentions that the man blames the station for the Clarence Thomas–Anita Hill hearing: "He specifically blames that on WBEZ. . . . He said that WBEZ brought Clarence Thomas down."

Gary laughs. "Another WBEZ success! Who is sitting on the Supreme Court today? Who cast the deciding vote against affirmative action? Another classic 'BEZ success."

While the Tetris music drones underneath them, the two hosts bat back and forth about whether or not pornography is de-eroticized on the Internet. They face each other, eyes locked, as if they're shooting the shit in some little bar instead of speaking into microphones.

The alleged pornographer then walks down chat-room memory lane, describing an instance in which a couple with a Polaroid camera posted an offer to perform any act, photograph it, scan the photograph, and send it back out. Our hero says he didn't quite believe it was true. He noticed a pen sitting on a table in one image, so he asked the woman to stick the pen to her forehead. A few minutes later, a picture of exactly that appeared on his screen. He freaked out: "I told someone to do something and they did it." The power, he says, "scared me."

The Larry on the phone turns out to be Larry Massett, the silver-smooth host of NPR's documentary program *Soundprint*. Massett, at home in Maryland, speeds around to various Web pages, discovering such things as the fact that there are forty-two ways to generate electric power from hamsters. He goes to a page called "Why Ask Why," which asks questions like, "When they ship Styrofoam, what do they pack it in?"

Ronnie, a listener, calls in. He enthusiastically doles out his web page address, making Gary, Mr. Power to the People, Mr. "Greetings, Fellow Workers," grumpy enough to deliver an irritated indictment.

"Another exhibitionist. Can you believe this?" He asks Ronnie, "Why is your life worth having on the Internet?"

Ira, incredulous, asks Gary, "What are you talking about? You are on the radio every week thinking you have something interesting to tell the forty or fifty people who listen to our program. How is this any different?"

Gary lamely responds, "I took an FCC test in 1974," while Massett pulls up Ronnie's "Cool Stuff" folder, which turns out to be a photograph of a park bench in Chicago.

Even though I confess that I am a bit of a technophobe, I like the *idea* that this Ronnie thinks he has something to say and puts it in plain view. Listening to the radio and the Internet collide, I can't help but give the Net some due. It's interesting for exactly the reason that this man doesn't need a license to "broadcast." Still, despite what we constantly hear about the fact that we live in a visual culture, I get sick of looking.

After mentioning a Web page with the wonderful title "Binge on Pain," Massett looks up an offering of Surrealist games in which a question is answered with a random

response. It sounds dumb, but ends up being kind of beautiful:

> *Is there a purpose to sleeping? An angry bullet.*
> *When is the best time to make love? Asleep at the wheel.*
> *What is the meaning of this question? Closed-door politics.*
> *Can you tell me the meaning of love? A desperate triumph*
> *underwater.*

Massett, sticking with the Surrealists, scrolls to something
called "Hypotheticals and Conditionals":

> *If these really were the best years of my life, then the truth*
> *would be known about permanence.*
> *If your finger was cut deeply enough, then no attachments*
> *would be left for an alliance among the wicked.*
> *If everyone wore handcuffs, then politicians wouldn't have*
> *to lie.*

Wrapping up, Gary assesses the Internet's influence on his
life: "I now know who Kate Moss is and what she looks like."
  "From several different angles," guesses Massett.
  Ira plugs Gary's documentary about homeless people in
San Francisco, which airs on *Soundprint* next week. When
Massett describes a homeless Web site, Gary notes that the
problem with finding it is that "it has no address."

As Ira and his girlfriend Anahed drive me home, I complain
about the show's horrid computer-game music considering
the Jonathan Richman CD Ira had brought to the studio.
He mentions that once he did an entire *Wild Room* devoted
to Jonathan, a tape of which, Anahed points out, just happens
to be in her glove compartment. It begins with an actor
named Michael Stumm, but he's identified later. He just
starts talking:

*Okay. So I walk into this record store . . . and I'm looking
through the used records. I'm a regular. Donovan, "Hurdy
Gurdy Man" forty-nine cents. Mott the Hoople. Gary Glit-
ter. A Velvets record.* [Jonathan's lovely gentle guitar starts
here, as if it's listening intently to the story.] *The guy
behind the counter motions me over. He's got this look on
his face. And he's holding these records in his hand. He's
got like three of them. He says to me, almost whispers in
my ear, "You know, Mike, you wanna buy these."*

He almost doesn't get the first one, the Ramones, because
he's "not really into Latin music." He buys it anyway, along
with two by Jonathan Richman and the Modern Lovers, and
heads home: "You know when you've got really good music
in your hand and you're going home, your hands, like, tingle.
You know [*grace note of a giggle*] you've got something cool."

He sets the scene: mid-1970s Milwaukee, cheap record
player. Decides not to get into his Ramones reaction here,
but assures us that it's "jaw-dropping."

He puts on the first Modern Lovers album. Describing it,
his voice takes on the cast of someone trying to describe
India or an exceptional meal: "I almost don't know where to
begin to explain the kind of thing that happens. How my
life changes. It's fabulous, fabulous teenage music. Let's not
forget this is 1975. There's not this kind of stuff on the
radio. . . ."

*First of all, you've got this guy right up front who sounds
like he has a very, very, very bad cold, singing about how
he's really, truly, in love with the suburbs. How he loves his
parents. How he meets his girlfriends on the astral plane at
night. And he means it. He means every single word of it. . . .
This stuff just smokes off my turntable. I'm kneeling in front
of my record player, uh, just wondering when, when this
good thing is gonna end.*

He finds the second record "if possible, even better. It's like
doo-wop music gone absolutely mad.

"Again, I play all this music. I'm kneeling in front of my record player thinking to myself, *if I don't move to New York in ten minutes, I'm gonna miss this!*"

Skip a beat. "One two three four five six!" It's "Roadrunner," Jonathan's greatest song, the best tribute ever to driving around with the (and the band hollers this continually, with extreme joy) "*Radio on!*"

And I hate getting home because the song's not over. One quick mumbled thanks to Ira and a rifle through a CD pile later, the song's on my stereo. You just can't skip the end of "Roadrunner." It starts out as a lark, a joy ride on Route 128 with a rockin' AM soundtrack. Then it turns into something like the theology of larks. The nocturnal highway acts as a veritable biblical wilderness where Jonathan chants a circular mantra of life and love and holy loneliness. "*Radio on!*" the band keeps yelling, as if to say, "Amen, brother!" And it's over as simply as the countdown that begins it, with a plain and neighborly "Bye-bye!"

It's the most visionary song I know.

Not on the radio in 1975? This stuff isn't on the radio now.

July 8.   **9:50 p.m. 1390-AM.**

I'm not even paying attention to this plug for Sheik condoms until its bizarre conclusion: ". . . but don't forget to pay for 'em. Or else some dime-store dick will get you for shoplifting. Sheik. Get some."

July 9.   **7:15 p.m. WLS-AM. Bruce Dumont:**
                                       Beyond the Beltway.

Dumont asks a caller—Sally from Margate, Florida—why she thinks that Congress rejected the Clinton administration plan for universal health care.

"All the congresspeople have wonderful health care paid for by the American taxpayers," she points out, adding that the United States and South Africa "are the only industrial societies that don't have it."

The discussion segues into political courtesy after Dana, an in-studio guest, accuses Hillary Clinton of "demonizing the 'profiteering' drug companies. I think civility is a good thing. I wish the White House would practice it, not just preach it."

Dumont, referring to the president's post–Oklahoma bombing call for more polite discourse, charges that the reason Clinton "wants to lower people's voices to have polite *MacNeil-Lehrer* discussions is that he will win MacNeil-Lehrer discussions." Dumont says this as a reproach, as if to say, "Oh sure, any wuss can talk things out."

A female caller complains that Mrs. Clinton's work with the health-care task force "became some sort of gender attack."

John from Richmond concurs; he's fed up: "The 1996 political campaign has already begun and it is underpinned in this lack of civility." He laments Jesse Helms' homophobia and wails, "Newt is calling women 'bitches.' What kind of future does this country have?"

July 10.   **7:00 p.m. WBEZ.** *Soundprint.*

Serving soup provided by something called the United Anarchists Front House, Keith McHenry is breaking the law. As cofounder of the Bay Area's Food Not Bombs, he's been arrested ninety times "in his long career of culinary activism." So says Gary Covino, producer of this documentary called *The Great San Francisco Food Fight.*

While furnishing the homeless with meals (without any kind of government or taxpayer funding) sounds like kind of a good idea, San Francisco city officials have consistently shut down the group's soup and salad tables because of the lack of permits and possible health-code violations.

Covino takes us to a Valentine's Day rally earlier this year at the Hall of Justice. The San Francisco Mime Troupe stage a sarcastic play in which the food-givers are pitted against cops. The dialogue (and I didn't know that mimes were allowed to speak) asks the basic question: "What's so bad about free food?"

The group's confrontation with police at the rally seems inevitable. "When it happens," Covino narrates, "it's fast and it's surreal. . . . A young member of Food Not Bombs sits on the courthouse steps with a plastic bucket of oatmeal. He offers a cup to someone nearby. Immediately four police officers swoop down and grab him." He says that another man holds up a bag of bagels, offers them, and is then grabbed by police.

Meanwhile, the mass of protesters are chanting, "Shame! Shame! Shame!" over and over behind police barricades.

Traffic noise at Civic Center Plaza: Covino outlines the history of the city's influx of the homeless since the 1980s. Mayor Frank Jordan, we're told, was elected on a platform of dealing with the problems of "dirty streets, panhandlers, the homeless." Jordan's victory speech bragged, "San Francisco is back on track, back on its feet, and we're gonna be proud of it again."

In October 1993, Jordan initiates the Matrix Program to clear the homeless out of city parks.

Terence Hallinan, a member of the Board of Supervisors, attended one feeding in which around a hundred and fifty police officers were harassing a dozen Food Not Bombs workers. He decided to take action:

> I just went out one day and got behind their table and started serving soup . . . the few people who I did serve, for them it was actual food on the table. It wasn't just an abstract thing. I saw the way these people ate that soup that I gave them and they were hungry people. And I know one person reached up at one point and grabbed my hand and when I looked at his hand, the poor guy, you could see the bones in his fingers and everything.

Cut to Jordan: "I apologize to no one for the Matrix Program." He calls the average panhandler "not a homeless person but an opportunist.... I apologize to no one for making it a police issue and dealing with it in a criminal-justice way."

Covino asserts that the Union Square area, a "tourist mecca," was swept clean of nontourists much to the relief of neighborhood hotels and businesses. Covino speaks to an antique dealer who seems sympathetic to the problem while maintaining that panhandlers in front of his store significantly slice his profit margin and, therefore, his viability.

Covino tapes a homeless couple, Randy and Janie, who describe their collection of police citations. "How would you like to get a ticket for eating a banana on a sidewalk?" Randy asks.

"What did you get charged with?"

"Eating a banana on the sidewalk!"

Covino finds Jordan boasting of the so-called Matrix teams, a group of social workers. He trails around with Paul, who approaches the homeless on the street with the question, "Do you need any services?" Invariably, the answer is no. When Paul tries to persuade one couple to put their names on a waiting list for a welfare hotel, they scream back at him complaints about rats and high rent in such places until he leaves them alone.

Aside from the obligatory Jordan citations, Covino nails down his fuck-tha-police point of view even further with a rabbi's insistence that human beings are "bearers of the sacred. Each of us carries the image of the divine with us into the world . . . by banishing them [presumably, the homeless] from our world, then we banish the divine from our world as well."

But if that's a little too heavy, a hipster rapper, in the process of serving food, delivers his own sermon in a grinning voice:

Take what you need. Give what you can. . . . Lend a hand. . . .
Strangers become friends. . . . We are brought together for
a reason, 'cause, hey, ensalada? That reason is 'cause we
love one another. . . . We complement one another. Yin and

*yang. Up and down. Man and woman. Rock and rollllllll!
There's another whole bucket of soup, folks! Never fear!*

Never fear.

But you pretty much have to fear listening to this, don't
you? Here you have an organization willing to bypass govern-
mental funding to help its citizens in need, accomplishing
something that (it seems) congressional Republicans keep
harping about (local involvement, avoiding the costly pitfalls
of so-called big-government programs), being harassed for
actually solving a problem. Maybe Food Not Bombs violates
health codes. But so does eating out of a Dumpster. When
citizens get arrested for eating a banana on a sidewalk and
handing someone else, of all things, a bagel, you have to fear.
You really do.

New York City

July 13.   **9:35 a.m. WSAU-FM.**

Even though I'm verging on broke from my Western travels,
I come to New York to pitch this book to publishers. (If
you're reading this, it must have worked.) I stay in Brooklyn
with my friends Steve and Mimi. It's sweltering.

Just as the morning's murky heat makes me feel like a
sludgy bucket of pulsating goo, the greatest sludge-rock band
in the world oozes out of the radio. They're humid, the
Melvins. I sweat more, if that's possible, and gulp some coffee,
as thick and black as they sound.

July 15.   **1:55 p.m. Dial scan.**

Hungover in my friend Susan's Manhattan apartment (air-
conditioned, thank God), I listen to the radio until I have
to leave for La Guardia.

Moving right to left from Pearl Jam's melancholy "Nothing
Man," past a murky jazz-fusion theme of the sort that accom-
panies those soap-opera Caribbean falling-in-lust montages,

I park briefly at "Wooly Bully" and its good old "*Watch it now!*" party banter. Onward to an Irish political prisoner's sister, a disco ballad, groovy hiphop delivered in an African tongue, a liturgical dirge, an ad that demands, "Go to the mall," Smashing Pumpkins.

And then, if not the saddest song in the world, then at least the saddest song yet, sung in Russian or Greek or some other icon-worshiping vernacular. I picture the singer as a babushka-clad Nico sitting in a dark little bar with a glass of something clear and strong in front of her. When she finishes, perhaps "expires" is a better word, the male DJ begins speaking the same tragic argot. His delivery is beautiful but heartbreaking, barely audible, as if he's giving a eulogy to an empty room for the woman he loved. Of course, she died in the revolution and . . .

A boy in desperate need of antihistamine sings that even though he was born in Iowa—"I-o-way," he calls it—he "heard the timber out in Oregon calling me." The lumberjack, maybe some unknown grandfather of grunge, sings like a pared-down, out-of-work Willie Nelson, too broke to buy an ounce or two of the vibrato that made Nelson famous. But he stops and the DJ says it *is* Willie—his first recording, made in a Portland garage in 1957.

One station over, a speed-metal band plays so loud and fuzzy that I can't tell if the station's in tune or not. On to weather (it's 100 degrees out, which is why I feel like the speed-metal band sounds). Then a rasta talking about "herbs" is asked by a psychic, "Are you touched by strange forces, curses, or evil spirits?"

3:00 p.m. WFMU 91.9-FM.

A crazed voice cries, "Now ladies and gentlemen! It's star time! They call me the Hound!" This is followed by a string of brash good-time songs that make "Wooly Bully" sound Sunday school–safe by comparison. Bubbling novelty rockers by kids who yell great dopey opinions like, "This party's swingin' now, daddy!"

Rockabilly–boogie-woogie–"Louie Louie" hybrids by groups like the Valiants or the Thunderocks or (my favorite) Little Hooley Herrera—songs I'll no doubt never hear again—broadcast from some time-warp cultural crossroads, i.e., New Jersey, though John Waters' beehive-bopping Baltimore seems more like it.

The Hound rattles around the mike, asking, "What the hell happened to the cart deck? It must be those Christians!" He announces this week's Macintosh Music Festival, a celebration of cybertunes, deciding that it's therefore "a good week to stay in—a lotta idiots in town."

The music is so great I'm about to miss my flight. On my way out the door he takes on Courtney Love: "She's amazing. She's relentless." Describing Courtney's assault on Bikini Kill's Kathleen Hanna at Lollapalooza this week, he sighs, "She's so dumb. You just gotta love that."

Chicago

July 16.   **9:19 p.m. WBEZ.**

Reluctantly ripping myself away from the air conditioner for a split second to turn on the radio, I hear crying-in-your-beer Dixieland jazz, funereal trombone wails and pallbearing clarinets. But any Chicagoan who heard the news today has death on the brain: Fifty-six people perished in Cook County this week due to the 100 degree–plus heat wave. It's so bad, according to the *Tribune*, that there's no room at the morgue; the county's rented a refrigerated semi truck to store the extra bodies.

July 17.   **8:40 a.m. WONX-AM 1590.**

Reading the paper at 8:39, I notice in the paltry "Radio Highlights" section that an AM station at the far right of the dial (figures) is interviewing Lynn Van Muizen in one minute. It says that "the newly elected president of the Michigan Militia talks about the future of the group and its public image." The station—at 1600—is in fact, so far right, that I can't pick it up. Expecting doom and gloom from Van Muizen and with a new front-page heat-stroke-casualty figure rattling around my head (a staggering 116), I feel hopeless. Even the milk in my coffee went sour. In the futile search for paramilitary updates, however, I stumble upon a polka, accordion and all, fueled by belly-laughing trumpets and tubas gone berserk. It sounds jolly, not to mention rip-roaring drunk.

There used to be a polka hour on KGLT Saturday mornings, hosted by this guy Steve. He told me once that a man called up, a real polka-hater, to tell him that his two young daughters were wild for the stuff. They'd get up on Saturday mornings and instead of hooting for cartoons, would jump up and down, plastering their father with demands of "Polka! Polka! Polka!" until he would finally give in, turning his Montana kitchen into a Kraków beerhall.

July 18.

Audio art–new music avatar Steve Peters wouldn't send me the tape of his Albuquerque radio show that I requested. This morning, I received this letter instead, explaining why, printed on his Nonsequitur Foundation letterhead:

July 14, 1995

Hi Sarah,

I once had a job working for Lever Bros., answering their 800 # and talking to people (mostly women) about Wisk, Snuggles, Surf, and other laundry and dishwashing products. At first it was really amazing to be inside the belly of the beast, to see how those insidious ad campaigns work (and they do!), to find out that people really care about this stuff (one woman was led down the long tunnel of light by the Snuggle Bear during a near-death experience) and how these huge companies relate to consumers. It was fascinating and kind of amusing for a few months. Then it got too depressing and I couldn't bear it anymore. Too scary. I suspect this is a little what your radio project will be like, so I wish you luck and courage with it—at least I was getting paid!

The radio show I do these days is really not very interesting. I do a "new music" show once a month on the local university NPR station, which is not so adventurous though it thinks it is. As a result, I have to play it pretty straight and stick to contempo classical. Sometimes I substitute on the free-form shows and can do a little more creative mixing, but I have to say that playing records is about the least interesting use of radio that I can think of at this point. I have some serious reservations about recorded music and mediated experience in general, and have lately been wondering to myself what would happen if I only listened to music in live situations, totally forsaking all recorded music. Of course there's a historical thing that recordings offer, but I kind of think that music should be more about community and presence and interaction and participations, and that recordings have devalued, mystified, and alienated music and musicians from audiences in a certain way.

I used to do a show at KAOS in Olympia and later at WFMU called Snapshot Radio (see the essay about it in the Cassette Mythos book) which used only recordings of everyday life, collected on cassette by myself and my collaborator Rich Jensen, and also sent in by listeners and interested people from around the world. It was like audio home movies: ambient recordings (natural or urban), conversations, social events like family picnics and parties and street demonstrations. At one point we did a tour, driving across the country, collecting sounds and making shows at community stations as we went along. Sometimes we did workshops at the stations and had people go around town making recordings which we'd use in that evening's show. All programs were collaged together live on the air, improvising with our little library of tapes. We never played the same tape twice, except on the tour. Some folks thought it was boring, but a lot of people really got into it, including (especially?) non-arty

*types, for whom it often evoked memories of times and places
in their lives that were different than their current experience. It was all quite humble and funky and unpretentious,
which is probably why they won't let me do it here on KUNM.
It just doesn't have that slick, NPR, yuppie-appeal factor
going for it. Since then I've made some pieces that are more
like "Radio Art," but they still draw on certain Snapshot
ideas. Of course one can't do the same work forever, but
I do look back on Snapshot with a certain fondness and
nostalgia.*

*Anyway, good luck with school, book, writing, jobs, etc.
Don't let all that radio listening turn your brains to mush
or induce feelings of incurable hopelessness and despair. I
recommend listening to Spanish/Mexican stations if they
have them there. Here they play rancheras, cumbias, maria-
chis, merengue, salsa, romantica, and Latin pop. Imagine
an English commercial format that played country, reggae,
jazz, big bands, oldies, crooners, and rock music and you'll
get the idea. Not to mention all that echo on the ads!*

Best,
Steve

July 19.   **11:05 p.m. WBBM 780-AM and WXRT.**

The news, and bad news at that: 436 people are dead because
of the heat wave. That figure is so incredible that the coroner
has been accused of making it up. Dr. Edmund Donaghue,
Cook County Chief Medical Examiner, defends the statistic:
"We stand by our numbers."

The plague brings all the apocalypse talk of my religious
childhood rushing back to me—the recurring dream in which
I get gunned down at the supermarket for refusing the mark
of the beast; the terrifying spring tornado-warning nights
spent in my grandfather's cellar in which I thought not the
wind but hoary demons from hell were making the door bob
up and down; that time at church camp I heard a trumpet
sound and thought the end was near, only to find out that

it was a recording on the PA system—just the normal kid stuff. And then, changing stations, another childhood memento, this one a little more light-hearted. On 'XRT's broadcast of the English program *Rock Over London*, Elvis Costello covers a kick-ass Waylon Jennings song my sister and I adored as children, "The Only Daddy That'll Walk the Line." Elvis camps out on the *on* in *only* until an almighty organ knocks him down like a fallen angel. Or a hoary demon—take your pick.

July 21.   **7:00 p.m. WBEZ.** *Soundstage.*

"I can go to the butcher shop and say, 'Are those the thoughts of cow?' " It's David Sedaris, referring to the way he connotes "cow brains" in his elementary French. He tells host Carl T. Wright that he's been taking lessons of late, though he dodges words and phrases useful to the traveler, preferring to look up verbs such as "to anoint."

He describes his recent seventeen-city book tour to promote his dark-humored collection of stories, *Barrel Fever*. On male television hosts of programs like *Good Morning Dallas:* "Most guys won't wear that much makeup until they're in their casket." Since none of them had actually read his work, he mimics a painfully slow sample question: "Now is it true [*pause*] that you, uh, write sort of wacky [*pause*] stories about human life?"

Wright, alluding to Sedaris's celebrity among the NPR crowd, asks, "You aren't the superstar that we think you are?"

"Uh. No. Sure am not."

Since 'BEZ is currently under the pledge-drive knife (or, as charismatic salesman Gary Covino will refer to it an hour later, "the beg-a-thon"), Wright asks Sedaris if he was an NPR member before he became a commentator. He says no, though he did pledge fifty bucks to *All Things Considered* when he was nineteen, even though "when it came to writing out the check I just couldn't bring myself to do it." Now a member, he suggests others pay up, not because of any moral obligation but because "you're allowed to be judgmental" toward the people who don't.

July 22.

You are what you listen to. Right? Friends who attended Lollapalooza's Chicago stop last week described (with no small horror) dozens, if not hundreds, of kids running around with Q101 rub-on tattoos plastered to their skin (one more apocalypse alert if you ask me). Paging through yesterday's edition of the *Reader*, the major local alternative weekly, I scan the personal columns—called "Matches"—in search of people whose boiled-down descriptions of self-identity include radio station preferences.

JUST FRIENDS: 0 out of 6.
WOMEN SEEKING MEN: 2 out of 104.
The "Dark-haired Beauty" enjoys the classy grab-bag rock station 'XRT, while "Ivory Seeks Ethnic" "grooves to [oldies stations] WGCI and V103."
MEN SEEKING WOMEN: 8 out of 184.
"Monogamous, Nonpracticing, BIWM" likes "museums and NPR."
"Pseudo Intellectual: North" is opposed to "TV addicts, Rush, organized sports/religion, cats."
"A Brave New SWM" goes for 'XRT.
"From Tux to Jeans," who moves from WFMT [the "fine arts" format] to [Top 40] B96, "can balance thoughtful conversation with Dave Barry–style playfulness."
"Writer at Heart but no appetite for noble poverty" prefers 'XRT.
"Sexy Jewish Male" champions public radio while "Nice Jewish Boy" also goes for NPR. Coincidence?
"Triathlete Guy, thirty-two" is triple-excited about 'XRT.
WOMEN SEEKING WOMEN: 0 out of 1.
MEN SEEKING MEN: 0 out of 45.
NONE OF THE ABOVE: 0 out of 50, but these people have things other than chitchat on their minds.

TOTAL: 10 out of 390. (Though one wonders which stations "Handsome Secular Humanist," "Former Mean Guy," and "Punker Turned Businesswoman" listen to.)

July 23.   **8:00 p.m. WUSN-FM aka "U.S. 99."**
                                              Country Flashback.

Merle Haggard's on the radio singing about how he's an incarcerated fuckup, despite the fact that "Mama Tried."

Haggard's easy to romanticize. We're told that he was "born the son of Dust Bowl–fleeing Okies" and that he spent nearly three years behind the bars of San Quentin. His songs are drenched in the despair of drunkenness, hard work, and death.

There's a working-class weariness in his voice that always, and I mean always, gets me down. The solution, a friend once said when he pulled me out of a dark Merle Haggard hole, is just to ditch him, turn him off, let him go. But he's one of my favorite country crooners and this hour-long tribute to his down-and-out oeuvre is honky-tonk heaven.

Host Nancy Turner hands out little Merle tidbits in between songs. She talks about a tour in 1969, the year my twin and I were born, literally Okies in Muskogee. In fact, I'm forced to think about Merle Haggard every time I'm asked for my birthplace ("You mean like in the song?"). Nineteen sixty-nine, the year the world went mad, the year of Woodstock, of the Manson murders, of Altamont, my sister and I emerge in the hokiest hickville on earth, the town "where even squares can have a ball." But I've never heard the story Turner tells.

It seems Haggard's band, on the road, passed a highway sign that announced "Muskogee, 19 miles." As it happens, my family lived in the minute town called Braggs, which posts just such a sign due to the fact that it *is* nineteen miles from Muskogee. Anyway, one of the musicians remarked, "I bet they don't smoke marijuana in Muskogee," inspiring the song that became a sort of anthem to the backwater silent majority.

But I'm not the only one in the family to comment on "Okie from Muskogee" of late. Earlier in the year, an Oklahoma City television station sent a camera crew to Muskogee to celebrate the song's twenty-fifth anniversary. My cousin Carolyn happened to catch the broadcast, her eyes popping out when she recognized our ninety-one-year-old grandfather with a microphone in his face, calling "Okie from Muskogee" something like "the nicest thing anybody ever said about this godforsaken town."

July 26.   **Review of Jerry Lee Lewis's**
                                       Young Blood* for *City Pages.

As far as I know, Jerry Lee Lewis, the soon-to-be-sixty rock 'n' roll Killer, and Kiri Jewell, the fourteen-year-old girl who testified against her tormentor David Koresh, have never met. But in my head, they've been talking for days, reaching only one conclusion: that there is still such a thing in the world as sin.

When a friend first told me the title of Lewis's new album, I smirked. *Young Blood*—does he still have it or does he just want to fuck it? Both, evidently. It's hardly surprising that Lewis has ended up as a dirty old man. After all, he was a dirty *young* man, forever doomed to live down his marriage to his thirteen-year-old second cousin, Myra Brown.

The title cut, a swaying boogie attributed to Doc Pomus and Lieber and Stoller, finds our hero swooning over a girl with a yellow ribbon in her hair, not so much a woman as somebody's daughter. He rhymes *bad* with *dad*.

But what song would the father sing? Would his voice seethe with disgust like David Jewell's, as I heard July 20 on NPR, voicing his bottomless contempt for Koresh, the serial rapist who violated his then ten-year-old daughter, calling him "a man of absolutely unparalleled evil intent"? Jerry Lee's impassioned performance of the song—he's still got it, whatever "it" might be—is a winking, macho, good-time pledge of his virility, ending on an exasperated, manly cry of "*Mercy!*" and a one-off piano keyboard sweep. One could imagine the failed rocker Koresh attempting this and much of the Lewis catalog; "Great Balls of Fire" comes to mind, or this album's introduction, the souped-up Hank Williams prophecy "I'll Never Get Out of This World Alive." In fact, rock 'n' roll's extensive obsession with underage girls and death could have supplied Waco's megalomaniac with a millennium's worth of material.

It is not Lewis's fault that his record arrived in the mail a couple of days after calm, clearheaded Nina Totenberg interrupted my breakfast. Totenberg reports that the first day of congressional hearings concerning the Bureau of Alcohol, Tobacco, and Firearms' torching of the Branch Davidian complex two years ago, "opened with expectations of drama and political profit running high." The Republicans see the focus on the disaster as a chance to embarrass the Clinton administration, while the Democrats are fidgeting about gun control. "But in the end," Totenberg points out, "it was not the FBI or the BATF, not the NRA, not gun control or militias that were center stage yesterday. That place was occupied by a fourteen-year-old girl named Kiri Jewell."

Even after that buildup, after Totenberg's warning (and she really is master of the expository), I wasn't prepared for the girl's unflinching voice. She said:

> I was wearing a long white T-shirt and panties. He kissed me and sat there. But then he laid me down. He took his penis and rubbed it on the outside of my vagina while he was still kissing me. I had known this would happen sometime, so I just laid there and stared at the ceiling. I didn't know how to kiss him back. Anyway, I was still kind of freaked out.

She takes one long breath. I know what our Congress looks like—mostly scraggly old men with pinched faces wearing imposing suits. Just picturing them all ganged up like that in front of you can make you shiver, even in July.

*When he was finished he told me to go take a shower. I
walked to the bathroom with my panties down around my
ankles. In the bathroom, I realized I was all wet and gooey
on my legs. That freaked me out more. I just stayed in the
shower for maybe an hour. When I came out, David was in
his jeans and the bed was made. He told me to "Come here"
again. This time he read to me from the Song of Solomon.
[Long pause.] I was ten years old when this happened.*

She says that people "need to know the truth. This is my
truth. It might not be somebody else's truth but this is what
I saw and this is what happened to me."

With this horror on my mind—not to mention my current
reading material, Simon Reynolds and Joy Press's book *The
Sex Revolts*, a deep search through the misogyny of popular
music so obsessive and far-reaching that now every song on
the radio sounds like one more addition to the conspiracy
against women, and therefore, real love—Jerry Lee may as
well have painted a big red target across his leering face.

But if young blood, the concept, makes my skin crawl,
Young Blood the album is still full of fine music. For Lewis
has always been a man with a pulse, an imperfect but great
American, a white-hot piano player and a singer barking at
the gates of hell. Though it's true what Mr. Modest claims
in his liner notes—"Jerry Lee Lewis can still ROCK AND
ROLL!"—I am less interested in hearing about how he can
still get it up than looking for the sad wisdom and mysteries
of age.

It's this poignant weariness that sighs over the sweetness
of "Miss the Mississippi and You," full of the sentimental
longing that sends provincials home or "One of Them Old
Things," an equally aching letter to his Louisiana parents.
While there's something beautiful about a fifty-nine-year-
old man who misses his mama and daddy, there's something
funny about his ode to "High Blood Pressure." Though he
claims that his heart rate climbs *"when you're by my side,"*
at his age, it could just as easily stem from decades of barbecue
and booze.

"*Ah, whiskey!*" he calls out, like Bob Wills himself, in the first few fiddle bars of the about-last-night song of regret, "It Was the Whiskey Talking (Not Me)." You can sense a pattern of abuse and apology in the song's flippant ending, the boys-will-be-boys demand that his woman give him a drink. For Jerry Lee's sake, and mine, and especially for the sake of Kiri Jewell—who must now equate sex with evil—I'll play another song Lewis recorded years ago: "There Must Be More to Love Than This."

July 29.   **8:55 p.m. WLUP-FM 97.9 "The Loop".**

Tony Fitzpatrick gives away a free Tom Jones T-shirt to a fourteen-year-old caller, chiding the boy with, "Tom Jones owns shoes that are older than you."

> Poetry is freewheeling. You get its impact by thumbing through any of the mass media.
>
> —John Cage, Silence

August 3. **WLUP-FM.** *The Richard Roeper Show.*

591-ROCK, 591-ROLL. This is the phone number, in case you want to call in with a response to Roeper's hideous commentary. But nobody replies to his mean mimick of Lisa-Marie Presley: "Of course she's stupid. Her parents were Elvis and Priscilla. 'I'm from Tupelo and I'm really stupid.' She's trailer trash with twenty-five million dollars. Gold-plated trailer trash."

August 4. **8:21 p.m. "U.S. 99."**

"*I might have been born just plain white trash,*" Reba McEntire growls, "*but Fancy is my name.*" It's her rise-to-the-top song, about moving uptown and turning into a lady, about becoming what her name says she is—*fancy*, meaning cultivated and ornate, acceptable. It is, in its own way, just as offensive as Roper's "trailer trash" slur last night.

Both points of view, Roeper's condemnation and McEntire's transformation, indicate a fundamental abhorrence of poor white roots. And even though Roper calls Elvis stupid because he was (like William Faulkner) born in Mississippi, he actually understood (and lived out) the complexities of his culture better than anyone. Consider the weary nod of recognition in his voice singing the near self-portrait "Long Black Limousine," in which the poor, hometown girl, like McEntire's Fancy, makes it big in the city and returns home in that swank car just like she always said she would (even though it turns out to be a hearse). It's a skull painting, a memento mori: No matter how high you climb, you always end up in the cold, hard ground, whether a nice rig drives you there or not.

Still, with Elvis, the point is living. And I think everyone agrees that at the point he became more legitimate, got Steve Allen–ed and Hollywooded and role-modeled to death, at the point in fact when he lost some of the down-home spirit that fueled the unfettered glory of his first recordings. (And you can hear it best in the freewheeling, free-associating hillbilly heaven of that magic Million Dollar Quartet recording at Sun Studios in which he, Jerry Lee Lewis, and Carl Perkins joy-ride through all kinds of songs, but especially the barn-burners of old-time religion.) And if that's trash, then park me at the landfill, because I've learned one thing from my own hick kin—the food's greasy enough to kill you at the table and the Queen's English will be led to the slaughter, but count on this: Those people can *sing*.

August 5.   **12:00 p.m. WZRD.**

Building the public-service announcement into a compulsive tower of babble, this college station (nicknamed "The Wizard") reads feature-length articles and editorials concerning public policy to its listeners. I've never made it all the way through a single one.

Today's tedium is read in honor of tomorrow's half-century anniversary of the bombing of Japan. Writer William Blum asks, "Is there any reason for the U.S. to apologize to Japan for atomizing Hiroshima and Nagasaki?" Reading over a grating bed of background noise that sounds like a slow-motion car wreck, the DJ narrates Blum's outline of the recent Smithsonian controversy. The censoring of the National Air and Space Museum's exhibit devoted to the *Enola Gay* enraged aged former flyboys who "took offense at the portrayal of Japanese civilians as blameless victims. An Air Force group said, 'Vets were feeling nuked.'"

Now, I live for metaphor, love turning one thing into another in my head and on the page, but this analogy strikes me, in this context, as astonishingly shameful. I mean, it's one thing to "feel" nuked. Actually *being* nuked is another, sadder story, now isn't it?

August 6.   11:00 p.m.–1:00 a.m. Q101. *Sound Opinions.*

Haven't you always wanted to be a fly on the wall when two rock critics get together to talk shop? Me neither. But this program, subtitled "the world's only rock 'n' roll talk show" (which is a lie since it follows a rock 'n' roll talk show called *Modern Rock Live*) and hosted by the *Chicago Reader*'s Bill Wyman and the *Sun-Times*' Jim DeRogatis, can be sort of charming, especially given its spot (in an admittedly crappy time slot) on Q101's slick corporate airwaves. Rough 'round the edges to a fault, it's a refreshing respite from the rest of the glossy liars here on "your rock alternative" announcing their excitement!—nay, their pleasure!—to give you—yes, you!—lucky listeners the chance to hear—that's right!—the exact same song we played thirty-five whole minutes ago!

They take a look-see through the news. Michael Jackson's flop record (which Q101 wouldn't touch anyway, considering that its artist is black, or used to be) *HIStory*, at number 12 on the *Billboard* chart is, according to DeRogatis, "sinking fast." Wyman calls it "the *Heaven's Gate*, the *Ishtar*, the *Waterworld*, of rock music."

And it wouldn't be news without a Courtney update these days. It seems she had another mishap.

Wyman: "I guess what happened is someone threw a shotgun shell onstage, while she was playing in Pittsburgh. She took offense, stomped offstage. An announcer said, 'A singular individual with a very sick mind threw something offensive onstage [so that Love was] unable to continue.'"

"See," DeRogatis responds, "I don't get her. Sometimes she jumps into the crowd and would kick the crap outta the guy and sometimes she storms offstage, 'unable to continue.'"

"Are you saying that she's kind of inconsistent and weird?" Wyman jokes.

And speaking of weird, DeRogatis brings up a telephone run-in with a Geffen representative named Dennis who chastised them for last week's airing of a soon-to-be (but not yet) released track off the forthcoming Urge Overkill album. Dennis is heard wheezing into DeRogatis's voice mail: "Have I done something that you feel you need to get me fired from my job? I don't know what to do to keep you from playing the record. Um. I thought you would do me a favor in the interest of seeing me thrive in my position here."

DeRogatis snorts, "I really don't care how well Dennis does."

"I'm confused," Dennis whines. "Call me back."

So of course it's downright de rigeur to play another new Urge song. This one's blurred and druggy and it's called "The Mistake."

Moving on to reviews of this weekend's live shows, DeRogatis has a bone to pick with his colleague. He's in a huff about Wyman's *Reader* preview of the Foo Fighters' show, a smarmy little blurb that pissed me off when I read it as well.

"You . . . had one of the most facetious, and meaningless and insipid and you know—"

"Don't mince words. Say what you want to say here," Wyman interrupts.

"You said two things which *infuriated* me," DeRogatis continues. "You said, 'I'm gonna compare the Foo Fighters to that old saw about the dancing pig. The wonder isn't how well he can dance, it's that he can dance at all.' Meaning, surprise, this guy's a drummer and he's leading a band now."

And, quoting the part he seems to hate the most, " 'It's essentially the nineties equivalent of a George Harrison record.' "

Wyman attempts to vindicate the analogy by replying, "George Harrison is cool. He was overshadowed by those guys. He's a talented supporting player in a band with a very talented person."

DeRogatis fires back that now Wyman sounds like he's on 'XRT (the more baby boomer–oriented station, which plays sixties standards alongside new releases) after Wyman claims that Greg Dulli (of the Afghan Whigs, who contributed a guitar track to Grohl's record) "is the equivalent of Bob Dylan appearing on [Harrison's] *All Things Must Pass*."

DeRogatis, enraged, asserts, "You have to make some sixties comparison to make 1995 valid for you."

Wyman's voice takes on an *Oh yeah?* tone: "You remind *me* of when Richard M. Nixon was nominating these mediocrities to the Supreme Court—"

"There you go, back with the sixties again."

Wyman rattles on about how the Senate kept rejecting Nixon's undistinguished nominations even though, as one supporter put it, " 'Mediocrity needs representation, too.' And that's what you are, the spokesperson for the people who are ahistorical and don't have any perspective on the past."

At the beginning of the show, DeRogatis promised—hoo boy!—to talk about "synthesizers and motorik beats and Kraut rock" with tonight's Euro guests—Tim and Laetitia from the electronic outfit Stereolab. They're real duds—two mumbling bottles of Nyquil. But DeRogatis is on fire with rapturous applause for analog seventies synthesizers, the clunky machines that "gurgled and burped and farted and wheezed." He wants (and despite Wyman's antihistorical characterization this seems to me by-the-book historical) to "track the evolution" from the German band Neu's electronic repetition to Stereolab's. He waxes on about Can and Kraftwerk, while Wyman asks the chanteuse Laetitia about her vocal stylings. She just mutters something about trying to "come to grips with what humanity's about."

Meanwhile, Albert calls in to say that he finds Kraftwerk (and I have to agree) "art wanky."

They let the guests play some records they brought with them. Tim introduces a "detourned" (in my art-school life, references to the Situationist noun *détournement* fly around as often as Pollock slung paint, but Q101 is usually détourne-free) song by a group called Culturecide. It consists of an out-of-tune cartoon character screaming along with Bruce Springsteen's "Dancing in the Dark." Only he's reading a different lyric sheet than the Boss, perhaps channeling Springsteen's inner voice. Lyrics like *"I'm just tired and bored with myself."*

Sometimes the listeners' calls on this show get a little too specific, and some callers (especially boys) ask guests boring questions along the lines of, "Who played tambourine on the fourth beat of the fourth bar of the fourth song on your fourth record?" Caller Frank wants to know with whom Stereolab's recording during their stay in Chicago and I'm sure whoever they are they're very nice people, but I don't care to know so I go to bed.

August 7.   **10:35 p.m. WZRD-FM.**

"Winter Wonderland." In August.

August 9.   **12:55 p.m. WJJD-AM.**
                                        The G. Gordon Liddy Show.

I'm listening to the self-proclaimed freedom fighter G. Gordon Liddy, when he interrupts his program to announce the death of Jerry Garcia. On one hand, there's a when-worlds-collide weirdness about the bald, unapologetic Watergate burglar Liddy briefly eulogizing the hairy hippie Garcia by extending condolences to Garcia's family. But even if their uniforms are different, Liddy and Garcia play on the same team. Or maybe they're cocaptains of the team, inspiring the same sort of vacant, Limbaughesque, old-guard hero worship in their followers. Because, really, a deadhead is just a dittohead who doesn't bathe.

The Grateful Dead's continuing influence over people my age and younger reeks of the worst kind of cultural posturing and fraud. Last month, they played Chicago. It would turn out to be the band's final concert with Garcia. I was walking up Michigan Avenue, on my way to the movies, in a throng of baby Dead fans, some of them half my age. They all had that born-too-late, relive the sixties, throwback look—longhaired, barefoot clones in tie-dye completely oblivious to how naive and anachronistic they really appeared.

Before I go on, two things. One, the art critic Dave Hickey once said that he can hate anything as long as he knows someone else likes it. (Meaning, it's not like I'm kicking some underdog's shins here. The Dead are more or less worshiped by countless people worldwide.) Two, much as I hate to admit it, I realize that there are people whom I love and admire in this world who do not share my venom toward this one rock band (though most of my best friends do). And these people maybe own one or two of the Dead's albums and perhaps caught a couple of shows where they got high as kites and had a good time and went home and proceeded to wear clothes designed in the last twenty years and listen to records that were not only produced in the last five years, but that sound like it. Really, no problem there.

But the Grateful Dead, as the fanatic fans always point out, are a way of life: someone else's. Twentieth-century teenagers, especially American ones, have been brilliant at creating their own culture, their own music, clothes, and point(s) of view. It's sad and fraudulent that the kind of wholesale worship of some historical way of life has settled over so many young people, infecting them like a noxious gas.

And I say all of this as someone who once had the misfortune to live in *Oregon*, the world's capital of all things Dead.

It's not that I'm against historicizing. On the contrary, as a historian, I'm all for it. If I have a thing against the Dead, I love the dead—grew up in the thrall of Shakespeare and Hank Williams and James Dean. And I adore the Rolling Stones. But there's a difference between cherishing "Satisfaction" and wearing Keith Richards' hair while doing Keith Richards' drugs. I don't want to be Keith Richards. I wanna be me. Not—like the neo-Deadheads—just another extra in an overblown costume drama about something that wasn't that interesting the first time around.

And maybe that's the rub. I guess I could handle it if the Grateful Dead's music was somehow passionate or inspiring or liberating. I could almost forgive all the lamebrains around me at the Stones' recent *Voodoo Lounge* tour who were having such a good time. Because the music sucked. Because now, the Stones suck. But once, they didn't. So maybe, all the people enjoying the crapola the band cranked out of that ridiculous stage while wearing (except for Charlie Watts of course) ridiculous clothes, everyone was playing some of their genius records (when the band knew how to play *and* how to dress) in their heads.

I switch to 'XRT, the one station in town that's sure to be obsessing, and hear that Garcia died of "natural causes" even though he was checked into a drug treatment center at the time of death. They play a tape of Garcia saying, "I would like to be thought of as a competent musician," and I guess he was that. But competent don't mean shit. They play some boring Dead song that goes on forever, full of noodling, pointless guitar. The song, like Jerry Garcia, is passive, placating, and irrelevant. And it's not that I'm glad he's dead (if anything, I'm dreading the deification process). It's just that I don't care. I never said a nice word about the man when he lived, so I need not start now.

11:51 p.m.

Ever been haunted? Intending to make a tape for a friend, I look through a stack of used but unmarked cassettes to find one to tape over. I pop it in the stereo and push Play, immediately hearing a voice resembling the denture-wearing grandfather character from *The Simpsons* saying, "Phil, Phil, remember me?"

"Phil," another old guy voice, answers, "No, no, I don't remember anything."

There's a downward-spiral-through-space sound in the background and the first old man says, "It's me. Jerry Garcia."

I'm spooked, but keep listening.

Seconds later, "Jerry" gets panicky, announcing, "Oh, oh my, oh my, oh my heart. . . . Quick—inside my buckskin jacket. That's my stash. The little bottle with the poppers. . . . [*sniffing noises*] . . . Okay, let's talk about old times before it wears off."

"Phil" asks, "Hey, remember our old band—the Dreadful Great?"

"Was that what it was?" "Jerry" queries.

"Oh, it was something like that. Those were the days."

It's the future, and dope is legal. They smoke a self-lighting joint containing opium, comfortable in the knowledge that "the comfort people will take you home."

As the cocaine helicopter flies over, I figure out that this is probably part of a drug-themed Negativland broadcast I taped a while back but never got around to listening to. I go back over my notes—Saturday, March 4, one to four P.M. on WZRD. The title: *The Dopey Show.*

August 10. 1:00 p.m.–3:00 p.m. WLS-AM and WJJD-AM.

Rush Limbaugh, research scientist:

A study by the Hadley Center for Climate Prediction Research in England says that sulphate particles, which is

the waste of burned fossil fuels, may reduce global warming
that some scientists predict will occur in coming decades.
So it may reduce something that hadn't happened yet. This
is great science, isn't it? This refuse may destroy what hasn't
been going on. But it may happen and it may destroy it.
We're all to be comforted.

Why don't I feel better? Who knows *what* he's talking about.
I hyperventilate thinking about the people who listen to
this show as news, who might be willing to chuck out the
overwhelming scientific evidence to the contrary all because
of this pronouncement. Who faxed him this tripe? His friends
at Shell? I imagine all the dittoheads dragging out their
aerosol cans en masse, spraying them into the air, because,
Hey, Rush said we could.

He doesn't stop there. "There is no such thing as global
warming, ladies and gentlemen," he says with seductive
smarminess. "I was right about feminism, I've been right
about this administration. I have been right about the ozone
layer. I tell you there's no global warming."

Hitting it home: "Now you can trust me, or you can ago-
nize. It's simpler to trust me."

Simpler. I guess that's one way of putting it.

While the bibliography to Rush's research paper is one source
long, G. Gordon Liddy, in a rant that's just as weird, drops
his macho swagger to turn schoolmarm for a few minutes.

"At any point in your preparatory education did you ever
learn how to diagram a sentence?" he asks a caller who wants
to talk about the quality of American schools.

When the caller answers yes, Liddy says, "I'm being told
these days, that they don't do that these days" (quite a
sentence, that), and wants to know if the American educational system is producing "someone who understands what
a dependent clause is."

The caller asserts, "I don't know how important that is."

He says that he thinks he's capable of expressing himself without knowing "what a dangling participle is."

Maybe so, but that's not good enough for Liddy. "Do you know how to use a semicolon?" It's a meaningless question, by and large, but as interrogatives go, I suppose it beats Rush "Why ask why?" Limbaugh's "This is great science, isn't it?" It's enough to drive someone to NPR. . . .

3:00 p.m. WBEZ-FM.

At a presidential press conference, Bill Clinton sets forth a plan that, in its seeming lack of any potential for political gain, is in its own way more bizarre than Limbaugh's quack science and Liddy's grammar patrol. He announces an executive order to ban teen smoking: "Today, three thousand young people will begin to smoke. One thousand of them will ultimately die from . . . diseases caused by smoking. That's more than a million vulnerable young people a year being hooked." He plans to "restrict sharply the advertising, promotion, distribution, and marketing of cigarettes to teenagers." These restrictions include requiring ID to purchase tobacco and the elimination of tobacco-promoting billboards near schools.

In the five minutes or so it takes him to outline the plan, he takes on the almighty tobacco industry (especially the Joe Camel cartoon character) and, by implication, advertisers, retailers, and tobacco farmers.

Referring to the latter group's cash crops, a reporter asks, "Are you writing off the South in next year's election? And isn't this a blow to other Democratic candidates in tobacco states?"

"First of all," the president replies, "the most important thing is that there is an epidemic among our children. . . . Whatever the political consequences, a thousand kids a day are beginning a habit which will probably shorten their lives. That is the issue. And I believe that is the issue everywhere." Tobacco farmers, he adds, receive "a paltry four and a half cents from a pack of cigarettes."

I can't think of a reason in the world to do this other than he thinks it's right. While it is meant to benefit children, children don't vote. Besides, most kids, even if they oppose smoking, abhor restrictions on their behavior. But even if the entire measure is a move rooted in Clinton's (thank God) lingering idealism, a reporter calls him on his hypocrisy:

"Mr. President, you noted in your speech in Charlotte yesterday that children follow what we do more than what we say and I wonder what you think the message is, when on the one hand, government cracks down on teen smoking and, on the other hand, it spends $25 million a year subsidizing the growth of tobacco, and when you yourself continue to smoke those big ol' cigars?"

"I smoke a handful a year," he confesses. "I probably shouldn't, but I plead guilty." And tobacco subsidies, he claims, are only the lesser of two evils, meant to preserve family farms instead of promoting corporate agriculture.

Meanwhile, I'm shocked. Shocked, really, that the president, my president, not only has an answer, but that he can actually string a sentence together. Hell, occasionally, he's even eloquent. For me, growing up with Reagan, every press conference was a nerve-racking exercise in embarrassment. Damn. You'd just sit there in a cold sweat, completely mortified that this man, this complete idiot, this out-and-out schmuck, was not only representing your culture to the world, but he was also in charge of your future, a future which, due to the influence of some of his lamebrained movie roles and cowboy nuclear ethic, he was basically eradicating. But in the movies, at least it was always the evil genius who planned to blow up the world; even though he had a black heart, at least he was smart. But with Reagan, you not only had to grow up fearing he *would* blow up the world, you had to (on the rare occasions he couldn't weasel out of facing the press) watch him squirm and sweat and guffaw like the blank doofus he was.

But I digress; only because at a Clinton press conference, I'm given the luxury of daydreaming, of being comfortable enough that he could find Peru on a map, say, that I don't have to hang on his every word, praying he won't fuck up.

A long-winded reporter asks, "Mr. President, the House has cut twenty billion dollars in discretionary spending for next year. Will they have to return some of those cuts to avoid you vetoing some of their appropriations?"

"Yes."(Eloquence needn't drone on forever.)

Glancing at the *Tribune* while I listen to this, I read that yesterday, the Senate voted to approve the National Endowment for the Arts another year, even though they slashed its miniscule $167 million budget down to $110 million. So right now, it's a black day in high-school art classes across the nation.

Almost all the art kids I knew as a teenager—the kids I admired, who changed my life, who saved my soul—were walking chimneys. Cigarettes, like art, were symbols to them, symbols of freedom. Everybody knew that smoking causes cancer and that artists starve, so the two acts took on a for-the-hell-of-it cast.

One hundred ten million dollars is a sham, a drop in the government bucket for which everyone in the arts community is supposed to get down on our knees in gratitude. Even the $167 million figure was still less than the U.S. spends funding military marching bands (though, I guess, that's art, too). But this is the clincher: Now, according to the article, "under a compromise hammered out on the Senate floor at the request of Majority Leader Bob Dole (Republican–Kansas), the NEA . . . would be forbidden to support obscene or sacrilegious projects and could not make grants to individual artists." (And "obscene" is what? And "sacrilegious" is what?)

So smoking is bad for you. And art is too. Plato didn't banish the artists from his Republic for nothing.

Great art is bad for government. But good for you. Which ends up, I think, being good for government. And I'm sure the reprieve passed with a lot of "Why art's good" debate. Senator Kay Bailey Hutchison (a Republican, even), who grew up in rural Texas, lauded the NEA-supported symphony and ballet which she enjoyed as a child. But that's just Culture, capital C.

Maybe I'm just rambling, dreading the fact that once

again, I might get stuck defending Mapplethorpe's photographs, their right to get funded, their Constitutional right to even exist, much less be shown. Which will be just one more instance when instead of talking about what really matters, namely the fact that the so-called X *Portfolio* of his, the one with "controversial" masochistic subject matter, contains some of the coldest, most formal images I know. In that they lack any of the gooey heat of sex, they're just not sexy.

Clinton supports the NEA, which is just one of the reasons that I voted for him. But last night, at my artsy class at my artsy school, my professor read aloud, with great passion and humor and gall, from Tzara's *Seven Dada Manifestoes* of 1916. It's an argument for real art (even though he can't stand the word), the kind of argument that's debated in the Senate chambers in my head:

Art was a game of trinkets children collected words with a tinkling on the
end then they went and shouted stanzas and they put little doll's shoes on
the stanza and the stanza turned into a queen to die a little and the queen
turned into a wolverine and the children ran till they all turned green
Then came the great Ambassadors of sentiment and exclaimed historically
in
chorus
psychology psychology heehee
Science Science Science . . .
But we Dada are not of their opinion for art is not serious I assure you and
if in exhibiting crime we learnedly say ventilator, it is to give you pleasure
kind reader.

Or, later, and more to the point:

*Freedom: Dada Dada Dada, a roaring of tense colors, and
interlacing of opposites and of all contradictions, grotesques,
inconsistencies: LIFE.*

So those words aren't on the radio. But they should be.

August 11.   **7:00 p.m. WBEZ-FM.** *The Wild Room.*

"Even though he was a man, even lesbian separatists on
Pacifica Radio had to pay respects to the King," Gary Covino
told me, referring to his experience driving through Washington, D.C., the day Elvis died.

This evening's *Wild Room* rebroadcasts an Elvis death
anniversary show produced four years ago by Covino, Ira
Glass, and Lynda Barry. Beginning with a version of "It's
Now or Never" sung in Latin, Covino asserts that Elvis-
worship exhibits affinities with Christianity. Correlations
such as the fact that Elvis was born "not in a manger exactly,
but the Mississippi equivalent of it," that he had an "immacu-
late mother and an ineffectual father," and that he could
perform miracles ("He made white people listen to black
music"). "There is the Elvis," he continues, "and the king
Judas who betrayed him, the evil Colonel Parker. There are
all these people touched by Elvis." People such as "Nixon,
the Pharisee."

Barry describes her "first Elvis experience." As a child,
she adored her pompadour-wearing Filipino uncle Dick who
would "imitate Elvis in a Filipino accent." She says that she
would listen to the *Blue Hawaii* album and touch E's lip on
the cover. One night, she whispers, she had a dream, "a
dream where I actually made out with Elvis and I was wearing
only a barrel." Later on she'll confide, "The thing is, before
that dream about Elvis, my only other erotic feeling had been
about Porky Pig."

They take calls and read from the *Weekly World News*
about Elvis sightings, then read from the "Elvis on Other
Planets Weight Chart." He'd weigh 99 pounds on Mercury

("Lean and mean!" gushes Barry) and 7,280 pounds on the sun ("Talk about a hunka burnin' love," says Covino).

After a George Jones song about pouring whiskey out of a decanter with an Elvis head into a Flintstones jelly jar up to Fred's rhymes-with-Elvis (*"The King is gone and so are you"*), Covino interrupts to say that he's looking for Deadheads to come on the show next week, especially tape-traders. After giving out phone numbers—his and Ira's—he warns, "Don't call 'BEZ. Don't call the station. No one here has ever heard of the Grateful Dead."

August 13.

Working on a project for school about artist Terry Allen, I listen again to his New American Radio sound piece *Bleeder*. It's the story of a Texas hemophiliac gambler on the lam, narrated by his wife, Jo Harvey Allen, in her gutsy drawl. The bleeder is a crook without a conscience with ties to the mob in New Orleans, has an ill-defined association with the Democratic party, was an acquaintance of Jack Kennedy's and, perhaps most of all, had a thing for women.

Describing the character's eventual funeral, Jo Harvey Allen burns up her delivery of what passed for a eulogy, a list of words in the bleeder's handwriting found scribbled on a napkin. She sounds like some kind of beat-poet-turned-preacher. Or vice versa: "I want a new tattoo. A snake. A mouth. A scarification moon. A total melody." His tattoo laundry list goes on to include "all the self-assurances that my decisions are true . . ."

Her words just fly out of the speakers, meaning nothing and everything at the same time, asking you what's on your tattoo, what matters, what you want.

A Bozeman friend who called this morning said the piece aired on KGLT this week. He sat out on his back porch and listened with the moonlight shining over the mountains.

Which is almost as nice as hearing it as homework with your face shoved against the air conditioner in Chicago's midday sun. Almost.

August 15.   **11:30 p.m.**

My cabdriver was listening to a man with a wheezing, high-pitched voice on the radio talking about Richard Rhodes' *The Making of the Atomic Bomb*, a book I read in a History of Science course I took in college. I did poorly on the mid-term exam, which covered Rhodes' material, because, as the professor scrawled on my paper, "Your understanding of how to construct an atom bomb is weak."

August 16.   **WJMK-FM 104.3.**

Elvis died eighteen years ago today, and I almost die myself waiting for this oldies station to play one of his songs. There's a contest involved, so that listeners call in when they hear it in order to win $100. At three-thirty, finally, I hear "All Shook Up," neither one of his shining moments nor a hideous slice of schlock. Barbara, from an insurance company, wins the dough, claiming, "I'm an oldtime Elvis fan." After she hangs up, it's on to "Paint It, Black."

After the waiting through hours and hours all day long of the Mamas and the Papas and the like, I'm worn out. Radio's great for surprise but lousy when it comes to fueling your own obsessions. That's what recordings are for. Wearing my Walkman, I walk to the train with the *Sun Sessions*. I'm giggling to the loose and thumping "Baby, Let's Play House," with Elvis's cries of *"Hit it!"* When he comes to *"Yeah!"* I smile and look up to see everything this song is not: a woman no older than me who looks to be about ten months pregnant inching her way down the street by clinging to walls, fences, anything she can. And maybe any other time than now, I'd look at her with wonder, maybe even jealousy, because pregnant women do look sort of magic, like they know something you don't. But right now, with this song, with this beat, I just speed up and think, "Better you than me."

August 18.   **7:00 p.m.** *The Wild Room.*

Before Covino and Glass get around to talking to the truly boring Deadheads they've brought into the studio, they read some of the mourning messages about Jerry Garcia's death from the Well, a computer bulletin board. They all sound stunned. One person's "tears are dripping," while another vows that "I grieve and I remain on the bus forever."

One man posted this anecdote:

> *Driving home tonight I was going across Golden Gate Bridge and I glanced back at Marin. As I topped the 17th Street Hill, I saw all of San Francisco spread out before me, rolling to the Bay. And I thought, this is Jerry Garcia's San Francisco.*

If Jerry Garcia's San Francisco embarrasses me, this morning's mail brought a missive from a Bay Area friend, and it speaks to another San Francisco that is equally dumb, only, if possible, more sinister. If the Deadheads mean to create a brainless neverland of complacency through their trippy Muzak, they at least talk up some noncapitalist ideal of hazy harmony (despite that three-quarters of the Deadheads with whom I went to college were trust-fund babies whose cars, bikes, and skis alone could finance my life for the next six years).

Enclosed in my friend's letter was a copy of a recent article from the "Next Generation" column of the *San Francisco Chronicle.* The section gives voice to high-school and college students who want to contribute editorials. This one, labeled "A Warning from the MTV Brood," was written by Amy Wu, a student at New York University.

It begins, "Politicians who want to attract young voters in the upcoming election could use a lesson from House Speaker Newt Gingrich. Gingrich recently appeared on an

MTV question-and-answer panel called 'Newt: Raw' and successfully wooed my generation."

Unfortunately, I missed this particular courtship ritual, but Wu claims that Newt's audience of suitors that day consisted of brainy twentysomethings who "asked hard questions" and "got straight answers." One of these relentless interrogators evidently asked about the status of funding for student loans. "Gingrich," Wu cheers, "came straight out and said, 'The government has no money right now.'"

The government, which has operated at a deficit for my entire lifetime, has somehow managed, on no money, to finance (along with student loans for millions of students, myself included) all kinds of costly, stupid programs. How many grants and loans could have grown out of all the billions wasted on the lamebrained Strategic Defense Initiative, for instance? Or tax breaks to gluttonous, gigantic corporations?

Wu says she got conned by Clinton in 1992 because she believed in his programs. "But now," she writes, "AmeriCorps may be cut." But who's cutting it? The air? No, it's mostly Republicans like her political paramour, Gingrich. She'll vote for a concept and then turn around and back up the man who plans to shoot it down?

But besides all that, Wu's championing of this just-the-facts brand of politics speaks to a larger, spiritually bankrupt mind-set.

Mario Cuomo said that "we campaign in poetry and govern in prose." But who the hell campaigns in poetry anymore? By campaigning in poetry, meaning to set forth a series of ideals, a conversation about who we want to be instead of the way things are, the talk of politics *can* give us something to shoot for. Amy Wu is arguing for resignation and acceptance, for shrugging her shoulders. She's not exactly saying yes to the system, in that she knows there should be better health care and more available student loans. But she's not saying no, either. It's something worse—she's saying, "Oh well." In her own way, she's no better than a dropout from "Jerry Garcia's San Francisco," in that she's given up on working on a better world.

That's not the worst part. Consider this sentence: "We twentysomethings can't be fooled." I'm embarrassed just typing those words.

One of the reasons I started this project was that, the year I lived as a taxpayer in San Francisco, I'd spend my day reading the newspaper (the *Chronicle* in fact), frying my brain at my job for eight or nine hours, riding public transportation, doing my own writing and research at night for another few hours, talking to my friends and family, etc. In other words, trying to balance an admittedly puritan work ethic with a sense of humor. Then I'd turn on the television news or open a magazine and read some dippy editorial about "my generation" and how I was supposed to be an uninformed, lazy, narcissistic cynic who never opened a newspaper and gave up on the world. And it's frustrating and condescending. I can see that it's this unsound concept that inspired Wu to write in.

But: I only conceived this diary as a means to say that I'm *just as* confused and overwhelmed as my elders, just as ill-informed and worried and perplexed and lacking in answers (but willing to look) as people twice my age. That's all. Every generation has its visionaries and idiots, its heroes and villains, and mine's no different. That's all. Christ—"we can't be fooled." To be human is to be fooled, is it not? Even Socrates told the world, "I know that I know nothing." While no self-respecting feminist would utter those words, she'd get the gist. Not that I *want* to be fooled, but the only way to stop that is to just kill myself right now. Fat chance.

Meanwhile, back on *The Wild Room*, the Deadhead tape-traders are playing some burdensome song from some burdensome show. (And I do admire the fact that the band lets the tapers set up their equipment to get good-quality recordings, thereby insuring high-fidelity versions of its big fat yawns.) The MTV brood's valentine to Newt, and now this: never-ending, listless drivel.

I turn off the radio and dial the 415 area code—San

Francisco. Not Jerry Garcia's and not Amy Wu's. Mine. If
it's still there.

August 19.   **11:30 p.m. WXRT. _Eleventh Hour._**

Sonic Youth, live. A gorgeous wall of noise hunkers down
into their catchiest song, "Kool Thing." At first, they're a
band, maybe a dinner party. Everyone's talking at once
because, you get the feeling, everyone has something to say.
All of a sudden, Kim Gordon throws down her napkin and
leaps up on the table, which turns into Mount Sinai, which
gets your attention. Before, she was stage-whispering some
small talk. Now, she's some kind of force of nature, kicking
nice goblets onto the floor, spitting up seeds of words that
sprout into some kind of burning bush of rage. "Male!" She
takes a breath. "White!" She gushes louder. "_Corporate!_"
It's etched in stone. "OPPRESSION!" She glares at the sky.
Roaring down the mountain, she delivers her own commandments, the first of which is "_Don't be shy._"

August 20.   **10:06 p.m. WFMT-FM 98.7.**

Republican presidential candidate Phil Gramm on the results
of the Iowa straw poll in which he, surprisingly, tied with
front-runner Bob Dole: "While Dole is loved and admired
[this _is_ news], people don't think he can change America."

August 21.   **8:00 a.m. WBEZ-FM. _Morning Edition._**

Last week, king-of-the-hill Bob Dole called the Iowa poll an
indicator of who would win the Republican nomination. This
morning, now that he tied with Gramm, he says that it was
only about "who could raise more money."

August 22.   **11:10 p.m. WCRX-FM 103.5.**

I was making a ninety-minute Jonathan Richman tape for a
friend. Imagine my squeamishness, after an hour and a half

of heartfelt, funny lyrics backed up by the warmest surfish guitar, hearing cries of *"Radio on!"* to turn the radio on.

Braced for evil or boredom or stupidity (or, more likely, all three) I find none other than my favorite song in five seconds flat—Neil Young's "Rockin' in the Free World."

It's more than a relief, it's a revelation. If Jonathan Richman crowds out some of the evil in the world by his mere existence, his nearly childlike honesty and gall, his call for "Parties in the U.S.A.," Neil Young looks evil in the eye. Young's song is one of the blackest I know, not embracing the world's ills, but pointing them out. Details like Styrofoam. The snapshot of the addict mother holding her baby. The baby who won't get life (*"fall in love"*), liberty (*"go to school"*), or the pursuit of happiness (*"be cool"*). The lyrics are drowned in the shit, the mess, the "kinder, gentler" lies of these United States. The title's words sound like a joke, a sneer, a sarcastic quip. The words tell you hell is other people, but not the sound, the tenacious guitars and drums whooping it up, laughing the darkest laugh there is. But it's an honest laugh, however bitter. And the words don't get the last word, the fervor of the noise does, and it sounds like nothing so much as the will to live.

August 23.   **12:15 p.m. WZRD-FM.**

There are two kinds of schlock: the kind that makes you laugh and the kind that makes you puke. William Shatner's (I'm serious) spoken-word version of the Beatles' "Lucy in the Sky with Diamonds" falls into the former category. For all its exclamation points and dippy intonation it still possesses a certain amount of verve, the kind of embarrassing gumption it takes for a grown man to not sing, but squeal, the words *"Marshmallow pies!"*

August 25.   **1:30 p.m. WZRD-FM.**

PJ Harvey's wonderful song "Dry": the most passionate song I know about the lack of passion.

August 26.   9:58 p.m. Q101-FM.

*What she lacked in vocal power and, at the moment, in skill,
she compensated for by a quality so mysterious and implaca-
bly egocentric that no one has ever been able to name it.
This quality involves a sense of the self so profound and so
powerful that it does not so much leap barriers as reduce
them to atoms—while still leaving them standing, mightily,
where they were; and this awful sense is private, unknowable,
not to be articulated, having, literally, to do with something
else; it transforms and lays waste and gives life, and kills."*

—*James Baldwin*, Another Country

I turn on the radio as the DJ is calling someone a "lunatic."
She must have been speaking of Courtney Love since her
banter is immediately followed by Hole's "Softer, Softest."
   Initially, it's melancholy as a rainy day, with slurred talk
about mother's milk. The chorus keeps the pace as Love,
really sounding lovely, commands that the witch be burned.
Then she kicks in, brilliantly grits up the delivery into a
simple explosion, like a letter bomb in a scented envelope,
"bring me back her he-ee-yead."

August 30.   2:00 p.m. WBEZ. *Talk of the Nation.*

Thirty-seven people were killed by a Serbian bomb in Sarajevo
two days ago. Host Ray Suarez listens to BBC journalist
Martin Dawes. Dawes describes the reaction to NATO's military response in a city, where, he says, eleven thousand are
already dead:

> *One woman I spoke to said when she realized what was
> going on, and it was by no means obvious to people—they'd
> never seen anything like this, or felt anything like this—but
> when she realized that this was NATO and U.N., Western
> military intervention, she actually burst into tears. And it
> wasn't tears of relief. It was tears for the dead who she felt*

hadn't needed to die. She felt that if something had been done earlier, then the thirty-seven on Monday wouldn't have died.

August 31.   **2:00 p.m. WBEZ.** *Talk of the Nation.*

Moving from Bosnia to Bruce Springsteen, *Talk of the Nation* broadcasts live from Cleveland to celebrate this weekend's opening of the Rock and Roll Hall of Fame. Ray Suarez is joined by the museum's administrators and they face a live audience along with the usual listeners at home.

Considering that the whole reason I thought we liked rock 'n' roll in the first place is that the best of it is anti-museum, anti-institution, anti-walls, meaning ethereal, loud, and unfettered, I find the entire idea ridiculous. I say this as someone who has worked in museums (including the National Gallery with its I. M. Pei East Wing), someone who goes to school at one now. Museums have their place, and that place is by nature conservative—to conserve culture and its artifacts. And rock has its share of artifacts. But Buddy Holly's grade-school report card (which I once saw at the Hard Rock Cafe in the National Gallery's neighborhood) has zero to do with his music. Tacking an object up on a wall changes things.

So I contaminate my project by calling in. The phone rings about forty-eight times. A woman answers and screens what I have to say. I tell her that I want to talk about Pei, who designed the Hall, whom I happen to think is about the least-rockin' architect in the known universe.

I'm instructed to turn down my radio, which means I have to listen through the telephone receiver, which is uncomfortable and only barely loud enough to hear. Just as I'm getting bored and trailing off (I'm on hold for maybe twenty-five minutes) I hear Ray Suarez, really the friendliest guy in radio, say, "Sarah joins us now from Chicago. Hiya, Sarah."

"Hi, Ray," I respond. "I was wondering if you guys were going to hire Tipper Gore as a guest curator." Silence. "But, uh, I was just kidding. I wanted to talk about I. M. Pei as your architect. I saw the photos of the building and it looked like typical I. M. Pei, cold, hard, climate-controlled, National Gallery–style beauty—"

Suarez interrupts, amused. "I take it you don't like that, Sarah?"

"No, it's fine. I'm sure his seriousness is part of what's keeping your fine institution from becoming a Hard Rock Cafe without the snacks." (Though, now that I think of it, the museum must sell food, which further blurs the distinction between the memento-displaying restaurant and the memento-displaying museum.)

"But I was thinking about what Pei's colleague Robert Venturi once wrote and he said, 'I. M. Pei will never be happy on Route 66.' And I think rock 'n' roll *is* Route 66, you know, it's where you get your kicks.

"I was worried about all this . . . I'm a little bit ambivalent about the institutionalization of this. But earlier in the show, you played Elvis and his singing just leapt right out of my radio. And I think that's the thing we have to keep in mind. Elvis Presley's voice can smash I. M. Pei's marble to dust."

This gets a laugh. Suarez asks the museum's Director of Exhibitions and Collections Management, Eileen Gallagher, to comment on Pei's work. She calls it a "sensational piece of architecture." Later on she addresses me with the fact that because "Pei is so well thought of by some people, Sarah, that he really brought us a lot of legitimacy, that we were a serious institution." This convinced artists, she continues, to give them stuff.

But that's precisely my point, this legitimacy concept. Rock's greatest moments, from "Blue Suede Shoes" to "Anarchy in the U.K.," were the very opposite of legit—spit on, censored, despised by the powers that be.

Suarez says that he heard that Pei, in preparation for the venture, took a "crash course in rock 'n' roll." As I'm picturing Pei holed up in his nice, neat office listening to "Let It Bleed," Gallagher responds in a jovial voice, "I think that I. M. Pei has gotten a great respect for rock 'n' roll as this project has gone on."

Suarez thanks me politely for my call, asking, "You think you're gonna come visit this thing?"

My astonishingly quick-witted answer is, "Uh . . . yeah . . . eventually . . . sure."

When Suarez asks for Clevelanders' opinion of this monstrosity in their midst, one man is irate, and waxes on about the immigrant Pei's life as "an American story," which is true, about how Pei fled China and ended up "giving something back to this country." "To me," he rails, "it's important, that, unlike the woman in Chicago [*me*]—we have immigrant bashing today—I think we're damn lucky to have it!"

Now I'm an immigrant basher because I find Pei too elegant.

But then, a guy (and he sounds guylike) stands up to opine, "Yeah. I think a good kind of building would have been a huge garage. Because most of rock 'n' roll . . . grew out of *garage bands!*"

Suarez calls it "a sharp-looking building" and decides that it's destined for icon status "in the way that you'll go to Kennedy Airport and find little tiny copper Empire State Buildings . . . you will probably find . . . little Rock and Roll Hall of Fame paperweights shaped in that distinctive—"

"We already have them," Gallagher deadpans.

Once upon a time, radio was a sound salvation. It played all
the time, in the kitchen, in the bedroom, on the pool deck,
in the car. The tinny pop chug-a-lug wired the air around it
with bright-minded echoes of retro romance and fakey fun,
filling up the empty blue space that envelops all suburbia with
the simplest of all possible remedies for boredom: a beat.

—*Gina Arnold*, Route 666

September 2.   **6:30 p.m. WXRT-FM. Rock and Roll**
                     Hall of Fame Concert, live.

I leave the house just as Jon Bon Jovi's murdering "A Little
Help from My Friends." When I get to my friends' house
for dinner, I make them listen with me for a few minutes.
As Bruce Springsteen starts playing, Julie (a technohead who
no longer listens to regular rock) says, "Oh yeah. I forgot
about guitars and drums."

September 3.   **11:00 p.m. Q101. *Sound Opinions.***

The rock crits tackle the Hall of Fame nonsense right away.
Jim DeRogatis says he was watching CNN when *Tribune*
critic Greg Kot appeared, "saying something about how ridiculous it was 'to build an air-conditioned temple to the devil's
music.'" He goes on to bemoan the institution's collection,
which includes "the first poem that Jim Morrison wrote when
he was ten years old."

While Bill Wyman commends the notion that the museum

might put some interesting or useful archival materials on line, he utters, "Let me tell you some of the silly things about this concert," which apparently lasted for seven hours. "Two words: Sheryl Crow. Another two words: Gin Blossoms. Two more, three more actually: Jon Bon Jovi."

That last name prompts DeRogatis to suggest that the museum place "one little picture of him behind glass somewhere in the hall that says, 'In the mideighties, there was this thing called "light metal," "hair rock." And it died. Thank God.'"

Asked if the concert included the blues, Wyman sighs, "Well, they'd say, 'We need to play some blues,' and they'd bring out Slash and Boz Scaggs to sing Jimi Hendrix's 'Red House.'"

This cracks DeRogatis up: "Renowned bluesman—Slash."

September 6.   **10:18 p.m. WZRD-FM.**

I have the Pacifica news on while talking on the phone. When I hang up, I look down at the scrap of paper I was doodling on and it says, "the United States are responsible for many miseries in the world." I have no recollection of writing the words and thus no idea about exactly which miseries I'm supposed to be guilty about.

September 7.   **4:00 p.m. WBEZ-FM.**
                                            All Things Considered.

I just finished my first day of teaching first-year art history to tomorrow's art stars. I am seized with the terror of responsibility of being in charge of two sections of people who have been in college for exactly four days. (Do you know what it's like when you say something and another person *writes it down*?) Since they haven't quite figured out what art school is like, I play them a tape of an alumnus, a role model you might say, describing it—David Sedaris's speech to the School of the Art Institute graduation ceremony last May, which aired on *Morning Edition*.

Describing his former life as a student here, he says that he muddled through his homework (assignments such as constructing a shopping bag out of fallen leaves) while listening to late-night radio talk shows:

On Sunday nights, a woman named Phyllis counsels listeners in regards to their sexual problems. To the unidentified premature ejaculator she suggests an exercise known as "the quiet vagina." . . . A student loan and now this. What a magnificent town.

He mentions his horror, the first week of classes, seeing his clone (even though he always thought of himself as "original") next to his locker. When Sedaris notes, "He's you. You *hate* him," the students look at each other and smile; one nose-ringed girl gives another nose-ringed girl a knowing glance.

Still, you can see that they recognize the possibilities of this place, of attending a school that allows what is perhaps the first commencement address in history to include the phrase "premature ejaculator."

Meanwhile, in the real world.

Waiting for one of my own classes to start, I go and listen to *All Things Considered* and they're not playing Sedaris today. An NPR news reporter says that the Senate Ethics Committee voted yesterday to expel Senator Bob Packwood, Republican from Oregon, from the Senate for sexual misconduct.

September 13.   8:50 a.m. WBEZ. *Morning Edition.*

According to Bob Edwards, "Nearly every town in America boasts a couple of bands that record their music at home in makeshift basement studios for friends and anyone else who might be interested." Hmm. Tell me more about this fascinating new trend.

Rick Karr (a young producer who works at NPR's Chicago

bureau) narrates this feature about Guided by Voices, referring to the band's "beer-fueled basement jam sessions" as
"their escape from the nine-to-five."

GBV, one learns, released six albums between 1986 and
'93. Karr announces that "the band's 1994 CD, *Bee Thousand,*
was even hailed as a classic by the less-than-cutting-edge
Rolling Stone."

"Less than cutting edge"—boy, that's a good one, coming
from NPR.

Meanwhile, GBV's low-key, lo-fi pop songs play under the
voices, including songwriter Bob Pollard, who's pushing forty
and recently quit his job as a fourth-grade teacher to pursue
music full-time. He talks with a bitter edge, sounds a little
bitchy:

> *You think I didn't get some [beep] for that from my parents?
> See, I taught for fourteen years. I've got benefits and every-
> thing and kids and everything's nice. And we have cars and
> I quit that, you know, gave all that up for rock? But now,
> everybody thinks it's cool. You know why? Because we're
> making money now. Money's everything. That's sad isn't it?*

Still, Pollard claims that even though he's no longer a teacher,
he enjoys being a role model for younger musicians. "It's
never too late to be a rocker," he says. "That's what kids dig.
Their uncles are up there drunk—drinkin' and rockin'."

It's a nice little story, but wouldn't you hate to be Rick
Karr? I wonder what he had to change to get this on the air,
to make it palatable for the *Morning Edition* audience. I met
him a few months ago and he sighed and told me that he
was talking about zines with one of his NPR bosses. She got
all excited and said that they should cover this remarkable
new development.

September 15.

I ditch everything to come here, for the hell of it.

Riding around town this morning, I ignored a Public Radio International documentary about photographer Richard Avedon. My friend drives me to Watts to see Simon Rodia's towers (which are shrouded in scaffolding). Later, we see the new Spike Lee movie, *Clockers*, in Hollywood. We leave the theater, get back in the car (always with the car in this town), and the same documentary is playing seven hours later. Which makes sense, considering the entire day has been as black-and-white as an Avedon portrait.

September 16.

Driving toward Pasadena in the sun, a news program cites President Clinton on welfare reform: "Work. Personal responsibility. Family." And I'm with him, I really am. Except for just now. The only reason I'm here is jailbreak. I'm ditching work, school, responsibility, haven't spoken to my family in days. I'll reform—on Monday.

September 17.

Walking through the unpopulated, gleaming corporate emptiness that is downtown L.A. after a visit to a sickeningly slick show of 1980s art at the Museum of Contemporary Art, I've got the creeps. I can handle being in the woods alone, but in the financial district of the country's second-largest city? It's neutron-bombsville down here, lonely and sinister. A Jeep pulls up to a stoplight and I'm thankful for a sign of life. Its radio's blasting Blondie's seamless, flashy, empty "Heart of Glass," which sounds all too reasonable.

I vow to stop complaining about the Midwest.

September 19.   **9:26 p.m. Dial scan.**

Women on men: "He could win the Olympics in serial killing," a woman says, while whiny new rock sensation Alanis
Morissette's obsessing if her old boyfriend's getting a blow
job at the movies (as if I care), at the same time that my
favorite bad girls, the Shangri-Las, are *vroom-vroom*ing about
"The Leader of the Pack."

September 20.   **12:30 p.m.**

Scanning an assigned essay—Bertolt Brecht's "Popularity and
Realism"—right before a class in a coffee shop on Michigan
Avenue, I stop at this passage: "The ruling classes use lies
oftener than before—and bigger ones. To tell the truth is
clearly an ever more urgent task. Suffering has increased and
with it the number of sufferers." Meanwhile, Elvis's "In the
Ghetto" blows a winter wind through the radio, filling up
the warm sunny room with the bitter cold tale of the Chicago
boy born to poverty, born, in fact, to die.

When that corny, sad song ends, ditsy Sheryl Crow stops
by to tell Elvis (and Brecht) to lighten up! To have some
fun! Get wasted at nine A.M.! Try it!

September 23.

Rolling my eyes past a classical DJ announcing Haydn (he
pronounces it "heighten," which is linguistically correct but
pretentious as hell), I land on a garishly funny noise that
takes a second to register. Putting the "cunt" back in *vacant*,
it's the Sex Pistols.

September 24.

I meet up with Bill Wyman and Jim DeRogatis to drive down
to Q101. They ignore me and gossip about rock-crit dirt like
crazy. When they remember I'm there, they implore me not

to repeat anything, which is like no problem at all since I have zero idea what they're talking about.

We arrive downtown and enter the lobby of Q101's building, which is tellingly named the "Merchandise Mart." We go up an elevator and walk through a dark hallway, past weird showroom windows of interior designers' furniture configurations.

The station itself (and as I go through the doors it hits me that I've never been inside a commercial station) looks totally corporate, like a picture ripped from an office-supply-company catalog—pale gray walls, maroon chairs, rooms of cubicles. We walk down a hall past framed gold records, some of them devoted to bands I like—the Meat Puppets, They Might Be Giants, Nirvana—and even though I've been here for about two seconds I just want to rip them down. I follow the two objects of my scrutiny into an (if possible) even more corporate looking conference room, where they sit at a long, oval table and whisper when they don't want me to hear what they're saying. A big board behind them is scribbled over with the remnants of some money-grubbing pep talk; phrases such as "retail spending power" and "big development" and "customer profiles" stand out.

Tonight's broadcast will be Jim's second-to-last. He's leaving the *Sun-Times* to become a *Rolling Stone* editor. His callers will give him shit for this later, but meanwhile, I ask him questions about moving to the, at best, dubious publication, which I can tell is just his favorite topic in the world. He mumbles something about changing it for the better, which seems like a good idea.

I'm brought some coffee in a Mrs. Fields mug and shown Lance and Stoley's trashed office. (They're the Q101 version of Beavis and Butt-head—only not as illuminating—who do the morning show.) The address of Urge Overkill's Nash Kato, rock star, is taped up on their bulletin board.

Right before eleven o'clock, we go to the studio. I'm placed next to the ill-mannered individual who answers the phone. He shares charming observations with me such as, "Excuse my language, but the best part of this job is that you get to be a dick to callers." How nice.

The ironic part of being here is that Phone Boy talks on the phone so loud, I can literally hear only every few words of the show.

I watch Bill and Jim through a glass window. They talk about Jim's imminent departure.

Caller Todd yells at him, "You sellout! You complete sellout!"

Another caller, Julia, has news about the R.E.M. show that ended minutes ago in which Patti Smith gave a cameo performance. Perplexed, Julia informs us that Smith "took off her shoes and socks for no apparent reason." When asked what Smith's song was, Julia answers, "Dancing Barefoot." Well, there ya go.

A certain Heather calls to say that while the crits' show "is very well prepared," they say "nasty, mean, horrible things about teenagers." Bill disagrees: "I'm in favor of rock-loving youths."

Jim gets sentimental about his recent Oklahoma City visit with the Flaming Lips. Observing them in the studio, "building songs from the riff up," he says, is "a magical process." He plays a beautiful, sad track from their new record, called "The Abandoned Hospital Ship," and gives the album an A-plus. "You are such a psychedelichead!" Bill exclaims, crying B-plus.

They play a station ID recorded by the lovely Mekons chanteuse Sally Timms, and Bill apologizes that "she was faced with the words 'Chicago's new rock alternative.'" Exhausted, my mind wanders for a while and I hear them saying something about, I think, Russian gulags, and it dawns on me that most of the time when I listen to this show, I'm in bed.

September 25.   **9:00 a.m. Q101.**

Samantha James, Q101's official English accent, announces
her engagement to Lance, the morning guy, the one whose
main job is to sit there and tell his dumber cohost, "Stoley,
I can't believe you said that," or variations thereof. James
calls her granny (her word) in England on the air and generally
turns the entire thing into a big ad for the station, accepting
congratulations from her callers all morning long.

September 29.

Every day, I take the train. And every day, at every stop, the
conductor (in a swirl of cackles and feedback and interfer-
ence) lays out the rules: "No smoking or littering or radio
playing." Every time I notice the command (and it's so ubiq-
uitous I mostly don't) I relax. Then my mind jumps for joy
enough to request an I ♥ COMMUTING button. No radio playing. The very idea is a relief, a respite, a refuge. Safe! it tells
me, because I am sick, sick, sick of that black box in the
corner lording over my life. Sick of writing down times. Sick
of call letters and station IDs. Sick of listening. Sick of paying
attention. Sick of getting home bone-tired and facing its
myriad crap. No radio playing, meaning that there's one place
in the world that's Linda Wertheimer–free. No traffic reports
with their endless (and to me, meaningless) overuse of the
phrase "coming in from Mannheim." (I have no idea where
Mannheim is and couldn't care less.) No Q101 twit announcing "forty minutes of nonstop music" and then proceeding
to butt in after every single bloody song to say "forty minutes
of nonstop music." No temperature at O'Hare or at the
Lakefront. No soul-station DJs calling each other "baby." No
"Denise," which one oldies station (over)plays every livelong
day. No offputting 'XRT segue from a good Elvis Costello
song into some evil Santana magnum opus. No Pearl Jam.
(And I like Pearl Jam, but those poor people! Even Pearl Jam
must be sick of Pearl Jam considering one is faced with a
choice of five of their many songs several times an hour.)

And while we're at it with the constantlies (hear ye, Q101), no Green Day Bush Nine Inch Nails Oasis Alanis Morissette SmashingPumpkins or (good God) Stone Temple Pilots. No talk-show hosts demanding of their feedback-drowned callers, "Are you standing close to your radio? Turn your radio down! Are you on a car phone?" No callers gushing to Rush or "It is I! G. Gordon" or whatever golden calf they're worshiping with one of two quips: (a) "I can't believe I got through! I've been trying for months!" or (b) "I can't believe I got through! I'm a first-time caller!" No country song that revolves around a cutesy double entendre that wears thin before you even hear it. No *Car Talk* in which Click says, "Don't listen to my brother," while Clack responds, "And don't listen to *my* brother." (Fine with me, I won't. Happily.) No college DJ that's, um, lost his, uh . . . where is it? . . . set list. No mean, tired attack on Courtney Love. No one attaching the suffix *-land* to Chicago, as in "Chicagoland" (in order to make sure that people in suburbs with different names will feel included enough to buy whatever useless item they're selling). No mention, *at all*, of Lake Wobegon. No rapid-fire machine-gun repetitions blasting out of the dance-music station like little headache bullets to my forehead. No *All Things Considered* theme song. Ditto *Morning Edition*'s. No (and this is the winner, hands-down) "Megadittos, Rush!" Have you ever heard anything more antidemocratic than that?

Not that the train's free of mean or stupid remarks. Two teenage girls kiss their boyfriends good-bye. After they detrain, the boys will refer to them for the next three stops as "them bitches."

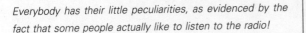

> Everybody has their little peculiarities, as evidenced by the
> fact that some people actually like to listen to the radio!
>
> —*Lester Bangs*, **Psychotic Reactions
> and Carburetor Dung**

October 7.   **12:30 p.m. WXRT-FM.**

Since the Pope's here visiting his American flock, I wonder
if he'll hear this song on his limo radio, Soul Asylum's "When
Does Life Begin." I guess he'd have an answer. Any good
religious patriarch would. But what if, and here's an idea,
everyone could decide how they feel about that one on their
own?

Not that everyone wants to; yesterday, I was teaching
medieval architectural history—Islamic mosques and Christian churches. I was hinting that these two religions, with
their restricted, controlled mandates of what to believe about
basically everything, were the beginning of the end of personal
freedom of thought in the Western world.

We were discussing the seventh century, when Islam
exploded, sweeping across North Africa in less than a hundred
years, leaving a trail of blood. An anxious student explodes,
characterizing my assessment of the Muslims' astonishing,
unprecedented conquest as "militaristic." "Well, yeah," I
reply. He saw it as racist. "What do you think," I asked him,

"people just changed religions basically overnight because they were really nice guys?"

His answer, and remember this is anything-goes art school, knocked me down: "Well, before Islam unified North Africa, people were just running around believing whatever they wanted!"

October 8.   **12:30 a.m.**

"Do you follow O. J.?" the cabdriver asks me, practically before I close my door. "Well I do," he begins, and boy does he. Not waiting for my answer, he launches a comprehensive diatribe about the trial and its participants (down to the first and last names of every single witness who has testified or is rumored to have been spotted within a twelve-mile radius of the Los Angeles County Courthouse) arguing on and on about the concept of "reasonable doubt" as if the existence of the phrase was a revelation. The radio news competes with his voice throughout his tirade. He must be listening with one ear, because the only thing that cuts off his discourse (and it does, midsentence) is the announcement that the Unabomber may have been apprehended.

8:00 p.m. Q101. *Sound Opinions.*

Bill Wyman tells his in-studio guests Billy Corgan and James Iha of Smashing Pumpkins that their new double album, *Melon Collie and the Infinite Sadness*, is "really something." Whatever that means.

Asked to justify the indulgence of the two-hour endeavor, Corgan jokes, "I felt like we really needed to do it before people started having babies and the drug problems grew." A few minutes later he'll describe it as "the emotions one person would go through in the course of one day."

It takes him a while to warm up to callers. When one named Debbie phones to ask him about his "influences" (and I have to say that I hate that word myself) Corgan answers with the unkind, "Can we electroshock you through the phone lines?"

Corgan waxes about the difficulties of fame, especially in this hometown context. One guy in a bar walked up to him and barked, "I heard you're anti-Chicago." "Well if I'm so anti-Chicago, why do I still live here?" Corgan fired back. "Well I don't care," says the guy, "'cause I'm from Detroit."

Caller Nikki asks about *Melon Collie*'s title change, which cracks him up. Corgan says that he never changed the title; it's just that *Us* magazine sent him a questionnaire about the album and he "made everything up." When Wyman recoils at this admission, Corgan sneers, "Like the press is based in truth, Bill."

Amber, a teenager whose band is holding a "vig-u-al" in her room to listen to their hero speak, asks, "How did you guys congeal?" They pass the phone around, and her guitar player tells Corgan that he learned to play with the *Siamese Dream* songbook, which Corgan calls "a horrible idea."

Wyman asks Corgan, "So what about Courtney Love?"— referring to their past relationship.

Iha responds, "She has a way with words."

Corgan says straight-out that "she has a right to her opinions."

Wyman wants to know if he thinks that she's out of control, if he's worried. Quietly, Corgan answers, "She's about the strongest person I've ever met."

This morning, I listened to a tape of the *Sound Opinions* interview Wyman and Jim DeRogatis conducted with Love in May. For about two hours, Love took calls, talked music (and a lot of dirt), and, in general, said what she thinks about all kinds of issues. My favorite part involves a conversation between Courtney, a caller, and the critics, discussing a show in which Hole opened for the self-important Nine Inch Nails at the University of Illinois–Chicago.

The caller, Scott, who had anticipated Hole's performance,

jabbed Love with the opinion, "Basically, it seemed like you were reading off a script."

She's surprised: "No. I was so into that show. I ruined my best dress, Scott. I ruined my best dress stage-diving."

Scott rebuts, "Well, that's what I'm talking about. It seemed like 'I'm going to smash my guitar here.' 'I'm going to stage-dive here.' "

Love asserts, "I would never do that by rote." Referring to the Nine Inch Nails component, she asks, "And you don't think all those automated lights where Trent [Reznor, the group's keyboardist and songwriter] lets the light show do all the work for him? . . ."

Scott argues that, according to an interview with Reznor, "he considers himself a lot closer to Alice Cooper as far as theater than Pearl Jam."

Love, indignant, shoots back, "No. He considers himself the biggest recording star since Elvis Presley, okay?" Laughs all around. "He's got the biggest ego, the biggest entourage, the most groupies, he's vile."

After Scott says that he's no acquaintance of Reznor's, he accuses Love of being wrapped up in her own self-image, which irks her: "Wait! I don't do interviews with MTV where I have six thousand candles behind me."

Love and DeRogatis urge Scott to get to his musical argument. DeRogatis claims he attended the performance in question and thought that "Hole kicked out the jams that night."

Still, Scott sticks to his guns: "For me, being on the other side of the arena—"

"Were you standing next to people going, 'What a slut!'?" she demands, also adding, "Were you standing next to [infamous Chicago producer Steve] Albini?"

"Yeah, I was hanging out with him, we had a beer."

Wyman: "Scott brings up an interesting point. . . . When you jump into the audience, a female rock star, you're exploding all sorts of conventions. It's an amazing thing to see. . . . When you do that every night or nearly every night, doesn't it lose its—"

"I figured it out," she interrupts quietly. "I was wanting to get passed like a football hero back to the back and back to the front." But she's concluded that it isn't a female thing, it's because of "the sexual aspect," since the sleazy Reznor gets torn to shreds as well, while tomboy rockers from Mudhoney and Pearl Jam are desexualized enough to get away with it.

Describing one experience singing her antirape song, she sounds at once angry and confused: "I was singing 'Asking for It,' I stage-dive, and I get raped! What?! Don't you see the irony?"

Here, her voice is drenched in guile: "For eight weeks, this thing would overcome me and I'd just *jump!* Where there were the most girls. And then I discovered at the Metro—"

"In Chicago," DeRogatis points out.

"—it was the *girls.* The *girls* were taking off my bra. The *girls* were taking out my hair . . . my barrette . . ."

"What did they want?" DeRogatis asks.

Love scoffs at the mention of one girl who molested her in the stage-diving process whom she drug onstage and beat up. When DeRogatis remembers reading this in the papers, she corrects him, "No, that was the other guy—the guy in Orlando. He's lying. I didn't beat him up. I beat her up but *[her voice trails off]* she didn't charge me with anything, so I can't talk about it." When Love demands that the girl explain "why you would do this to another female" the girl "had nothing to say."

"People want a piece of you," DeRogatis points out.

"I mean, they want a piece of me quite literally."

When DeRogatis brings up the fact that Love "kept a piece of Kurt," Love orders that he "shut up about that." He asks if her motives for saving pieces of her late husband's pubic hair are the same as her fans' search (on her body) for souvenirs.

"Your husband's dead!" she hollers. "You wanna, like, keep him . . ."

"Yeah," DeRogatis queries, "but what are these people

going to do with your barrette after they walk out of the show. Isn't it the same thing?"

"No! They're not married to me. I don't owe them anything. I gave them a record. It's a good record."

"Ah!" DeRogatis rebuts, "but they have an intimate relationship with you. You talked to their concerns. Maybe you hit something that's really important in their lives, you're talking for them in a way that nobody else does. They might feel just as close to you. You never met them, but they know you."

"I don't have sex with them," she answers, which takes care of that.

This four-way conversation between the young male caller, the two male critics, and the female artist, draws and quarters me: as a woman, as a critic, as a radio listener, as a fan. On the one hand, Love is indicting her female fans for participating in violating behavior. On the other hand, Love makes a lot of remarks throughout the interview that aren't exactly drenched in girl power, especially her newfound insistence on avoiding interviews with female writers; as a female writer I find that reprehensible—just plain lame. Also, while the two critics present seem sympathetic to the female struggle, I seem to have spent my entire life listening to boys talk about music. And sometimes, no matter how smart or untrivial or meaningful the boy might be, the sheer aesthetic presence of a masculine voice engaged in record talk can get on my nerves. Because there are so many males talking, all the time, about everything, on television and on the radio, that I just get sick of men. I love men. Most of my best friends, the fact of which I'm still trying to figure out, are men. But it's like the old food argument: You like strawberries, you even love strawberries; you just can't eat them every meal; that's how you get sick.

Hole's last album meant a lot to me. *Live Through This*, I believe, is smart, complicated, heartfelt, pissed off, and full of gall. It spoke *to* me—not, as DeRogatis says, *for* me. Would

I pick up, say, Love's earring off the floor at a show? Probably, as a curiosity. Would I rip it off her ear as she passed by me through the crowd? Absolutely not. As she says, she doesn't owe me anything, she gave me a good record. And if I keep a little piece of her, I'll put it where I keep Proust and Salinger and the Shangri-Las. That's enough, and it's a lot.

Meanwhile, back on the radio, Love's old friend Billy Corgan is confronted with Ozra, the editor of a local high-school paper. She talks about futile struggles to get in touch with Corgan via his publicist for her article "In Search of Billy Corgan." In order to glean primary material she ended up contacting his old friends, which resulted in the publication of embarrassing Corgan anecdotes and photos.

"You know what we call that, Ozra?" interrupts Wyman. "Good reporting!"

"It won awards," she adds.

Discussing the ills of commercialism, Corgan defends fame and fortune as a subversive route. "The best way to get this stuff off the radio," he opines, referring to Nirvana's toppling of Mariah Carey, "is to put something else on. . . . The only way to change the music industry is to make money."

When Wyman asks about their upcoming tour, and the ongoing debate about Ticketmaster's monopoly, Corgan whines, "Pearl Jam farts and it's on *MTV News*." He calls the Ticketmaster crisis "one sore thumb in a screwed-up body," implying that there are so many horrid things about the commercial music world already, why bother changing this one, itty-bitty complaint? He says that Pearl Jam, who has led the battle against Ticketmaster, should just charge less money themselves.

"They did," Wyman reminds him.

Corgan, perhaps realizing that he's wrong, drops it, and moves away from context to the commercializing effect on the music itself, the way "shocking, moving, exciting" set

lists have turned into "Okay. Where do we put the MTV
hit? ... We forget how bad music can actually be.... We
used to compete with Nirvana. That was good. That was
viscerally good. Now we compete with imitation Nirvana."

I'm no great Pumpkins fan but their songs on the radio
always sound honest. *Of course* I'd rather hear Billy Corgan
on the radio than Michael Bolton. And radio does seem to
come down to that, eventually—who do you hate most? Or
least? But this un-punk notion of competition bursts from a
Mariah Carey soul, a cutthroat, Top 40ish attitude about
what successful music is. Courtney Love, in her interview,
shares this notion, claiming a desire to sell more records than
Trent Reznor as a form of personal validation. Everyone with
any kind of claim on the mythic "underground" shares varying
forms of ambivalence about the issue. But, ultimately, music
has always represented not just the works of genius but also
a form of community, and not just a community of fans.
Nirvana, at the peak of their popularity were unkind to Pearl
Jam (bad) but also rapturous about so many of their peers
and ancestors (good), from great old punks like the Raincoats
and the Buzzcocks to hometown comrades Mudhoney.

Eddie from Urge Overkill drops by the studio to tape a
segment of the syndicated program *Modern Rock Live.*

"Those crazy Chicago rock stars!" Wyman exclaims,
"Don't you guys all live in the same big house?"

But Eddie wants to add his two cents about the Ticketmaster issue Corgan just dodged. He quite rightly complains
about the fact that, wanting to attend a recent PJ Harvey
show, Ticketmaster "added four bucks per ticket, plus three
bucks just to pick up the phone."

The rest of the calls are weird. One boy talks about singing
a Pumpkins song at his high-school homecoming dance,
much to the delight of his date. "That wimpy lyric thing
always works for me," Corgan admits. Another boy speaks
with all the brainless hero-worship of a Limbaugh listener,
while yet another thinks that the singer should cap his teeth.
The same boy decides that "Billy, you are incredible, you are
an idol—"

"I'm a Billy Idol?"

"—but James—you are a tolerable person."

Wyman mentions that the "tolerable" Iha, along with bass player D'Arcy, has launched a record label with "D'Arcy's sister's husband" called Scratchie Records but they can't play any of them now because "Q101 doesn't have a working turntable." A radio station? Without a turntable?

In the middle of a dark pop Pumpkins song that I don't recognize, the show gets cut off by an ad for a drum shop, and is therefore, the end.

October 10.   **12:00 p.m.**

I sit in the art-history department office at school and listen to the radio with the two women working there. Everyone holds her breath. O. J. Simpson is found not guilty.

                                    10:50 p.m. WZRD.

My mother calls to say that my grandfather has two days, if that, to live. After crying in silence, I turn on the radio, just for some noise. But the radio's already throwing earth on his grave: A children's choir sings a cappella, followed by Gregorian chant—masses for the dead. "Sugarfoot," the tough old coot would scold me, "don't bury me yet."

October 14.   **7:23 p.m. WLUP-FM.** *The Liz Wilde Show.*

Wilde announces her guest lineup for this evening, including "the guy who just wrote that Tom Cruise autobiography."

October 16.   **4:00 p.m. WBEZ.** *All Things Considered.*

Today, a million men were marching, but I can only think of one. A people gather to recognize their history, make plans for the future. But the last real link to my own past up and left this earth only hours ago. And as I sit through the minister

Louis Farrakhan's propaganda, the *ATC* hosts' bland repartee and to the dozens of sane, encouraging, Million Man March participants who try and get at what this day means to them, I can only half pay attention.

This morning, my grandfather died. He wasn't even born in a state—Oklahoma was still Indian Territory in 1904 when he first drew breath. No more of his stories about my Swedish grandmother who died before my birth. No more updates on Cherokee tribal politics. Then again, no more diatribes about how he wants me to become, of all things, a high-school French teacher. No more telephone rants against my—to him—frightening urban lifestyle amidst the "opium dens of San Francisco" or the "gangsters of Chicago." Still, without him, I feel a little weightless, a little more alone, cut off.

And Farrakhan says:

> We came because we want to move forward toward a more perfect union, and if you notice, the press triggered every one of those divisions. "You shouldn't come, you're a Christian." "That's a Muslim thing." "You shouldn't come. You're too intelligent to follow hate." "You shouldn't come. Look at what they did. They excluded women, you see." They played all the cards. They pulled all the strings. Oh, but you better look again, Willy. There's a new black man in America today. A new black woman in America today.

Well, where are the women? Quite honestly, nothing makes me more nervous than the idea of a million (or as the Park Service estimates, four hundred thousand, men of *any* color, shape, or size gathered together. Any woman is well aware that a group of more than three men you don't know, convened in any configuration is, whether real or imagined, a threat.

But Maya Angelou is speaking, in her dignified voice, like the mother of us all: "My brothers and sons and grandsons and cousins and nephews, the night has been long. The wound has been deep. The pit has been dark, and the walls have been steep."

A few minutes later, Noah Adams, truly the whitest man

on the radio, speaks from the National Mall. The words he says, in themselves, are kind and loving—"The sun's warm and a cool wind comes down along the Potomac River, making the flags dance and swirling the charcoal smoke from the barbecues"—but emanating from his pinched throat they fall cold and flat to the ground, where they are trampled by real people.

Elizabeth Arnold, reporting from the Capitol Building (where Congress is conveniently on vacation) cites President Clinton's speech in Austin this morning, in which he "praised the march's message of responsibility, but said a million men can't make up for one man with a message of hate." She goes on to make the hardly astonishing observation that "racial issues have not been near the top of the Republican Congress's agenda" and that Republican "presidential hopefuls have had nothing to say about race." Except for Phil Gramm, who contributes this stupid, baffled sound bite:

I think—I don't know anything about the sponsors or anything else, but anybody who is focusing on people living up to their responsibilities to their children and their spouses, that's a good thing. Other than that, I don't know anything about it.

Moving right along, the wicked stepmother Linda Wertheimer interviews Leonard "Mr. Spock" Nimoy. After he says, in character, the word "fascinating," Wertheimer—the true Vulcan among us—makes one of her unsuccessful attempts at sounding human: "It gives us all a cheer to hear you say that. *[Yeah, right.]* Say it again." When he does, she replies, "I love that."

"Oh, good," Nimoy responds.

"Oh, God," I'm thinking. "Beam me outta here."

Meanwhile, back on planet Earth, a reporter named Claudio Sanchez hooks up with some college students heading toward the march early this morning. He notices something astonishing: "All men hold hands, spanning a six-lane street. Police escorts lead the way as young women scream their approval." I like contemplating this picture, and turn off the radio before its beauty gets spoiled by Wertheimer's snooty diction. Because today, there's only so much I can bear.

October 19.   **11:50 p.m. WXRT.**

Out the window, the night sky is a man-made pink—beautiful but toxic, postapocalyptic even. Then R.E.M. sings its energetic "It's the End of the World As We Know It" as I put on my slippers. For some reason, like them, I feel fine.

October 20.   **4:55 p.m. WXRT.**

Waylon and Willie sing a song I've never heard, simple and sweet, about a woman with whom they don't see eye-to-eye. It's the loveliest country song I've heard on the radio in a while, stripped bare of the usual glitzy smiley faces pasted across the face of country tunes staring out of hit radio these days.

   I grin after I realize what this is; you know things are bad when the best country song on the radio is a Pizza Hut commercial.

October 21.   **1:10–1:25 a.m. Rock 103.5-FM.**

In a cab on the way home from seeing the Chicago Film Festival screening of *Not Bad for a Girl*, a women-in-punk documentary (featuring L7, Lunachicks, Hole, Babes in Toyland, et al), I giggle about the teenage riot grrrl band (didn't catch their name) who shrieked a song called "Elvis Costello Has No Soul." The radio's on and during the entire fifteen-minute ride the station plays no women's voices at all, just a DJ talking about tickets for an upcoming concert, ad after ad (including one for a "Ladies Night" at a local club), ending on a Stone Roses song that starts as I pay the driver.

October 21.   12:00 p.m. WZRD. Church of the SubGenius:
Hour of Slack.

Unexplained collage: a man (you know those voices that sound as if they're wearing a tie?) says, "This is a program about knives. How to sharpen them, set them, adjust them, replace them, align them, maintain them, analyze them, sharpen them, set them, adjust them [*where have I heard this before?*] replace them, align them, maintain them, analyze them. In short, everything you ever would want to know about keeping the knives in John Deere forage harvesters in cutting trim."

Cut to another man, speaking matter-of-factly: "I can recall his headless body was found dangling from a chandelier. So, mistakes will happen, won't they? Now, if you'll forgive me, *BOING!* Now, if you'll forgive me, *BOING!* Now, if you'll forgive me, *BOING!* Ah ha ha ha! Aha ha ha ha ha ha!"

Woman: "Program complete. Enter when ready. I don't think wine will do it. I don't think acid would do it. Some other time maybe. My mind has expanded as far as it can go. Any more, and it'll pop, you know what I mean?"

When a man asks, "How are you feeling now?" another man responds, "I put that gun in your mouth, soldier."

"There is nothing like being at the heart of it all," exclaims a woman: "The dead center. The pulsating vortex. The gravity spot. Where the very air sings with the electric current of split-second decision-making. It is there that you will find the unparalleled intensity of comrades-in-arms on the front lines before the masses. Where are they? *Who* are they?"

And Ivan Stang answers, "Uhhhhhhhhhhh . . ."

9:00 p.m. WXRT.

"Come As You Are" segues to the sickly, embarrassing waste of time called Hootie and the Blowfish. I can forgive a stupid name, I guess, maybe, possibly, sometimes, if the music's good, but this sugary, limp, lobotomized, whining, fake rock song about crying for no good reason is the worst kind of

status quo, suck-up, frat boy–friendly, stadium-ready crud
that gets under my skin until I'm crawling with that woolen,
itchy boredom that corrodes any thinking person's psyche.

"Can eight million Hootie fans be wrong?" asks the DJ in
reference to their astounding, inexplicable, infuriating record
sales. To which I say, in several languages, HELL YES.

October 22.   10:00 a.m. WBEZ. *CBC Sunday Morning.*

A documentary about the feminist ethics of an all-girl school
employs a recurring Green Day riff in the background. If
they need a rock song to signify "teenager," why didn't the
(female) producer pick a girl band's music?

October 23.   The Riviera Theatre.

Hometown rockers Smashing Pumpkins give a worldwide,
live broadcast of selections from their new album, *Melon
Collie and the Infinite Sadness.* They play two whole songs
before the power goes out, disappointing fanatical Italian
Pumpkins fans who got up in the middle of the night to hear
this. Eventually, things work out (minus the light show) so
that bald Billy Corgan (dressed in a shirt emblazoned ZERO)
and band can deliver their usual brand of energetic but too-
long songs. But not before my friend and I are forced to
witness the unsmooth attempts of two junior high school boys
to pick up a too-bright-for-them Belgian exchange student.

October 25.   8:30 a.m. WJJD-AM.

You know you're in trouble when an old carny like Howard
Stern questions your ethics:

*I'm gonna give him the benefit of the doubt. Let's say ol'
Rush walks out with five-hundred thousand dollars. This is
a guy, at this point, who has made millions of dollars. Why,*

why does he need five-hundred thousand dollars to sell his audience a tape recorder that has nothing to do with anything? Why does he need that? I mean, be generous. Go wild. Don't hawk the tape recorder. Skip it. Say it's not worthy. It's almost like a desperation in this business. Nobody believes it's gonna last. He plans like a guy who thinks he's gonna be on the radio for another six weeks. Because he knows at some point, the bottom's gonna fall out.

11:45 a.m. WLS-AM.

Rush, claiming to possess "talent on loan from God," introduces caller Cheryl in Little Rock. "Oh! I'm so nervous," she squeals. "*Giga*dittos from Little Rock, believe it or not, Rush."

He thanks her.

She's tried to call so many times, can't believe she got through, blah, blah, blah, such an honor, etc. She was out shopping with her two sons for a birthday gift for her husband, "and my seven-year-old looked over, and he goes, 'Oh look, Mom, there's Rush Limbaugh.' And I thought, 'What?' And I looked over and there's a whole table with your ties and they were both going 'Oh! Yeah! We've gotta get these! You know how Dad loves Rush Limbaugh!'"

Rush deadpans, "And you found them colorful, stylish, vibrant, and affordable."

"Well yes, actually, some of them were a little bit too vibrant for my taste, being a nice conservative that I am, but we loved 'em!"

Boy, can you imagine dinnertime chez Cheryl this evening? Hubby comes home, blushing with pride after catching his spouse's contact with his hero, pumped up from the jealous glances he got all day from the guys at the office. "Honey, can I kiss the mouth that spoke to Rush? Whisper sweet nothings into the ear that heard his words?" Cheryl will consent, undress him until he's naked except for the Limbaugh tie knotted coquettishly around his throat. Maybe

they'll have a little ménage à trois of the mind, fuck each
other in the name of Rush, conceive a child, and name him
Ditto, just like their dog.

October 26.   **8:00 a.m. WBEZ.** *Morning Edition.*

Few things could make me more nervous than waking up to
Bob Dole throwing around phrases such as "historic
moment."

Elizabeth Arnold reports that the Congress is noodling
around with this insane seven-year balanced-budget plan (I
don't think that I could balance my own little-bitty state
college–debt budget in seven short years) from "finishing
work on the thirteen bills that will finance government this
year. . . . Yesterday, Dole urged reporters to focus on the big
picture."

"This is all the little details," Dole admonishes. "The big
thing is we've got this big package that's gonna fundamentally
change the direction of this government of ours and it's
gonna pass. That's the story. All this other stuff belongs at
the bottom."

"All this other stuff" includes the fact that, according to
Senate minority leader Tom Daschle, "This is an income
transfer from middle-income people to upper-income people." Senator Jay Rockefeller remarks that "all this other
stuff" includes "a mind-boggling raid that will cut health-
care benefits, increase senior costs, and threaten the very
existence of hospitals." "All this other stuff," Arnold says,
involves "hidden provisions," including "reduced fees for
grazing, transfer of forest land for ski resorts, opening up the
Arctic National Wildlife Refuge in Alaska for oil drilling—
all as special-interest giveaways."

It seems that an impasse is in order. Arnold says that
Republican leaders aim to force the president's hand. If he
vetoes the budget plan, they won't "extend the government's
borrowing authority. But from the White House yesterday,

the president called the tactic 'economic blackmail, pure and simple.' He repeated his pledge to veto the budget bill."
Then what?

October 28.   **9:55 a.m. WLUW-FM.**
Live at the Heartland Café.

I overslept. I meant to listen to this Loyola University talk show hosted by Danny Postal, a man I met at a reading earlier in the week. I catch the last few minutes of his eager interview with the author of a book called *Against Capitalism*. "We must have you back," Postal exclaims.

I could have dreamed this, but I'm pretty sure that the ten o'clock folk-music program's title is *Other People's Problems*. At least that's what it sounded like—droning Korean something-or-other that requires a minimum of three cups of coffee to sit through, which is three more than I've had.

12:23 p.m. WZRD-FM. The Church of the SubGenius:
Hour of Slack.

Finally, roughly five-sixths of the way through the year, do I hear Hank Williams. Too bad some weirdo had to die to get Hank to the people. Eulogizing SubGenius preacher Doctor Legume, who's evidently now with Bob, Reverend Stang plays the frenzied gumption of "I'll Never Get Out of This World Alive."

October 29. 10:00 a.m. WBEZ-FM. *CBC Sunday Morning.*

One of those deeply labyrinthine, CBC long documentaries recounts the story of a drunk-driving Canadian man who killed his two best friends. Instead of serving prison time, the man received a suspended sentence of eight hundred community-service hours. He goes to high schools to tell his story, to relive it constantly before others. His guilt is palpable

through the speakers, drenched in a tangible desire for suicide, for his own death. But it isn't his voice that gets to me.
It's one of the dead boys' mothers', explaining to a judge
that he was her son's best friend and that (and here I lost
it) she asked him what clothes her son should be buried in.
The overwhelming grace of forgiveness in her statement
makes me cry.

This is real life. But WBEZ wrenches me away from it to
their version of real life, or at least the real world: fund drive.
They pitch to the Canadian contingent, lamely. They want
your money "if you've spent time in Canada. If you're still
Canadian. Whatever. Give us a call." Then a francophone
comes on and begs in French for *"votre générosité."*

Back with the CBC, a collage of voices weighs in with
thoughts for and against tomorrow's referendum concerning
Quebec's independence: "It's brought Canada together" . . .
"When will these self-serving, saltwater cowboys stop sucking
the government teat?" . . . *"Trop peu, trop tard"* . . . *"Le
sovéreignité de notre pays! Le Québec!"* . . . *"Ensemble, ensemble, nous sommes solidaires."* . . . "I'm a Canadian and I'm
very upset about this whole thing."

I'm an American, and I'm upset, too. As a true New World
mutt, a Swedish-Cherokee-French-English person who has
lived in five states and the District of Columbia, it's hard
for me to imagine anything more than a general sort of
nationalism. So even as the great-great-granddaughter of a
Confederate soldier, the French Canadian desire for succes-
sion confuses me, strikes me as petty and self-important—
cloistered.

Host Ian Brown, an Anglo born and raised in Montreal,
delivers a bewildered but brilliant editorial of separation anxiety. Filled with "impotence" in the face of History, Brown
points out:

> It's often said by politicians on a campaign or by football
> coaches before a big game that we make our own history,
> that it's personalities and not principles that move an age.
> The "you just have to get out there and do it" philosophy.

But in fact, that's only true in special and rather narrow
circumstances. When opportunity and events and the will
of enough people coincide.

He launches into an analysis of the Canadian fur traders'
influence on the French Revolution. Their capital, he says,
created "a new class of uppity arriviste bourgeois business-
men" who were in the right place at the right time. "The
French made their own history then as some people in Quebec hope to today."

"But," and it's a big *but,*

if the magic circumstances aren't in place, then we never
get the chance to make history to our liking. Then our history
makes us. And history becomes an impersonal tide that
swamps us as its victims—an avalanche you either float
down on or get buried by.

Here, he changes pace, describing his Montreal childhood:

I spoke English and French. I had English and French
friends. I lived there. It was my home and my family. It is
also the foundation, the distinct *foundation of my memory.*
The countryside, the testicle-clenching winters with the elec-
tricity down, the odd, thrilling trip to the Forum to play in
a peewee hockey championship, various people. . . . Those
were some elements of "my Quebec," if you'll pardon the
expression.

His voice becomes a crescendo of desperation, filled with
life-and-death longing:

Now, a group of people, the forty-six or forty-eight or fifty-
two percent of the people of Quebec, want to take away that
part of my history. You can say I'm being illogical. Even
with a separate Quebec, memory is something you always
own. And to a Quebecker who lives there now my pique
must seem indulgent. But that is the way that the threat

feels. As if nonelective surgery was being performed on my brain against my will. And what makes it worse is that I understand the impulse of the sovereigntists. I understand the appeal of creating a new country that needs you. Even if another part of me resists the theft of my past and the sense of who I am. Resists it and wants to shout, "You can't take that away without paying for it somehow!" . . . But what can I do? Should I beg? Should I implore Quebeckers, my old neighbors, not to cut out of my head and my chest the idea and the ideal that for me is the essence of this country, a decent moral dream?

Brown continues, yelling (perhaps in vain) at History as the masculine force that could divide the country "no matter what the outcome of the vote Monday":

And I suspect History isn't listening. And even if he is, and History does seem very male to me these days, and maybe even handsome and maybe even one-legged. Even if history is listening, he doesn't want to hear. So what to do?

Earlier in the essay, Brown mentioned Pierre Trudeau as a "terrifying specter." Those two small words, in describing a past national leader to the nation he once led, are opinionated, full of freedom. Can you imagine NPR's polite, play-it-safe, don't-fuck-up Bob Edwards describing Ronald Reagan that way on the air? I cannot. But Brown deepens the complexity of his argument by bringing up what he calls a "rumor"—that Trudeau, who had refused to comment on the referendum because he feared making matters worse, "went up north to look at the water."

What to do?

If Trudeau went "to look at the water" because, as Brown remarks, "the water stays the same, even though the course of the river changes," Brown gives us this lesson: "Revolutions never lighten the burden of tyranny. They just shift it, as someone once said, to another shoulder."

This troubled eloquence of Brown's commentary lurches

back and forth between the personal (peewee hockey) and the world-historical (French Revolution) in step with the public/private schizophrenia that great radio exploits, bringing you broadcasting's greatest gift: someone who speaks your language.

Brown calls the lived-out, bilingual solidarity of his childhood "a decent, moral dream." Those are simple words, but these days, the idealistic sentiment is painfully rare. In this, the year when public discourse seems hell-bent on replacing decent, moral dreams with the meanest sort of pathological goals, I drink coffee on Sunday mornings, and let Citizen Brown remind me that there is still something to shoot for—something like the concept of Nation.

October 30.   **8:55 a.m. WBEZ-FM.** *Morning Edition.*

Usually, I wake up at a glacial pace, but this morning I squirt over to the radio to hear about Quebec. And the 'BEZ fund drive inches forward for what seems like forever. Bossy Nina Totenberg tells listeners to pledge "NOW." Cutting back to the locals, they describe (and I'm fairly sure they're not joking) Nina's recent *singing* appearance on A *Prairie Home Companion*. Maybe she'll start crooning her Supreme Court coverage (but what rhymes with Scalia?).

Finally, at nine o'clock, the news. The referendum failed, but only by a less than two-percent margin.

NOVEMBER

> But I can't listen to music too often. It affects your nerves,
> makes you want to say stupid, nice things, and stroke the
> heads of people who could create such beauty while living in
> this vile hell.
>
> — *Vladimir Lenin*

November 3.

A friend just handed me a photocopy of a poem from the
journal *Documents* (#6), written by someone only identified
as "Sparrow." When I saw the title—"Nine Days Without
a Radio"—I started salivating. Nine. Whole. Days. This late
in the year, I'd settle for nine whole hours. Sparrow has made
a list of his or her 216 hours of radio-free living, deciding
"without a radio, one *becomes* a radio," and that "the virtue
of being a radio is that one plays one's favorite songs." I
believed that once, but now I'm not so sure. Even when the
radio's turned off, my mind replays what it's heard over and
over: lately, the first eight notes announcing *All Things Considered*. I wonder how many days without a radio it will take
to get *my* songs back? I used to bounce around to my inner
Fastbacks. Now I just mope along, imprisoned by an all-too
appropriate Smashing Pumpkins line that goes "Despite all
my rage I am still just a rat in a cage."

November 4.   **1:00–4:00 p.m. WZRD. Negativland's**
                                                 Over the Edge.

Under the weather, I take some cold medicine and try and
concentrate on this once-a-month collage show produced by
the California media-critic band. This one, I think, focuses
on the subject of gender, but I keep drifting in and out of
sleep. I wake up as someone is saying, "Hitler wore khakis."
Or maybe I dreamed that.

November 6.   **10:30 p.m. WXRT.**

I hang up the phone. A friend just told me her excruciating
abortion story, questioning her decision, and describing the
ways her body changed during her brief pregnancy. I scan
the radio manically for forty-five minutes, up and down and
back again past Bach and Pearl Jam and Randy Travis, looking
for some kind of answer. I never find one, only R.E.M.'s
"Everybody Hurts."

November 9.   **9:06 a.m. Q101.**

Outside, it's snowing. I listen to substitute DJ Robert Chase
(who doesn't have his own Q101 show, I guess because he
has a brain in his head) while I grade art-history essay exams.
Regarding a twelfth-century sculpture of the Hindu god
Shiva, one student writes, "She has many significate [*sic*]
meanings in religion." How thoughtful of him to spare me
the boring, pesky details.

But just as I sigh, enter "Smells Like Teen Spirit," loud.
So I just put down my red grader's pen and as the song ends,
Chase pretty much sums up my sentiments, with a well-
placed, good-hearted, "Yeah!"

November 11.   **12:00 p.m. WZRD. The Church of**
                                  the SubGenius: *Hour of Slack.*

The Reverend Stang is talking up his show's international
Internet access. The other day, a friend said that soon, anyone

with a minimum of equipment will be able to function as a one-person radio station, broadcasting through their computers to the world. I love the "In My Room" implications of this, thrill to the notion that someday I could listen in on some Australian teenager's musical collage or live concerts of someone's Alabama aunts or secret diary readings by twelve-year-old girls.

November 13.   **1:13 p.m. WJJD-AM.**

Overheard on the *G. Gordon Liddy Show:* A listener claims, "I'd put one of those shotgun shells in my .45 if I was gonna shoot turtles or snakes."

November 14.   **8:00 a.m. WBEZ.** *Morning Edition.*

Mara Liasson reports that the U.S. government has shut down, except for "essential" services such as air-traffic control and food inspection. She says that Republicans "trooped down to the White House last night" after President Clinton vetoed two temporary spending measures which would keep things running. The Republicans are "offering to discuss dropping the Medicare provision if the president agrees to their play to get rid of the deficit in seven years and so far, he's not."

Host Bob Edwards, sounding drowsy, asks, "Uh—any hope for progress now?"

Liasson responds that "the stalemate could last some time." On the other hand, she points out, "One good sign is that Bob Dole did indicate that they had made some headway at least in the sense, as he put it, that no one is going to beat each other up. He said, 'We know this is serious business.'"

Bob, bored, queries, "Well, how did this happen? Why is government about to shut down?" Interesting that he doesn't say "the" government, as in specifically, this here American one, but rather "government" sans article, implying the breakdown of the entire concept.

Liasson reports that the White House has enlarged the challenge beyond the nuts and bolts of dollars and cents into a larger symbol:

> *This is a defining moment for him. . . . This is a way that he can prove that he is standing firm behind his principles, such as not cutting Medicare, education, or the environment. And polls show that the American people by about two-to-one think he should veto the Republicans' budget plans and at least, for now, the public appears to be blaming Republicans for this impasse.*

Bob: "Thank you, Mara."

November 15.   **8:30 a.m. Q101.**

"Lump," by the band called Presidents of the United States of America, is lovable enough—a little too goofy, but its heart's in the right place. But if they really wanted a punk name, symbolizing the hated and/or the despised, they'd call themselves the Congressmen.

At 10:35, there's a a test of the Emergency Broadcast System. Perhaps in light of the government shutdown, they should change the usual public safety notice to something like, "In the event of an emergency, the government is unwilling to expend its resources to help you out. Suffer, you suckers!"

November 16.   **11:30 p.m.**

Walking home from the train, I look up at a gigantic Q101 billboard in a triptych format. The left third of the board is white space, save for the Q101 logo plastered in the center. The right third contains one word, split in half and stacked on top of itself: ALTER sits on NATIVE. But it's the center panel that astonishes me: the colossal, writhing head of Kurt Cobain (I think from the Nirvana video for "Heart-Shaped

Box") engaged in a piercing scream—his eyes cast in that deer-in-a-headlight stupefaction, his mouth, open as if to receive dentistry. It is an image of unadulterated anguish. As advertising, it's remarkable. It offers none of the youth, fun, or freedom traditionally associated with rock 'n' roll; it offers only pain. Oh well, I guess the Christians have used this ad campaign for centuries and it seems to have worked for them.

November 18.   **12:30 a.m.**

Just as my cab passes a street called "Mozart" a new song comes on the radio: the tuba duet version of *Eine Kleine Nachtmusik.*

9:05 a.m. WCKG-FM 105.9. *Breakfast with the Beatles.*

The Beatles sing about love and things getting better and sunshine while I scan the newspaper headlines: GOP REJECTS DEAL and FIRM ACCUSED OF SCRAPPING SAFE CIGARETTE and THREE IN FAMILY SLAIN and VOTE COULD CHILL BID FOR BOS-NIAN ACCORD.

November 20.   **8:00 a.m. WBEZ. *Morning Edition.***

The government is, for now, back in business. But Cokie Roberts points out that shutting down things like the Grand Canyon was "embarrassing."

Seattle

November 21.   **6:40 p.m. Dial scan.**

Visiting friends on the Thanksgiving break, I sneak off to the radio:

"For years independent booksellers have claimed that pub-lishers give a higher discount to chains such as B. Dalton. All of this is a violation of the antitrust laws." . . . Ad for a TV movie: A woman says, "The only freedom is in forgiveness." A

man replies, "Then I guess I'll never be free." . . . "Time for
caroling! Time to reflect! To worship! To give thanks!" . . .
Harmonica solo in a Tom Petty song. . . . "Any journalist
who's censored should quit?" "Yes, exactly." . . . "I was just
noticing on the listener comment line where it said, 'Hey,
how about a little more Santana?' " . . . "God bless you. I'm
gonna take an hour tomorrow and tell you about the greatest
Bible software I've ever seen." . . . And, finally, some Seattle
music by way of "Purple Haze."

November 23 (Thanksgiving).

An ad on the radio: "Tonight, let's give thanks for all the
wonderful things this country has produced. Like the smash
hit movie *Home Alone!*"

Chicago

November 25.   **9:54 p.m. WLS-FM.**

I hear chanting out the window. The Neighborhood Watch
is on the corner by the crack bar screaming, "NO DRUGS!
NO GANGS!" over and over. I turn on the radio to drown
them out and find my favorite (after Elvis) childhood Christmas record, Gene Autry singing "Rudolph the Red-Nosed
Reindeer," which is followed by a schmaltzy-bad version of
"Have Yourself a Merry Little Christmas" and a song about
guardian angels that is really more than I can stand.

November 28.   **8:30 a.m. WBEZ. *Morning Edition.***

I spent all of yesterday escaping the world in my favorite
place—Art Land. I wrote a record review, saw weirdo artist
Paul McCarthy speak (and show his indescribably sick video
making fun of painter Willem de Kooning), and read a Raymond Chandler novel, *The High Window.* I forgot to read
the newspaper and couldn't face the radio. Apparently, while
I was enjoying this aesthetic exile from reality, the president

addressed the nation: He's sending troops to Bosnia to enforce the recent peace agreement. And sometimes, like now, I find my life a little irrelevant. What good did my opinions on the new Amps record do anybody? I felt this once before, when I had to take the GREs at the Naval Academy in Annapolis. On the break, I was feeling depressed about my math abilities, so I went outside for some air, only to witness some boy younger than me telling his parents that he was being shipped off to Somalia.

November 28. **Book review for *New Art Examiner: Phantasmic Radio* by Allen S. Weiss (Duke).**

While reading Allen Weiss's *Phantasmic Radio*, I listen to the radio; not the phantasmic one, but the plain old, everyday, rock 'n' roll kind, with banter and ads and weather and tunes less than four minutes long. The DJ says that it's ten o'clock and Kurt Cobain murmurs "Come As You Are," proving Weiss's point:

Radiophonic airspace is a necropolis riddled with dead voices, the voices of the dead, and dead air—all cut off from their originary bodies, all now transmitted to the outer international and cosmic airwaves only in order to reenter our inner ears in a "mad Totentanz.*"*

People die. It's radio waves that live forever.

Weiss's thin but dense book consists of four essays devoted to Antonin Artaud's radio rant *To Have Done with the Judgment of God*, John Cage's *Imaginary Landscapes* (in which the radio acts as a musical instrument), Valère Novarina's *Theater of the Ears*, and Gregory Whitehead's audio artworks. But Artaud can't seem to sit still in his own little chapter and promptly haunts the entire enterprise—especially his notion of the "body without organs," manifested in radio's characteristic disembodied voice.

To deny the body is to deny death, which is to defy the

creator. Since Artaud's previous theological forays resulted in perky blasphemies such as "I jerk off on the cross of God," it's hardly surprising that on the eve of its scheduled broadcast in 1948, French radio pulled the plug on *To Have Done*. Unwilling to pardon Artaud's French, they called it obscene. The work's scatological heresies ("Is God a being? If he is, it is made of shit.") were not aired for another twenty-five years, three-quarters of a century after Jarry's famous outing of the word *merde*.

If Artaud sought to challenge nature, John Cage vied with culture, setting out to liberate sound from music by celebrating wildcat noise and silence. Cage's composition, Weiss writes, becomes "any sound event whatsoever." His analysis of *Imaginary Landscape No. 4* of 1951 for twelve radios—"where silence arrived in ironic stealth"—asserts radio's potential for radicality, behaving as an "active musical agent and not merely as a passive transmitter."

It is this insistence on action, along with an obsessive quest for freedom (from the limitations of the body, recording, representation, and language) that allowed me to ignore the occasional pitfalls of his writing style, which betrays subtle signs of too much time spent reading all those overly brilliant French theorists who can't write a sentence. His preoccupations with madness, poetry, glossolalia, screams, and sound itself are justified (I'm hard-pressed to imagine more interesting subjects), but readers seeking a healthier dose of thoughts on broadcasting per se will be disappointed: too much phantasm, not enough radio.

November 29.   **10:00 p.m. WXRT.**

Bob Costas interviews Bruce Springsteen about his new record, *The Ghost of Tom Joad*. But the most moving piece of the broadcast comes when Costas asks Springsteen to defend himself from accusations that he's "too mainstream." It turns into a kind of verbal cover version of Jonathan "Radio on!" Richman's "Roadrunner":

A lot of the things that I really liked were very mainstream. The stuff that moved me and changed my life were mainstream records. They were from people who came from outside of the mainstream but changed the mainstream to accommodate who they were by the force of their abilities and their talent and their ideas and their presence. Those were the artists that I admired a lot. Whether it was Dylan, hey—before "Like a Rolling Stone" you couldn't sing like that and get on the radio. You couldn't get on the radio like that. I've also said that the same thing before Nirvana came out with "Smells Like Teen Spirit," you couldn't sound like that and get on Top 40 radio. . . . I think I was essentially a child of Elvis Presley initially. . . . The thing that meant a lot to me when I was young were the things that came across the AM radio. I didn't live in an environment where there was a lot of cultural education. You weren't exposed to things that were outside of the mainstream for the most part. So the mainstream was what you had. In your small town, what came across the radio was—I found it very liberating.

A good radio program deserves the same critical attention as a good book or a good film. . . . With an analysis of radio, the serious criticism of broadcasting could begin, and with it, the serious reforms.

— **R. Murray Schafer**

December 2.   **8:10 a.m. Q101.**

In a temporary fit of self-recognition, a DJ from "your rock alternative" spouts: "Repackaging the same old songs and hoping you'll think it's something new—it's Q101."

December 4.   **8:45 p.m.**

The radio has become such a compulsive, constant companion that I've been home for around two hours, made three phone calls, cooked dinner, read a magazine cover to cover, and now, there's a grating guitar instrumental coming out of the speaker and I don't even remember turning the thing on.

December 6.   **9:10 p.m.**

After sitting through George Strait's version of "All My Exes Live in Texas" on country station "U.S. 99," I stumble across a man calling Mix 101.9 to dedicate a song to his lover.

"We've been having some problems lately," he claims, because he has to spend time with his ex. When the DJ asks why, he answers, "She's expecting. . . . I just want to tell Jamie that my exes are my exes and she's the only one for me."

December 7.   **10:00 p.m.** *The Mike Walker Show.*

Washington Post media critic Howard Kurtz, plugging his book *The Media Circus*, discusses recent news about news. He brings up the recent flap over the fact that CBS refused to allow *60 Minutes* to air an interview with a former Brown and Williamson tobacco-company executive.

"Well, guess what, kids!" Walker exclaims. "Last month Larry Tisch, CBS owner, purchased six cigarette brands from Brown and Williamson."

Kurtz responds:

> *It does raise some very troubling questions. You see now what happens when . . . the Disney Amusement Park or General Electric, which makes nuclear reactors, or other big corporate citizens owning television networks. It brings all kinds of possible conflicts and, I think, makes news . . . less important. And therefore, they're willing, I believe, to take fewer risks when it comes to taking on important interests who might, for example, stick some lawyers on 'em.*

Walker, after pointing out that he has no hard evidence, opines, "After keeping this interview that would have been harmful to a tobacco company off the air and the same network owner goes out and buys six brands of tobacco from that tobacco company, little suspicious, wouldn't you say?"

Kurtz agrees. "That's a good way of putting it."

December 8.   **12:30 p.m.**

Walking out on the creepy, deserted carnival that is Chicago's Navy Pier (picture a frozen Ferris wheel looming out of the icy lakefront), I arrive at the new headquarters of NPR affiliate WBEZ. I enter a nondescript foyer, see that 'BEZ offices are housed on the third floor, and decide to take the stairs. The third-floor stairwell door is locked. The station's call letters, however, are not painted on said door, but rather written in ballpoint pen on a yellow Post-it note.

After backtracking to the elevator and being screened by a receptionist, I am led down a clean, new corridor to the small office and cubicles occupied by Ira Glass and his crack radio crew.

Ira has quit his old job at NPR, as well as *The Wild Room* (Gary Covino continues solo), and is producing a new radio series funded in part by the MacArthur Foundation and the CPB. *This American Life* is a one-hour program that tells stories grouped around a common theme. Tonight's show features "Nightmare Vacations."

While 'BEZ's old studios on Clark Street had a crusty green cast, their new space has a bright gray newness decorated in the Corporate Anywhere style. As an added bonus, every door is numbered in both Arabic numerals and Braille.

Ira and production assistant Peter Clowney are huddled over a computer sound-editing program I have never seen in the flesh. The screen is divided into horizontal bands. Over and over, a woman's voice comes out of the computer. She says, "My mother was an optimist. No—I mean *really* an optimist." Later, I'll learn that it's columnist Sandra Tsing Loh describing a childhood vacation to Ethiopia.

I'm horrified and fascinated at the same time. I love watching tape being physically cut and spliced together, the discarded pieces draped around the floor like mud puddles. On the other hand, Peter cuts out an obtrusive breath in about two seconds flat. (The razor-blade approach would take, by my calculations, about thirty seconds if the editor's fast.)

They insert a pause after the phrase "Pearl of the Red Sea," and Ira's off to record his own story.

I follow him into a sleek, clean modern studio. While he sets up his tape and papers, I look through a glass window looking out onto the studio next door. Then I look again.

Comedian Jackie Mason is being interviewed there and the
two people asking him questions are laughing.

Ira's assistant Alix Spiegel (who it turns out is one of
those strangers I always recognize on the train—once we
even had a several-stop-long discussion about childbirth)
brings him, again, something I've never seen. It's called a
minidisc and it looks like a tiny version of a normal two-and-
a-half-inch computer disc. It works like a CD, and Alix has
used it to restructure a Hawaiian song into a ten-second
instrumental–thirty-second vocal–six-minute instrumental around which he can organize his monologue. After con-
ferring with Alix, who goes to yet another studio to monitor
a computer, Ira looks down at his old-fashioned manuscript
with a pen in hand to prepare to record his narrative.

"The thing about Hawaii," he says, then looks down, mutters under his breath, plans his pronunciation strategy, mumbles, "oh, and that could be," ruffles papers, scribbles notes.
"Okay, Alix, roll," he asks, and takes a huge breath.

*The thing about Hawaii, is that before you go, all anyone
will tell you is that it's paradise. That is literally the word
everyone uses. "Hawaii?" your friends say, and shake their
heads, as if in a dream, "Paradise."*

*After four separate people said this to me, I started to
wonder about brainwashing and kickback schemes. "Thank
you for flying Air Hawaii. In the future, if anyone mentions
the word 'Hawaii' to you, and you respond with the word
'paradise,' you win five hundred frequent flyer miles or a
discount on a Hertz rent-a-car."*

*A couple of days before my family went, I mentioned
the trip to my therapist—normally the most pragmatic,
clearheaded, reserved person. Even he got that faraway look
in his eyes. For me, suddenly time seemed to move in slow
motion. I watched his lips slowly wrap around the syllables
[in slow-mo] "It's paradise," and launch into a rhapsody
about snorkeling. It was like a scene from* The Manchurian
Candidate.

He delivers the program's introduction, identifying himself, and informing listeners of the Tsing Loh and David Sedaris stories to come. He asks the question, "If an American family can't get along in paradise, what hope is there?" Cut to ukulele (the aforementioned ten seconds) and a singer crooning about his little gray Hawaiian shack. While the music plays, Ira bounces his head around and dances in his chair; it's a catchy song.

That was the first of three takes through those paragraphs, which change subtly as Ira ad-libs. When the ukulele winds down, he jumps into the rest of the story, talking about a recent vacation he took with his mother, father, sisters, and nephews. Dissecting the quandary of the adult child visiting home—he says it transcends race or class—he calls it a "cultural problem. It's as if, somehow, in growing up, we've become a part of a different culture. We end up with different ideas about what's nice, what's interesting to talk about, what things mean, what's pleasurable."

The fact that his parents turn on television morning shows as soon as they wake up, confounds him, since, "To me, this noisy vapid clatter makes it impossible to think, impossible to feel anything." But he sucks in his discomfort because he wants to "feel closer" even though Paradise "brought the cultural difference between us to the fore." Besides their complete lack of interest in any form of traditional tourist activities, he notices that "they wanted to re-create their suburban home" to the extent that "they brought their own breakfast cereals with them, to Hawaii."

They focus, he claims, on the "personal habitat" of their rented condo:

The sliding glass doors weren't the heavy, nice kind. The bathrooms weren't as nice as my mom would like. And rather than spend more time with us, she'd steal away for hours, visiting this hotel and that, comparing the accommodations.

This all sounds pretty gripey and childish on Ira's part. Later in the story, he'll note that his parents probably felt the same way about him. He concludes about his petty criticisms that, "this is no way to treat your aging parents." But there is real sadness in his voice when he says, "Me, I don't think that heavier sliding glass doors and better bathrooms would make us feel closer. But it's not like I have any better ideas—about how to feel close."

His voice drops a little and pulls back from its earlier, tangible air of self-doubt:

C. S. Lewis once wrote—and it's maybe not original to him—that there is no heaven or hell, that in the afterlife, all that happens is that you continue to be the person you are, and develop in that direction for eternity. And for some, it's heaven, for some it's hell. Paradise shares this quality with the afterlife. For some, a vacation in paradise is paradise. For others, it's much more difficult.

This slides immediately into a killer whiff of Frank Sinatra's "Nicer to Come Home," which is so brassy and great that it threatens to upstage Ira's heartfelt yarn. He fades down before the hilarious ending, the part where Frank comes home to his slippers and his pizza.

Ira, Alix, and fellow producer Nancy Updike gather around a computer in another studio. His words are transformed into the hills and valleys of a graph on the screen.

The whole reason I wanted to come down and watch them work, instead of just listen in the privacy of my apartment, was Ira's description of his crew's group dynamic. He called it a "love fest." And I can see what he meant. There is a real respect and rapport between them.

The three of them sit and listen (Clowney is still at work in a small cubicle editing parts of the Sedaris odyssey) over and over to different bits. They don't just edit out the extra *"you know"* or the redundant *"pretty much"* that distracts from the flow of Ira's story. They have an egalitarian dialogue, which, from where I'm sitting, acts as some kind of metaphor for the way meaning is constructed. Words and phrases are cut out that "don't work"; they hold on to the portions that are "poignant."

Still, it becomes increasingly difficult for me to stifle my urges to partipate in the process. I do manage to bite my lip and "observe," but when they consider letting go of the fragment about sliding glass doors (Alix calls it the "your mom and architecture section") I have to hold my breath. That was my favorite part and I imagine the audience hearing about the therapist and not (for me) the crux—"I don't think that heavier sliding glass doors and better bathrooms would make us feel closer." But in the end, they reinstall the doors and boot the shrink.

We all traipse back into the last studio and listen to Sedaris's hitchhiking narrative. For some reason, they listen, like twenty-five times, to a particular sentence which gets stuck in my head: "We smoked it and they popped in an eight-track of the Ozark Mountain Daredevils."

Popping in Tsing Loh's story again, they balk at its harsh, scratchy timbre. Nancy realizes that she recorded the entire piece at the wrong speed and there's not enough time before the seven o'clock deadline to fix it. I have to witness her tense "I'm sorry" moment and she looks as if she wants to disappear. Ira handles it gallantly with a low-key kindness, reassuring her, "That's what happens with new technologies," telling her that he's made the same mistake himself.

He leaves the room and Nancy's eyes are still full of tears. She stretches out her arms into a crucifixion pose and tells me, "I'm the technological asshole of the group."

Ira comes back and says, "It's WBEZ. When this comes out of people's radios, they won't blame us." He pages through a Hawaiian tourist brochure and razor-blades a small square of paper out of it, handing it to her saying, "You don't have to worry about anything with the radio station because . . ." Nancy laughs and shows it to me. It says: WE'LL STAY AT THE VOLCANO AS LONG AS YOU LIKE.

At 6:25, they're frantically hacking seconds off of Ira's piece. A radio blares from someone's cubicle and it's tuned to *All Things Considered*. I hear Rick Karr's name—Ira's old

NPR bureau coworker downtown. Karr writes a friendly little postcard from Chicago, walking up to the bureau's roof at the Union Carbide Building on Michigan Avenue. He describes the view (he can see into architect Helmut Jahn's drawing room) and says that it's the last time he'll go up on the roof to dust snow off the satellite with a brush from Ace Hardware—they're going digital. It's all very sweet and peaceful.

Just as Karr signs off, I hear the crazed crew screaming, "Yep! Yep! Yep! That'll work."

At 6:45, they finish editing and start dubbing Ira's ten-minute piece that starts the show, thus clearing the deadline with a whopping five minutes to spare.

December 9.   **12:50 p.m. WFMT-FM.**

Just as I swoop past something that sounds suspiciously orchestral, I stop cold. What's that? A banjo? A thrilling, brassy noise with trumpets and cymbals swells into cabaret melodies. Someone belts the word *"ma-ha-gon-ney"* and I realize it's Kurt Weill's collaboration with Bertolt Brecht, the opera *The Rise and Fall of the City of Mahagonny*, and, therefore, turn it up. Just as someone is singing about searching "from house to house" I look into the liner notes of my Weill tribute CD *Lost in the Stars* for the historical scoop.

Mahagonny premiered in Leipzig in 1930. Paul M. Young and David L. Hamilton write:

> *The Nazis had bought blocks of seats to the premiere, packing the house with whistle-blowing, stink bomb throwing brown-shirts who successfully disrupted the performance. The second night of the performance the house lights were left on and the walls of the theater were lined with police.*

Picturing this, the ungodliest upright piano (surely music sounding this drunk on whiskey can't be a pouring out of a pompous grand) erupts into an out-of-control tinny spree lurching into the great "Alabama Song."

At intermission, Robert Marks from the New York Public Library for the Performing Arts plows into historical context, informing us that "The libretto evokes a decadent city where unbridled self-interest leads to moral and social collapse."

I'm not exactly a Met-head myself, but what I heard of the first act came off downright juicy. But smack dab in the middle of Marks's refined banter, he kills off the Met with one quick blast, playing a 1956 recording in German by the original riot frau, Lotte Lenya. Gone are the operatic curlicues. What's left is a tough, harsh, half-spoken, half-sung gut bomb that puts nonsinging singer Lou Reed to shame. Backed by banjo and trumpets and rolling her r's as if she's parting the Red Sea in the course of a breath, she soars up to a lyrical climax like a bad-girl Valkyrie and then, silence, back to lecture, which is so irritating, that without realizing what I'm doing, I actually speak to my radio, hollering, "Let 'er sing, god damn it!"

But blah, blah, blah and on and on about re-creating the "aura of the opera's first night. In this case, of course, without the riot."

Of course.

Now, the CEO of Texaco (the corporation underwriting this series) goes into his "we are delighted" to use this public broadcasting time to suck up to music lovers in hopes that they'll buy our gas and forget about all the bad things we've done or plan to accomplish.

After Mr. Capitalism 1995 finishes, we return to the announcer who glosses over Brecht's devout socialist practices (those eccentric artists!) to pump up the (by comparison) aesthete Weill. Weill, it is said with a wink, remarked, "I'm not interested in composing Karl Marx. I like to write music."

Bravos resound for the reentrance of conductor James Levine and the strings saw back and forth. I listen to the hurricane approach.

11:00 p.m. WXRT. *Eleventh Hour.*

Nirvana live recording, from a thick, throbbing performance in Del Mar, California. As loud as a monster truck but as fun as a Tonka toy, they crash into some of my favorite songs, like the screeching joy of "No Recess" (a song I've played a lot as a refuge from this radio shadow). But the crowd goes insane at "Smells Like Teen Spirit," and it's even more extreme than the *Nevermind* version, turning gutsier as it goes on. Cobain screams the word *"libido"* and then says it in sound, so that by the end, you're churned into a whirlpool of pure want. After the cries of *"denial"* at the end, which are just about the most raw, human noise I've heard all year, it's all that I can do to keep on listening. I could turn off the radio and smash it right now. But they dive straight into that lovable *"Gramma take me home"* song, so I listen to the whole thing, which varies from some of their nice, respectful covers to those glorious passages of pure noise, which sound even better once I remember that this is the station currently playing the hell out of the dreary new John Hiatt album.

December 11.   **10:10 p.m. Q101.**

Q101's James Vanosdol and that silver-tongued individual known as "Whipping Boy" (sometimes, affectionately, "Whip" for short) interview the overrated, overanalyzed hit factory known as Alanis Morissette. James asks,

> *In retrospect, is there anything you wish, since this all really kind of snowballed for you, is there anything you wish had kind of happened differently? Or are you just overwhelmingly happy about the way everything has been mapped out for you?*

And the smug Canadian diva replies:

> *I'm overwhelmingly happy. I guess the most gratifying part of all of this is that if it inspires one person out there who's*

*eating macaroni and cheese on the floor feeling desperate
and alone, writing a song and thinking that he doesn't want
to sell out or she doesn't want to sell out so they don't want
to get in the industry. The only thing I can say about that
is that, you know, I didn't have to compromise anything. I
didn't sell my soul. I didn't write anything I didn't wanna
write. I didn't say yes to someone I wanted to say no to.
And with that personal sort of success, along with it came
the sort of external adulation and I think you can have both.*

No one I trust would talk that way, employing (as a synonym
for *music*) the painful word "industry" or the desire for "adulation." Now, I want to like her, want to support anybody's
girl-power impulse, want to appreciate her freaky, unladylike
twitches that I watched not long ago on *Saturday Night Live*.
And it's not that her hit songs' explicit sex talk particularly
turns me off. It's just that, ultimately, she's whiny (which is
different than the funnier puissance of "cranky").

Q101 plays Morissette's I'm okay–You're okay song "Hand
in My Pocket" but I flick it off and put on PJ Harvey's current
release, *To Bring You My Love*, a record that, compared to
Morissette's twice-an-hour anthems, has gotten just about
zero airplay on this station. Harvey's just as anxious and
nervous as Morissette, but there's a well of power there, a
deep source of strength and guts and blood that's missing
in Morissette's pinched whimpers. The big uproar about Morissette is that she's a girl who sings about blowjobs at the
movies ("putting the sin back in cinema-going," as Bill
Wyman wrote). Big deal. But there's a difference between
whining and wailing. While Morissette's standing around
with one hand in her pocket, Harvey's fingers are flying around
all over the place—praying, reaching, slapping, clawing her
own skin. Morissette is full of resignation, telling us that it's
all gonna be all right not as relief but as a lie. Harvey gives
us no such small hope in her words, but her deep sound
offers the prospects of desire in her album's last line: *"Bring
peace to my naked, empty heart."*

Mancow Mueller, most famous for his ongoing war of words
with the only slightly more charming Howard Stern, reads
an article about his show to his sidekick, Irma:

> *"Mancow draws from an ignorant fan base, the same group
> of people that likes Beavis and Butt-head and 2 Live Crew.
> Mancow's audience should be set up for mass extermina-
> tion."* Well—the guy's a Nazi? Mass extermination? 2 Live
> Crew? They're like black rap, hardcore stuff.

After scrolling through the lineup for tomorrow's show (Robin
Leach, soap star Susan Lucci, porn star Nikki Tyler, the
inventor of the Chia Pet, and a woman who sold her husband's World Series tickets), Mancow calls his pal "Turd,"
who's doing a live remote from the Tower of Cars monument.
"We have a scale," Mancow asserts. "We are weighing car
warts. Irma, what is a car wart?"

"A car wart is that sludge, snow, junk, that kicks up off
the tire and is stuck underneath your car, a big chunk of it."

"Absolutely. Now we're weighing that."

Turd reports that a man named Bill wins the contest with
a twenty-four-pound wart. Mancow asks the lucky Bill, "Hey
dude, do you have any kids?" Bill, who has three children, is
awarded a cash prize, but only if he spends it buying Christmas gifts. Bill agrees.

Not particularly in the mood for this, I skip over to WNUR,
where I recognize my friend John Corbett's voice. He plays
some Coltrane, and its haphazard textures act as a radiant
soundtrack to the random snowfall out the window.

December 14.   2:00 p.m. WBEZ-FM. *Talk of the Nation.*

Since the government shuts down tomorrow at midnight,
again, Ray Suarez tracks the progress of the Republican
majority's year: "The new members [of Congress] came to

Washington saying, 'No more business as usual.' Is this what they had in mind?"

He is joined by two freshman representatives, Dick Chrysler (Republican–Michigan) and Chaka Fattah (Democrat–Pensylvania).

Gary calls from Buffalo:

I think it's very wrong that the Congress holds the budget process hostage by what they want. I think that our president has more than shown that he's willing to compromise. He's actually been called names because of that . . . I think that it's a total shame that . . . we spend more money to pay for the wastage of the shutdown of the government than . . . the NPR and the NEA funding. That was relatively small amounts of money, yet the Congress is willing to throw away, I heard, $115 million a day that it costs us to shut down the government. [NEA annual budget: $110 million.]

Suarez echoes Gary's point, that federal employees will still receive compensation for the jobs they're not doing. He asks Fattah about his constituents' response. The Philadelphia legislator says,

They see it for what it is—it's foolish. . . . The disagreement isn't about the spending . . . it's about . . . the entitlements. The Republicans have failed, really, I think, to completely understand that the American public does want a balanced budget. But any old balanced budget won't do. They want a budget that still reflects appropriately American ideals and what we consider to be our values as a country . . . to get to a budget that is fiscally balanced but also morally balanced as to our responsibilities.

Chrysler, on the other hand, claims that 86 percent of his constituents asked him not to "cave."

Fattah, as a freshman in the minority party, probably has about as much say in how the government is run as Socks the White House cat. He recognizes this opportunity to speak

his mind and he just seizes the microphone to spill his guts.
It's his moment:

> *I want your listeners to listen up. Listen to what the Republi-*
> *cans are saying. They're saying on one hand, "We want to*
> *balance the budget, that's our number one priority. We're*
> *willing to cut back on what might be needed for higher*
> *education for your children in terms of Pell grants. We might*
> *be willing to cut back on the rate of growth in food stamps*
> *because we want to balance the budget. Except, before we*
> *even start to balance the budget, we want to give away $245*
> *billion . . . to some of the wealthiest people in the country.*
> *And then, on our way to balancing this budget, we want to*
> *increase defense spending by $7 billion over what the Penta-*
> *gon even says it needs. . . . And then, because we have to*
> *balance this budget, and it's difficult, we wanna do it quickly*
> *. . . [Chrysler gasps and sighs] over the next seven years so*
> *we have to cut even more deeply into these programs. We*
> *say this calmly as if there's no consequences." . . . For the*
> *eight thousand kids that worked in summer jobs in Philadel-*
> *phia this year, there won't be one summer job next year. . . .*
> *So I want people to listen to what's being said and under-*
> *stand that the reason why we have an impasse, is we have*
> *a difference of opinion about which way this ought to go.*

Chrysler fires back that $170 million of the $245 billion "goes
to families that have small children." Doesn't Donald Trump
have small children? He adds, "Seventy-seven percent of it
goes to families who are earning under $75,000 and there
are no cuts." I'm not sure that I know anybody who makes
$75,000 a year. The poverty level in this country is well below
$20,000.

When Suarez tells Chrysler that the president has been
more than willing to compromise, so why don't the Republicans "give a little," Chrysler gets metaphorical:

> *Think of it this way. The Republicans are in New York City,*
> *the Democrats are in Los Angeles. When we settle this thing,*

probably about the end of next week [yeah, right], *we'll be some place in New York State. We've been to Arizona and Utah for forty years. We're gonna stay no further west than Buffalo on this one because we think that's what the American voters want us to do.*

"So we're not gonna get to your district in Michigan?" Suarez asks.

"No further west than Buffalo."

December 17.   10:00 p.m. Q101. *Modern Rock Live.*

Dave Grohl and William Goldsmith from the Foo Fighters field calls on this syndicated program from listeners of alternarock commercial outlets across the country with names like "The Buzz," "The Edge" (four of these), "The Laser," and "The End."

Christina phones from Detroit. ("My wife's from Detroit!" Grohl exclaims.) She wants to know if they expected their record "to be as successful as it is."

"You know, we thought it would be *more successful,*" Grohl jokes.

The way I see it, Grohl is one of the most lovable rock 'n' rollers of the nineties. I have fond memories of that Nirvana concert on New Year's Eve two years ago in which, at the stroke of twelve, MC Bobcat Goldthwait, dressed as a diaper-clad Baby New Year, was lowered from the Oakland Coliseum into Grohl's loving embrace.

"When we were doing interviews," he says, "people were like, 'Now, God, isn't it strange for you guys to play these 500–1,000-capacity venues? Isn't it weird?' It's, like, No! It was weird when you had to go up and sit in front of 6,000 people. That's weird."

After a spin through Grohl's great "This Is a Call," John in Tulsa, in all seriousness, asks, "What was your greatest musical achievement?"

"My greatest musical achievement? Um—probably play-

ing in Nirvana. That was probably it. That was quite a big
deal."

"I would say so, yes," adds host Tom Calderone.

When listeners call in to ask about the meanings of specific
songs, Grohl mostly answers, "Nothing," but, finally, he counsels one caller to "Read into it, man!"

He's asked by a boy named Kevin if he's ever stage-dived.
Dave answers, "Yeah," while William says, "No," which sur-
prises Dave.

"You haven't?" he asks.

"Uh-uh."

"Really?"

"No," William assures him.

"I thought you were punk rock, man!"

"Well, I always had too many spikes on my leather jacket.
I didn't wanna hurt anybody."

"That's what it was: 'I was afraid my Mohawk was gonna
poke someone's eye out.' It's all fun and games until someone
loses an eye. With a Mohawk like mine . . ."

After Calderone breaks in to plug Sony shower radios, the
boys laugh and burp in the background. Then Dave's mom
calls to say she just put up the Christmas tree. "You're using
the same stand, right?" he asks.

"Yeah, the big heavy one," she answers. After that, she
makes fun of his disorderly room growing up: "It was a
legend."

"Mom, I miss you," Dave whimpers. We're told that this
will be his first Christmas away from home. He yells, "Here
come the waterworks!"

December 18.

On what was arguably the crummiest day of the year, when
Newt Gingrich is named *Time* magazine's Man of the Year
(even though he's being investigated by the House Ethics

Committee regarding misuse of campaign funds and whopping book royalties), when I had to watch not one, but two,
friends cry, I roam around the radio range past paranoid
preachers, college-station sludge, Mariah Carey with (bonus!)
Boyz II Men, a gripey Bulls fan, the washed-up Ozzy
Osbourne, news that the Communists won a lot of votes in
the Russian election. Then I hear a catchy little blow-job
line I've always liked from "Walk on the Wild Side." Boy,
you know you're in pain when the closest thing you can find
to a friend on the radio is Lou Reed.

**Hubert Horatio Humphrey International
Airport, Minneapolis/St. Paul**

December 20.   **9:10 a.m.**

On a layover en route to spend Christmas
with my family in Montana, I notice that this place is like
one giant Garrison Keillor gift shop. In my ten-minute walk
to change planes, I pass up three opportunities to purchase
various articles of prominently displayed *Prairie Home Companion* merchandise. Flipping through Keillor's novel *WLT:
A Radio Romance*, at one newsstand, I stop at this paragraph:

*Hank, the future of broadcasting is eavesdropping. We could
use hypnotism. Ordinary people could be actors of the sub-
conscious. Their dreams and all the night thoughts people
think—put it on the radio. Of course, it'd be obscene and
against the law, but, you wouldn't try to change the law,
just change radio. Put out a signal so a person needs a
decoding machine to receive it. Put it beyond the law. Radio's
fading fast, Hank.*

Aside from the Orwellian, invasion-of-privacy overtones of
this passage, the suggestion of hypnotism (I sat through that
Werner Herzog movie where he hypnotized the actors and
it was a vacant bore), and the fussy, spy-boy nonsense of a
"decoding machine," I like the phrase about "all the night
thoughts people think." But there are no night thoughts on

A *Prairie Home Companion* and nothing "obscene and against the law" that cracks through that show's choking cheerfulness, its lobotomized barbershop harmonies and dippy duct-tape jokes. Forget fading fast, Keillor's moved on to wearing thin.

Waiting to board my flight to Montana, I get out the Walkman, anxious to hear some of the good Minneapolis rock 'n' roll radio I've heard so much about. I only pick up two faint stations playing "White Christmas" and Whitney Houston. I check the batteries and it's like a little Love Canal in there, yellow and corroded as if the batteries needed a hankie. I take them out and get crusty toxins on my fingers. For an instant I fantasize about draining what's left of the acid into the pristine waters of Lake Wobegon but I settle for rinsing in tap water and waiting around for my thumb to fall off.

<hr>

Bozeman

12:35 p.m.

When the plane breaks through the clouds and I see the Bridger Mountains, I know I'm home. Amy, my twin sister, picks me up in the car her husband just inherited from his grandmother—a gigantic 1966 Buick Skylark that looks all the more huge with my tiny sister behind the wheel. Its vast dashboard sports a perky-looking radio with chunky buttons mythically named the Son-O-Matic. It reeks optimism, like it might screen out sad songs to the point that you'd just hear Donovan all day long. I'll never know, since it no longer works. But maybe after spitting out "Mellow Yellow" for three decades, it deserves some silence.

December 21.   **8:50 p.m. KEMC-FM.**

A woman on this NPR affiliate is fielding questions and she sounds familiar. After five minutes, I realize that it's Gloria Steinem. She's asked about the controversy surrounding one of her pet projects—Take Our Daughters to Work Day. People keep hounding her about the boys, what are they supposed to do, shouldn't they get the same professional inspiration as the girls, isn't that sexist, etc. I think that the day is a good idea, but I always smile when I hear about it, imagining what my gunsmith father would have taught me as an eight-year-old looking for career advice. Thanks to him, at that age I already possessed a nongirlie world of firearms and machine-shop vocabulary, full of words and phrases such as "blueing tank," "lathe," "checkering," "muzzle loader," and "drill bit." Maybe my sister and I could have sat around his shop and listened to endless deer-kill stories while wearing little hunter's orange outfits, or leafed through back issues of *American Rifleman.* Just last night, I was helping him look for a photograph of my great-grandfather and I happened to lean over a standing gun rack next to his desk in such a way that approximately nine rifle barrels were aiming straight at my face. Not exactly, I'm guessing, what *Ms.* magazine had in mind.

In answering the query, however, Steinem quotes Eleanor Norton, who responded to the question "Why is there no 'Take Our Sons to Work Day'?" with the reply, "'For the same reason that there's no White History Month.'"

9:00 p.m. KGLT-FM. *The Blues Tradition.*

For as long as I can remember, Dr. Ray Pratt has played blues on Thursday nights. Right now, he reads a PSA for the Swim Center. The school district–owned cement pond is hands-down my least favorite place in town. I shiver as several years of gym-class anxiety attacks flash before my eyes. The PSA reminds listeners about Kayaking Night at the pool. I can picture the outdoorsy attendees, more than one of whom will change directly out of ski clothes into a swimsuit. They'll paddle around and swap tall tales of their day on the hill, and to them, every day on skis is a good day.

Dr. Ray plays gospel music for an hour and it's beautiful

but depressing as hell. I get gloomy and start missing Chicago, where I've never heard the word "kayak" uttered, not once.

December 22.   **12:00 p.m.** *AP Network News.*

The Christian Coalition, it is reported, is attacking NPR for a supposedly anti-Christian remark expressed by Romanian commentator Andrei Codrescu on *All Things Considered.*

Now, I'm as opposed to fatwahs as the next person, but if only the Christian equivalent could force the ironymeister Codrescu into hiding, along with Robert Siegel, Linda Wertheimer, and Noah Adams.

December 23.   **9:55 a.m. KGLT.**

Rik James, the down-to-earth, lovable (if overly talkative) host of the tried-and-true *Bluegrass Traditions*, spins a suitably folksy Christmas. Johnny Cash drawls through a down-home spoken-word yarn called "Christmas As I Knew It." He says that things were tight that year in Arkansas. Mama sewed his sisters dresses out of flour sacks and Johnny whittled his brother Jack a whistle, that kind of thing. But if his family had it rough, the sharecroppers across the way had it worse. So Jack and Johnny leave some coal oil and hickory nuts on the poorer clan's porch.

A couple of the sappiest sort of tears roll down my cheek. Maybe it's because I'm vulnerable before coffee, but I swear, every time I spend more than five minutes around my kind-hearted mother, I quite simply go soft.

December 24.   **10:00 p.m.**

This afternoon, I listened to NPR's automobile-maintenance call-in show *Car Talk* as I ate lunch. At the beginning of the program, Click said to Clack (or was it the other way around?) that they don't just answer questions, they also appreciate comments, so that if, say, "some guy in Montana" calls up

with an opinion, they're more than willing to listen. I found
the Montana reference slightly odd, but I've become accus-
tomed to the fact that the state's geographical location is
often referenced as the American synonym for "outer Mon-
golia."

I turned off the radio and went Christmas-shopping just
as a woman was asking for advice about the sort of car to
buy her college-bound son.

After dinner, my brother-in-law was reading this morning's
paper and noticed an AP story from Helena titled "Patrol
Chief Matches Wits with *Car Talk* Hosts." Evidently, I
missed the appearance of Montana Highway Patrol colonel
Craig Reap, who offered a rebuttal to hosts Tom and Ray
Magliozzi for calling Montanans "moronic" because of the
state's recent elimination of the highway speed limit.
According to the report, brother Tom claimed that "the
first prize for dimwittedness goes to the wonderful state of
Montana. . . . It's moronic. I mean, let's face it. . . . These
guys, what the heck are they thinking?"

The previous page contains more NPR hate mail describing
the on-air apology Andrei Codrescu was made to offer the
Christian Coalition on Friday. His offending remark described
a theological pamphlet. He said, "The evaporation of four
million [people] who believe in this crap would leave the
world a better place." The article goes on to say that *All
Things Considered* turned down a Christian Coalition request
for two minutes of airtime, which seems, even for NPR,
kind of wimpy. So now, the zealot lobby plans to push for
elimination of federal funding of public broadcasting. Of
course, they'll have to stand in line. . . .

But can you imagine how the *Montana* branch of the
Christian Coalition must feel?

December 25.   **11:00 a.m. KGLT.**

I host a nerve-racking hour of my friend Barrett's show, playing tapes of some of my favorite radio moments of the year.
Besides the obvious perils of going through nearly two hours

of that Courtney Love interview and picking out the most engaging bit, the technological component makes me jumpy. I'll never miss the button-pushing, levels-monitoring, organizational aspect of doing radio. I still have those DJ nightmares where the turntable is on one end zone of a football field and the records are in the other, so that every segue requires a brand-new touchdown's worth of running.

December 26.   **6:00 p.m. KMMS-FM.**

I turn off an AM preacher giving a sermon on Elvis (did you know that despite his fame and fortune *"even Elvis was lonely"*?) in time to hear DJ Colter Langan playing a request. He pleads for forgiveness and I know why: Lynyrd Skynyrd breaks into "Free Bird" and before I have time to wince, I answer the phone and hear a voice twelve times more annoying than the music. It's the most condescending woman in the world inviting my parents to a party. I get stuck answering those what-are-you-doing-with-your-life-you-young-person questions for the entire length of the song, and it's a *long* song, believe me.

December 27.   **6:00 a.m.**

I spend the first few conscious minutes of my twenty-sixth birthday hearing a blaring country song about how much nicer the world would be if everyone had a front porch. I'm thinking how much nicer my birthday would be if I hadn't fallen asleep reading on the couch downstairs last night so that I would miss my early-bird father's clock radio.

December 28.   **1:30 a.m.**

The word *room* has two, seemingly opposite meanings, connoting enclosed spaces as well as infinite ones, claustrophobia and freedom. A crowded room. Room to move. One-room apartment. Elbow room.

There are rooms built up out of four little walls, rooms of
a cramped and stifling smallness that are still so comfortable,
or at least so intimately known in their casual usage, where
your head goes traveling—little Grand Canyons of the mind.
In those spaces, the ones where we work, anything is possible.

I spend the last few minutes of my birthday in the production room at KGLT. I've missed the smell of it. I still do,
since right now it reeks of ashtray thanks to Barrett's tobacco-
rule-breaking, but never mind.

It's been remodeled since the first mornings I spent here
the summer I was eighteen, putting together newscasts with
a complex figure named Dave Bailey, who always showed up
bearing gigantic cups of coffee from the Kwikway at the edge
of campus. He was years ahead of his time, a punk rocker
who joined ROTC. I assume that these days junior Air Force
types might listen to Soundgarden in their free time, but back
then no one got the Dead Kennedys/Die for Your Country
dichotomy of Dave's life.

Then he got religion. One minute he's quoting Jello Biafra
and the next it's Jesus Christ. (Not such a big leap, looking
back.) He started wearing knit pullovers literally overnight,
but it took a few weeks for the shaved-off hair on the sides
of his head to grow back in.

So I've had a fair share of interesting, caffeine-fueled conversations in this room. But maybe the best conversations
the room made possible were between tapes.

My favorite electronic tête-à-tête occurred between Kim
Gordon and Gertrude Stein right before the 1992 presidential
election. Engineer Darin Crabtree and I were producing a
series of women-and-voting PSAs. The best one spliced
together the suffragette opera Stein wrote with Virgil Thomp-
son called A *Woman of Our Time* and Sonic Youth's "Kool
Thing," so that the female chorus exclaiming that they can
vote! cuts to Gordon's down-with-the-patriarchy rap.

But Barrett, who spends more time in this room than
anyone, is good at making recordings talk to each other at
the twentieth-century cocktail parties he hosts between his
ears. Obsessed with that you-know-it-when-you-hear-it entity

known as Good Tape, he's willing to sabotage the linear coherence of his radio stories in order to include those rare moments—maybe just a few thrilling words—when someone says something so true or beautiful that it stands outside any narrative, unforgettable.

We listen to his work in progress, a collage of songs and speeches about the atomic age. *All Things Considered* was supposed to air it tomorrow, but they turned it down. I can see why. There is no he said/she said narrator to identify Harry Truman, no affected reporter watering down the power of Bob Dylan's "Talking World War III Blues." There are inclusions that have zero to do with the bomb but everything to do with postwar public life. Case in point, some of the best Good Tape I've heard, of a reporter who gets gassed at the '68 Democratic Convention in Chicago. The man starts out objective, describing the release of tear gas and the police donning of gas masks. By the end, he's blinded and has to be led to a nearby gas station by a protester to wash out his eyes.

Barrett's weak justification for this stunning but non-atomic segment involves some mumbled reference about how the media itself becomes a story. The project is a beautifully orchestrated train wreck, with slick cuts from orators ("Remember orators?" Barrett asks. No, I don't; they all got killed off before I was born.) like Kennedy and crooks such as McCarthy to apocalyptic songs by hillbillies who pick and grin all the way to the New Jerusalem.

In short, the piece has room, the kind of thinking and singing that can lead you out of doors and into the world. Too bad *ATC* almost always turns it down—the world. It's where their listeners live.

Chicago

December 29.   8:00 p.m. WBEZ. *This American Life.*

Ira Glass is discussing "pivotal moments," those seemingly insignificant split seconds that can change a life forever. He describes a woman named Evan Harris who used to work in a mail room. One day, while alphabetically sorting mail with her coworker Shelly Ross, she asks, "Shouldn't *Q* be further toward the back of the alphabet?"

He notes that unlike the all-purpose, popular midalphabet consonants like *M* or *P*, *Q* belongs down with the oddballs like *X* and *Y*. "*Q*," Ira says, "makes demands and sees that they are met." (I have no idea what that means, but it sounds poetic.)

Harris's list of *Q* words leads to the one that, for her, alters everything—*quit*. She started thinking through its implications: "Potential quits seemed to be everywhere." She quit her job, her boyfriend, then her city. She and Ross started publishing a zine devoted to the topic called *Quitter Quarterly*.

She gets obsessed, starts reading world history as a series of quits, develops theories, even defines the "stages of the quit," which are "(1) You think about it. (2) You think about it some more." She bases her belief in the quit on two concepts: "Nothing lasts forever" and "You have to be doing something." "Quitting is about being willfull," she asserts. And better yet: "The point of quitting is to move in the world."

To move in the world. It's a seductive phrase. I can see her point and start to think about big quits. Abolition of slavery—good quit. Repealing Prohibition—ditto. But quitting Saigon—too late. And what if you quit honoring a fair treaty or quit subsidizing family farms or quit funding student loans and school lunches?

Quit happens.

It's an ambiguous word, *quit*. The dictionary throws around *forsake* and *free*; *depart* as well as *abandon*. Quitting piano lessons is one thing, a father who quits his child is another. Some quits are liberating steps in the right direction, others are gutless, selfish, indefensible cop-outs.

On the quits that should have been, Ira introduces some of the strangest bickering I've ever heard, culled from a CD called *Shut Up Little Man*, recorded in San Francisco in the late 1980s by Eddie Lee Sausage and Mitchell D.

Sausage and D. initially started taping their neighbors Peter and Raymond's arguments and brawls to use as evidence in case one man killed the other. While it is unclear if the two men, both now dead, were a couple or merely roommates, their disputes are rife with profanity (of the truest, ugliest sort) and homophobic slurs, often ending in the creepy command, "Shut up little man!"

Sometimes, one has the pleasure of meeting those sage, elderly men with deep, profound eyes and soft, knowing voices. And then there are these two: demeaning, sinister, crotchety assholes with nothing better to do than humiliate each other to death. Their dialogues contain, Ira sarcastically comments, "warning signs about when it is time to quit a relationship."

They engage in a confounding duel simply because one cuts his toenails and the other doesn't want to watch. The rapid-fire obscenities turn the radio version of their fights into a sea of beeps, creating sentences such as "You're a stinking *BEEP* piece of *BEEP*."

Evidently, the homophobia works in weird ways, making women's names into the worst sort of insult: "Okay, Mabel, try, try Mabel, try Alice. . . . You haven't proven anything Sally . . . Sally June, Abigail May . . ."

It's the kind of talk that makes you embarrassed to be human. You can quit genders and quit living, but your species, you're stuck with that.

December 30.   **12:00 p.m. WZRD. Church of the SubGenius: *Hour of Slack.***

Maybe they'll burn him at the stake. That's what religions do to heretics, don't they? All year long, Church of the SubGenius clergyman Ivan Stang has been preaching on and on about getting some slack in the name of Bob. Slack this. Slack that. But Stang is a backslider of the worst sort—a workaholic, an overachiever. His travel schedule alone must be grueling. This year, he's everywhere, like some kind of subcultural gadfly, attending various SubGenius devivals, touring with the cartoon metal band Gwar, appearing at the Chicago Underground Film Festival, hosting book-signings, turning up in interviews, and running the Church's Internet and radio ministries.

Stang begins today's show with a ranting collage of impressions of all the people who want something from him, from the SubGenius T-shirt they ordered three weeks ago, to the bands who want him to air their songs. The way I see it, he's stressed out. Which means he doesn't practice what he preaches. Slack, my ass. I bet he even wears a wristwatch.

1:50 p.m. WLS-AM. *The Rush Limbaugh Show.*

Douglas, a brand-spanking-new conservative convert, is telling Rush, "You make a lot of sense. . . . Newt, I support him 100 percent. Great guy. I don't care about his attitude. I don't care how he says it. I like what he's saying. You know, it's my money . . . I want my money! Pass the Flavor-aid!"

(Okay, I made that last one up.)

"That's just incredible," Rush replies. "Six months ago you used to be a liberal?"

"You don't know. You don't know. It's fantastic."

Rush notes, "These sorts of transformations are not very frequent. The psychological record is not complete to make a study of this."

"Well, sir," Douglas begins, and I hate it when men call each other "sir" in the middle of (what passes for) a conversation:

I knew Rush Limbaugh. I didn't like Rush Limbaugh. Never read a book, never heard a program. . . . I knew you were conservative. Just wanted to listen because I didn't like my military going everywhere with no money. [What planet is he living on?] *And everything else fell into place. Fiscally. Socially. It all makes sense. And I'm a happy guy right now.*

"What a great Christmas gift!" Rush exclaims. (Your very own zombie!)

"Speaking of Christmas gifts," Douglas adds, "again, listening for six months, just walked in the door, picked up the phone—first time I ever tried, first ring and here I am!"

At two o'clock, the *AP Network News* cites Bob Dole on this, the fifteenth day of the partial government shutdown. Looks like an agreement will wait until next year: "We're getting fairly close, I think, to the big issues." Congratulations. President Clinton follows with, "Every day, twenty-five hundred people can't get guaranteed home mortgages. Every day, thousands of young people looking for college loans can't apply for them. If ever we needed a reminder that our government is not our enemy, this is it." Amen to that. This is followed by Newt's New Year's resolution: "To listen more carefully and try to be more thoughtful." Like that's a tough track record to top.

Back to Rush:

> *You're tuned to America's truth detector, you people, the doctor of democracy, the majority maker. You know who named me the majority maker? The House Republican freshmen. They gave me an award when I went down to speak to them last December in Baltimore. You know what they call themselves? They call themselves the "dittohead caucus." And I am one proud puppy because of all that.*

Keith, of Green Bay, Wisconsin, calls to say that he is "turned off by both sides of the budget battle." But Rush soothes his fear of the future: "There is no dirty water on your horizon [because it's already in the foreground], nobody will starve [sigh of relief], senior citizens are not going to be kicked out of their homes [they'll just be carried out in body bags when they starve]."

And later, this wisdom: "The Democrats have become the party of the welfare state."

On the Democrats' vision of a "future" state of the union:

> *It is an America in soup lines, an America going to soup kitchens. It's an America that's homeless. It's an America*

that is destitute, forlorn, and racked with poverty and pesti-
lence. I mean that's the America they see. Because that's
the America they think needs their assistance and help.
That's what they see as their return to power. They want to
see a devastated America.

How does this man, this New Yorker, get to his studio every
day? Is he air-lifted from skyscraper to skyscraper without
touching the ground, without hitting the streets? The scene
he describes is not, as every urban dweller who's left her
house knows, a prescription for some sort of dystopian future.
It's where we live. And it's where Rush lives, too, if he'd only
peer through that stinky cloud of cigar smoke that evidently
blocks his vision. It's not some prophetic America that's
homeless, it's the just plain, everyday one. Racked with poverty? Something like 15 percent of Americans don't even
have health care and what are the repercussions of that ten,
twenty, thirty years down the line? Pestilence? This means
plague, and what is AIDS if not the black death of the here
and now? It's not just the America that some puny political
party might "think" needs its help. We're there. Every day,
walking down the street becomes some kind of excruciating,
endurance test of compassion. And, in my case, that's just
from looking around my own working-class neighborhood
and the capitalist byways of downtown Chicago. I don't even
venture where the city's hardest-hit. The fact that this man
is spreading this garbage across the country that, for better
or worse, I still love, is so repulsive and so false, that I don't
think I'll ever quite wash the stench of his lies out of my
head. Just listening to him, all year long, has damaged me,
and because of it I'm just a little more sad, a little more
cynical, and a whole lot more fed up. And to think of the
overwhelming influence this "proud puppy" has over legisla-
tors, besides the thousands of his listeners, makes me want
to throw up, preferably all over one of his stupid, ugly ties.
There's talk of a return to civility in public discourse.
The nice-girl part of me says fine, but sometimes, civility's
overrated. After all, wasn't Chamberlain just being civil at

Munich when he should have screamed, at the top of his lungs, that he couldn't even stand to sit in the same room as that incarnation of Satan? But no, he politely signed the death certificate for a goodly portion of the Western Hemisphere. And no teacups were broken and no tablecloths were stained. Only the world paid his tab later in madness and ashes, and it was an ill-mannered, uncivil, impolite mess now, wasn't it?

I say fight fire with fire. Which is not to say fight stupidity with greater stupidity. The American left has got to come up with a broadcaster with some kind of pizzazz who can verbally decapitate this moron. But soon.

December 31.

Just writing that beautiful word, December, alongside that radiant number, 31, gives me the giggles. Free at last from this radio hell. Now I know how Galileo must have felt a few years back when the Catholic church finally de-excommunicated him, thereby liberating him from centuries of purgatory.

12:10 a.m. WNUR.

A DJ signing off: "Enjoy this. It's Willie Nelson." He then completely fucks up the cue, fumbling around for a few seconds with setting the needle. (At least his station owns a record player.) "You don't think anyone's ever cued up like that on-air? . . . I had the speeds wrong. This is 89.3, WNUR-FM. And, uh, stick around." A piano whirs and Willie, or at least his chipmunk alter ego, starts singing "Always on My Mind." The speed is still wrong, which is too bad; it's a lovely song.

When and if the announcer figures out the goof, he has two options—wordlessly fix it (the yellow-bellied route in my book) or 'fess up and move on. The bumble continues for—I timed it—forty-two seconds, a radio eternity. Finally, the speed clumsily slows down.

"Good call, Sam. We've been playing that whole song at a way-too-fast pitch. So that's why Willie Nelson couldn't have his customary beautiful voice."

Another voice in the room, perhaps the aforementioned Sam, shouts, "That's how we get more music on WNUR."

"Exactly," he replies. "Basically, we can squeeze in three or four songs by the end of the day because we play everything at about 105 percent of actual speed." Then he speeds it back up again for a split-second, just for fun, returning to the right one.

It's one of those "baby give me one more chance" kind of songs, the one that Elvis sang to Priscilla after their breakup. But today, my divorce from radio becomes final and the three words now on my lips are not Auld Lang Syne but DON'T LOOK BACK.

8:45 a.m. WBEZ. *Weekend Edition.*

Not wanting to miss the last *CBC Sunday Morning* of the year, I inadvertently catch the final moments of this NPR yawn. Liane Hansen is interviewing self-proclaimed saloon singer Bobby Short about his gig tonight at New York's Carlisle Hotel. It's a horrible way to wake up, to Short's affected speech and foppish anecdotes about the glamour drain these days: Recently, he was dining in "one of New York's finest restaurants," where, gasp, his fellow diners (and he says this with well-I-never indignation) "weren't even properly dressed."

9:00 a.m. *CBC Sunday Morning.*

Ian Brown (and he's giddy with respect) interviews the grandmotherly voiced Doris Lessing about her new novel, *Love Again.* The conversation turns into a kind of treatise on the emotional force of music.

Lessing says that people are unaware of music's psychological influence:

The kind of music we listen to affects us very much. We treat it as if it's so much wallpaper or, I don't know, the sound of bathwater running, but in actual fact, we listen all the time to very powerful music, as if it has no effect on us at all.

She mentions living through "the most appalling grief" in her sixties and that she still doesn't "know what it was about." Brown asks, "Do you know what brought it on?"
She replies:

Oh, I know what brought it on—it was a severe overdose of a certain kind of music, to my mind. And I saw a very interesting remark the other day. You know the agony columns? I saw somebody saying to a woman who'd lost her husband . . . She said, "In the next two years, be careful not to listen to any powerful music, because that's going to tip you back into grief. I thought, well, there you are; it's not just me.

Brown asks, "out of curiosity," what music brought on her agony, and she says that it was medieval troubadour songs. (Don't you hate that when you break up with somebody and every three minutes on the radio there's yet another thirteenth-century French ballad reminding you of your lost love?) Still, Lessing assures us, "It's very powerful stuff."

I can agree with Lessing about the oft-overlooked energy of music, but I don't think I understand her insistence on it as a source of real, deep anguish. For me, only the opposite is true. Music doesn't cause my grief—sometimes, it's the only thing that saves me, offers perfect moments of relief. Of course there's bad music—deadweights of malice or mediocrity or lack of passion. But bad music doesn't make me grieve, it only makes me angry, which can be a creative, productive experience, especially in my line of work.

There's that wonderful moment in *Let Us Now Praise Famous Men* where James Agee asks you to put your ear against a speaker and listen to Beethoven or Schubert (though

I never understood the Schubert part) on the radio and crank
the volume all the way up and

stay there, breathing as lightly as possible, and not moving,
and neither eating nor smoking nor drinking. Concentrate
everything you can into your hearing and into your body.
You won't hear it nicely. If it hurts you, be glad of it. As
near as you will ever get, you are inside the music; not only
inside it, you are it; your body is no longer your shape and
substance, it is the shape and substance of the music.

　Is what you hear pretty? or beautiful? or legal? or accept-
able in polite or any other society? It is beyond any calcula-
tion savage and dangerous and murderous to all equilibrium
in human life as human life is; and nothing can equal the
rape it does on all that death; nothing except anything,
anything in existence or dream, perceived anywhere remotely
toward its true dimension.

Agee cites the self-confident Beethoven, who claimed, "He
who understands my music can never know unhappiness
again." Lurking beneath the egomania of Beethoven's statement and the strangeness of Agee's ear-torture exercise, is
the most reassuring solace in the world, the notion that a
small, black box in the corner of a room can cast out grief
and death like some kind of miracle.

4:25 p.m. "Rock 103.5."

I nervously scan through the radio dial for hours, having faith
that I'll know the ending when I hear it. And it's not the
news (though Yassar Arafat has advised his fellow Palestinians
"to respect their Israeli neighbors," an unheard-of sentence
not so long ago), or a preacher on fire with Isaiah ("And
justice standeth afar off, for truth is fallen in the street") or
a systematic end-of-the-year eulogy for dead entertainers. No,
what I can only take as the equivalent to a sign from God,
my favorite song, Neil Young's "Rockin' in the Free World,"
comes on at 4:25. This, I decide, is it.

I turn it up, James Agee—loud, pour some Jack Daniels in a glass and sit in a chair to listen. When the song ends, I get up, turn off the radio, pour the rest of the whiskey into the glass, and sit back down—to think. About all of it, all year long. All the days I listened for hours and hours and had nothing to say. All the stupidity, the hatred (especially my own), that one day in April when I couldn't muster the guts to even turn the damn thing on, sat in this very chair and drank this very brand of whiskey until I couldn't see straight, playing Young's live album *Weld* over and over again until I cried myself to sleep. And now, I polish off my drink and just listen to the quiet and whatever fills it—the pulses of the heater (it's cold outside), children playing on the sidewalk, cars driving by. And then I get up and put on my second favorite song.

Later on, I'll have dinner with a friend. We'll go hear the Mekons, who were never on the radio (and the radio needed them). And tomorrow is another year. I'll sleep very late and stop taking notes. I'll cook up a pot of black-eyed peas for luck; God knows we'll need it. But right now, I'll hum along with this song about thinking and wishing and hoping and praying—"Wouldn't It Be Nice." Wouldn't it?

acknowledgments

While the radio was often lacking kind, intelligent, funny voices, my life was full of them.

I thank first of all my mother, Janie, for her compassion, my father, Pat, for his humor and my sister, Amy, for her heart.

I thank these people for their friendship, conversation, tapes, radio tips, and hospitality: Lucy Atkinson, Stanley Booth, Jay Brooker, Ian Brown, Julie Campbell, Shane Campbell, Gary Covino, Eric Danzer, Jim Fitzgerald, Nicole Francis (who bore the brunt of my neurosis), Susan Frei (for the glamour), Ira Glass (who was gracious), Regan Good, Harvey Hamburgh, Carson Herrington, Tim Jag, Mimi Jorling, KGLT, Rick Karr, Jim Kehoe, Brandon LaBelle, Ben Lloyd, Joanne Mannell, Jenny Marcus, Chris Martin, Katie Martin, Donald McGhie, Patsy Pehleman, Steve Peters, Christopher Pinet, Tom Sloan, Steve Smith, Ursula Smith, Matthew Sontheimer, Lisa Wainwright, and critic Bill Wyman (who started out as someone to write about and became someone to talk to).

Barrett Golding was radio buddy number one.

Jack Dew, Claire Needell, and Wendy Weil at the Wendy Weil Agency were helpful and enthusiastic.

Some of the reviews and features I published in *High Performance, New Art Examiner,* and Minneapolis's *City Pages* are scattered throughout the book. I appreciate the corrections and camaraderie of editors Jacki Apple, Linda Frye Burnham, and Steven Durland at *HP;* Kathryn Hixson at *NAE;* and Will Hermes at *CP,* who went beyond the call of duty. Besides being a true friend and an encouraging colleague, he read this manuscript and made invaluable suggestions.

Simon Anderson, who always listened, was my advisor, teacher, friend, and partner in anti-art crime. Besides the fact that he recommended many improvements on this random treatise, he always laughed at my jokes.

Finally, this book would not exist without Greil Marcus. There is no real way to thank him for his generous efforts on my behalf. I can only say that his writing and his friendship have changed my life, and that he understands.